THE LORD OF THE RINGS

THE MAKING OF THE MOVIE TRILOGY

THE LORD OF THE RINGS

THE MAKING OF THE MOVIE TRILOGY

BRIAN SIBLEY

HarperCollins*Publishers*

For
IAN HOLM
whom I first encountered when he was 'Frodo'
and we were setting out together on a radio journey
'There and Back Again'.
Twenty-one years later, he is now 'Bilbo'
and we are still exploring Middle-earth!
With admiration and affection
BS

HarperCollins*Publishers*
77–85 Fulham Palace Road,
Hammersmith, London W6 8JB
www.tolkien.co.uk

Published by HarperCollins*Publishers* 2002
1 3 5 7 9 8 6 4 2

ISBN 0 00 713567 X (trade paperback)
ISBN 0 00 712302 7 (collector's hardback)

Edited by Jane Johnson and Chris Smith
Designed by Barnett Design Consultants
Production by Graham Green
Colour origination by Saxon Photolitho, UK
Printed and bound in Belgium by Proost NV

Contents

Foreword

The day *The Lord of the Rings* opened at the Embassy Cinema in New Zealand's capital, Wellingtonians woke to discover that overnight their city had been re-named by government decree. To honour the achievement of their local film industry, Wellington was for one unique day exchanged for 'Middle-earth' on sign-posts and public buildings. By the evening a red carpet stretched the length of Courtenay Place in front of the Embassy, scene of multitudinous celebrations as the audience crowded in to the premiere. Those of us who couldn't be there had already caught the Kiwis' excitement when we saw that Tolkien's characters were on the end-of-year postage stamps, advertising New Zealand's enterprise worldwide. When a film employs more workers than any other industry in the country, there is reason for celebration.

For those of us who were drafted in from abroad to participate in the film-making, this local identification was a real encouragement. A year away from home was less daunting when everyone hearing the British accent knew at once, 'Oh, you are here for *The Lord of the Rings*'!

We also encountered an obsessive concern for the outcome of Peter Jackson's translation of novels into cinema, and not only in New Zealand. The internet was buzzing with questions, half-answers, guesses, hopes and fears from Tolkien's admirers. My response to this enthusiasm was to set up my own public journal, 'The Grey Book' (on www.mckellen.com). Reading this book now, I realize how inadequate my observations were, so if you want to experience what it was really like making *The Fellowship of the Ring*, *The Two Towers* and even 2003's *The Return of the King*, you have the most authoritative source in your hands.

When Peter Jackson and his partner Fran Walsh first talked to me about their project, I was a Tolkien ignoramus (as I don't consider a single reading of *The Hobbit* as a teenager to count very much!). They came to my home in London some months before shooting with a file of Middle-earth images and the trilogy's initial screenplay. They left behind a sense that a great journey was afoot and that my ticket to ride was the chance of a lifetime. Brian Sibley's book captures the excitement perfectly.

Ian McKellen

NEW LINE CINEMA AND ENTERTAINMENT FILM DISTRIBUTORS CORDIALLY INVITE

Mr. Brian Sibley

TO THE WORLD PREMIERE AND TO THE PARTY AFTERWARDS

THE LORD OF THE RINGS
THE FELLOWSHIP OF THE RING

Prologue
The Long-expected Party

It is like a scene out of a movie. To be specific, it's like a scene from one of those Battle of Britain films of the 1950s in which the intrepid young airmen are being given a last, stiff-upper-lip, briefing, prior to scrambling to their planes…

True, the setting and characters are rather different – we are in a sumptuous suite at the Dorchester Hotel in London and those being briefed are stars – but the *mood* is spot on.

It is lunchtime on Sunday, December 9th 2001 and New Line Cinema's Tracy Lorie is taking the cast of *The Fellowship of the Ring* through the schedule for the next day's world premiere at the Odeon, Leicester Square.

Around the table sit Christopher Lee, Ian Holm, Orlando Bloom and Weta Workshop's Richard Taylor and Tania Rodger. Everyone is more or less exhausted from two days of non-stop media interviews – as many as fifty a day – and far too tired to do more than pick at the generous spread of fruit, cheese and pastries. At the other end of the room, Elijah Wood and family are lounging on sofas and armchairs along with Dominic Monaghan and Billy Boyd.

The rest of the cast – Liv Tyler, John Rhys-Davies, Viggo Mortensen and the two Seans (Astin and Bean) – are still at it in other suites up and down the corridor: attempting to answer the same questions over and over as if they've never heard them before; trying to think in those much-desired sound-bites; remembering to

smile. Ian McKellen is somewhere above the Atlantic on Concorde, en route from New York; and, as of now, no one is sure whether Cate Blanchett – who gave birth to her son, Dashiell, only three days ago – will be attending the premiere or not.

For those who have made it to the briefing, there is much to take in: the times of departure by car from the Dorchester and arrival in Leicester Square; arrangements for partners, relatives and guests; and the procedure to be followed once at the Odeon Theatre: 'You'll make your way along the red carpet, past the press corps in the pen to your right but, *please*, do not stop –'

With a perfectly straight face, Elijah asks if it is permitted to wave? 'By all means acknowledge them,' he is told, 'but please don't stop and *don't* go across to the public barriers on the other side –'

'Oh, I was just going to ignore *them!* ' jokes Elijah: a jest that is rewarded with a headmasterly frown from

Christopher Lee: 'It's actually *very* important that we don't stop to chat or sign things, or we'll be there, literally, all night!'

'After all,' continues Tracy, making sure that the point has gone home, 'the film *is* three hours long and so *must* start no later than 7.45.' More instructions follow: once inside the cinema, everyone is to make their way upstairs for a round of television interviews: 'The cameras will be arranged in a large semi-circle and you will be divided into two groups: one moving left to right, the other, right to left…'

Ian Holm sits, saying nothing, with his hands together, the finger-tips pressed thoughtfully to his lips.

'After the interviews,' Tracy goes on, 'everyone will go back down onto the staircase for a cast photograph before being escorted to the front of the stalls so that Peter can bring you on stage and introduce you to the audience.' Richard Taylor grins at me across the room with the obvious relief of someone feeling glad *not* to be a star! 'And, when *that's* over, you will be conducted to your seats and the film will begin. Afterwards –'

'The Party!' someone interjects. But the infinitely patient Tracy has one or two *further* instructions: about the order and timing of cars from the cinema to the reception at Tobacco Dock in London's East End.

Here there's another interruption, as Orlando Bloom raises a question about how he is going to meet up with his mates who are coming as guests.

Once that has been settled: 'And so we come to what happens when you arrive at the party –' At which point, Elijah remarks hopefully: 'Well, it's *just* a party, isn't it?' Not quite, it seems! There is to be *another* press line-up and *more* interviews. Altogether, it sounds as if it is going to be a long, tiring and, possibly, stressful evening.

A quiet finally descends on the room. And it is only then that Ian Holm looks up and says, in a soft voice that drops like a stone into the well of silence: 'Hmmm… and the rehearsal is – *when?*'

As it turns out, the event – even *without* a rehearsal – goes like clockwork. It is a bitterly cold December evening, but the crowds have turned out in force, shunning the blaring music, garish lights and dizzying rides of Leicester Square's Christmas Fair in order to applaud the stars as they make their way along the red carpet to the theatre.

The hobbits are in snappy suits and stylish open-neck shirts (smart-casual with the accent on smart), the wizards, as befitting their status, have opted for a more conservative look with collars and ties. And whilst – not too surprisingly, perhaps – Cate Blanchett *isn't* there, Liv Tyler most certainly *is*, wearing a scarlet Alexander McQueen trouser-suit with a fiery lace train. The photographers are ecstatic and Liv looks calm and unflustered, though she later confesses to having spent most of the day in fittings for the *ensemble* and to feeling, in consequence, decidedly nervous.

Peter Jackson, either in deference to the occasion or because of the weather, has spurned his customary attire of shorts in favour of a

purple shirt and black trousers. Never totally at ease with being on show, Peter nevertheless strides confidently along with the beaming smile of a man who, for all his modesty, suspects that his movie is about to become a hit on a fairly phenomenal scale!

The fans, many of whom have been loyally waiting for hours, seem oblivious to the icy winds whipping across the square and whistling round the statue of Shakespeare. They are too busy identifying who's who ('That's Viggo! He's Aragorn'), feverishly snapping photos, cheering and screaming: 'We love you, Elijah!'

Interspersed with the film-makers, who are largely *un*identified by the crowd (but courteously clapped nonetheless), is a tranche of British celebrities – comedians, soap-stars, TV presenters and the like. Among those rumoured to be on the guest-list are Bob Geldof, Claudia Schiffer, Richard E. Grant, Jude Law, Sir Richard Branson and Sir Cliff Richard. Some are spotted, others are not.

Sean Bean (contrary to instructions, but then he *had* missed the briefing) happily works his way along the line of fans, shaking hands and giving autographs until – to the groans of those still further off – his publicist finally shepherds him resolutely towards the theatre entrance.

Above the doors to the Odeon is the legend 'ONE

RING TO RULE THEM ALL' and a row of large hoops – symbolic rings – that burst into flame and flare dramatically in the night air.

Inside, the cast carry out their duties to perfection and, eventually, the waiting audience (already well steeped in popcorn) give them a rapturous welcome on stage along with Executive Producers Bob Shaye, Michael Lynne and Mark Ordesky, Producer Barrie Osborne and the man whose night this truly is, Peter Jackson.

For those who might have wondered, Peter explains the choice of London as the venue for the world premiere. A classic of modern English Literature – the book of the twentieth century, according to some – the epic was the work of a British writer who had talked of creating a new mythology for his homeland. '*The Lord of the Rings*,' says Peter, 'was written here and it is right that the movie which we based on that book should be shown here first.'

There is more applause, the lights go down, the curtains open and the film begins...

The voice of Galadriel comes drifting out of the darkness: 'The world is changed, I feel it in the water, I feel it in the earth, I smell it in the air. Much that once was, is lost – for none now live who remember it…' The mournful, yearning notes of Howard Shore's opening composition, 'The Prophecy', swirl around the cinema, carrying us back to that lost age, to a time before 'history became legend' and 'legend became myth'. And so the spell is cast. A hush of anticipation falls over the fifteen hundred privileged guests gathered in the cinema.

As an audience we give an exceptional performance: we respond to everything, we miss nothing! We laugh at the antics of Merry and Pippin, shudder at the hiss of the Ringwraiths, are on the edge of our seats during the flight to the Ford. We recoil in horror when Bilbo makes an unexpected bid for the Ring, jump when the cave troll appears suddenly from behind a column, weep at the fall of Gandalf and the passing of Boromir. Though it's extremely un-British of us, we even find ourselves cheering as Aragorn decapitates the leader of the Uruk-hai with one deadly sweep of his sword!

Nearly three hours later, the film reaches its almost downbeat conclusion, with Frodo and Sam making their way down the stony slopes towards the shadow-filled realm of Mordor: 'Sam, I'm glad you're with me…'

There is a moment's silence and the cinema becomes a maelstrom of delighted whoops, yells and roars that almost drowns Enya's closing rendition of 'May it Be' and repeatedly punctuates the fifteen minutes of closing credits.

By midnight we have been shuttled across town to Tobacco Dock, to be greeted with glasses of Mulled Cider & Orange and bags of Hot Chestnuts as well as the spectacle of rustically-attired chefs roasting a pig on a spit, and the prospect of a never-to-be-forgotten party. But for the stars there is another walk along another acre of red carpeting, through another lightning-storm of flash-bulbs…

It's back to work for Peter Jackson and the cast: giving interviews, mixing-and-mingling, somehow managing to find new quotes for the press. Christopher Lee observes: 'We made three remarkable books into three remarkable films'; Ian McKellen says: 'It's like a Fritz Lang epic!'

The young members of the cast work as hard and tirelessly as anyone and, hours later, Elijah is still moving among the guests, chatting away, as if the party were one of Frodo's own gatherings at Bag End and he were the host.

The former tobacco warehouses – now converted into a vast, retro-chic venue – have been magically transformed by Dan and Chris Hennah (shown right), of the film's art department, into various Tolkienesque locations. We wander through Rivendell and Lothlórien sampling a Middle-earth menu that includes 'Baked River Anduin Salmon', 'Barliman Butterbur's Famous Sausage and Mash', 'Gandalf's Secret Recipe of Pan-fried Guinea Fowl' and (alarming thought) 'Hot Hobbit Pies'!

There is a bar from the hobbit's inn, 'The Green Dragon', constructed to three-foot-six-scale and requiring patrons to stoop in order to reach their beer and another, inspired by 'The Prancing Pony' at Bree, built from a hobbit's perspective, so that even the tallest guests have their noses well below the level of the counter! There are stooks of corn, baskets overflowing with apples, and trees hung with lanterns recalling the homely Shire. But there is also the monstrous trio of grimacing stone trolls beneath which the hobbits camp on their way to Rivendell and, surrounded by billowing smoke and illuminated by multi-coloured lights, the towering figure of a mounted Ringwraith that looms high above the dance floor.

For the throng of guests it is an evening of unalloyed fun. What else could it be with plenty of good ale on offer as well as second helpings of 'Rosie Cotton's Chewy Treacle & Honey Tarts with Clotted Cream'?

But for those who have been working on the project: cast and crew, writers, craftspeople, technicians and producers – and, most significantly, for director Peter Jackson – it is far more than just a party: it is a milestone on a journey that began almost six years earlier…

True, it is a journey that is still far from over – three more premieres (in New York, Los Angeles and Wellington), and, after that, two more films to be completed – but it is a day, an evening, a night and a party that has been anticipated with as much enthusiasm and, perhaps, a degree of anxiety, for even longer than the hobbits of Hobbiton had awaited Mr Bilbo Baggins' eleventy-first birthday party.

It is scarcely an event that has allowed much time for reflection, but there have been moments, Peter confides, when he has looked back to an ordinary - yet extraordinary - Sunday morning in November 1995: 'I was lying in bed thinking about what to do next. At the time I was working on *The Frighteners*, but whenever you're making a movie, half your mind is thinking about what you're going to do when this one's over.

'And of course the first thing I thought of was *The Lord of the Rings*! Why not make a film along those lines?' He pauses, gives an incredulous shake of the head and laughs. 'I never for a moment thought I'd end up filming the book itself - and yet that's exactly what we went and did!'

How that passing idea took form and eventually became one of the most startlingly ambitious projects in the history of cinema, is a tale for another book: the tracking down and acquiring of the rights to Tolkien's novel; the process by which Peter and his co-

scriptwriters, Fran Walsh and Philippa Boyens, crafted a trilogy of compelling screenplays from the thousand-page epic; the enlisting of established Tolkien illustrators, Alan Lee and John Howe, to work with Wellington special-effects house, Weta Workshop, in shaping a filmic vision of Middle-earth; and, last but not least, the finding, in New Line, of a studio willing to give financial backing to this inspired, if wildly insane, undertaking!

Meanwhile, in the pages that follow, we embark on a creative journey that, like the quest in the original book, has demanded determination and endurance, as well as an openess to the happy quirks of serendipity!

Lucky Man

'I am somebody who really loves what I'm doing!' Peter Jackson is reflecting on what he sees as his fortunate lot in life: 'I grew up with parents that were doing a job of work because that's what you had to do in order to earn money.'

Peter's father was a wages-clerk with Wellington City Council; his mother worked in a factory. 'In that situation,' says Peter, 'your only real joy in life comes from your weekends and your three-week annual vacation. The rest of the time, it's about working to pay your twenty-year mortgage. That's why I feel incredibly lucky every day that I am doing something that I really love doing…'

Peter was born on 31st October (Hallowe'en) 1961 at Pukerua Bay, on the North Island of New Zealand. He took his first steps towards his film-career when, at an early age, he borrowed his parents' Super-8 cine-camera and started making his own experimental home-movies. Inspired by stop-motion animation of the kind used in the films of Ray Harryhausen, Peter made his first short film, featuring a cast of animated clay dinosaurs.

By the time he had reached the age of sixteen, Peter's fascination had extended to live-action horror films and he was heading up a film crew comprising his school-mates and making his very own vampire movie! At twenty, he was working as an apprentice photo-lithographer, but – still dreaming of a career in movies – had saved the money for a 16mm camera and was devoting all his spare time to making his first amateur feature-film. The result, completed four years later in 1987, was *Bad Taste*. Screened at the Cannes Film Festival it won awards and

accolades and became the launch-pad for his career.

Bad Taste was followed, in 1989, by *Meet the Feebles*, a backstage drama on the set of a TV puppet-show that could be read as an outrageous lampoon of the ever-popular *Muppet Show*.

In 1992 came *Braindead*, a spectacularly grisly zombie-flick splattered with an superabundance of gore and guts. Whilst *Braindead* quickly achieved cult-status, it was an unlikely precursor to Peter's next film, *Heavenly Creatures*.

Released in 1994, *Heavenly Creatures* was based on the Parker-Hulme murder case, the story of two schoolgirls (played by Kate Winslet and Sarah Peirse) whose obsessive relationship and constant retreat into their private, fantasy realm eventually leads them to murder one of their mothers. An art-house movie that widened public awareness of Peter as a film-maker, *Heavenly Creatures* earned him and his partner, Fran Walsh, an Oscar nomination for Best Screenplay Written Directly for the Screen.

Peter's next ventures, both in 1996, were *Forgotten Silver*, a spoof-documentary on the 'lost' career of a pioneering New Zealand director of the silent-movie era; and *The Frighteners*, a psychic detective-story starring Michael J. Fox. Producing the innovative computer-generated special-effects for *The Frighteners* was to spur Peter's imagination in the direction of making a fantasy film – a road that would, eventually, lead him to Middle-earth.

'Making *The Lord of the Rings*,' says Peter, 'is something that is quite amazing! It's a special book and a special project and there's never a day goes by when I don't think it's a real honour to be doing it!'

This belief in his good fortune, coupled with his affection for his late parents who – despite the constraints of their own hard-grafted lives – always gave Peter their unstinting encouragement, resulted in the director's moving dedication on the closing credits of *The Fellowship of the Ring*: 'For Joan and Bill Jackson: Thank you for your belief, support and love…'

The PJ Philosophy

Peter Jackson is not just a passionate film-maker: he is also proud of being a New Zealander, a Wellingtonian and, in particular, a resident of Wellington's Miramar region, as evidenced by a letter from Peter to the City's Mayor, Mark Blumsky in September 1998: 'As you know, I am a Wellingtonian through and through and I am proud to have been able to bring this project not only to New Zealand but to our own Miramar. It is clearly international recognition of how good the Wellington brand of Kiwi is. And people from all over New Zealand are going to come here and experience our best-guarded secrets: our city and our great way of life.

'Film-making is very much a co-operative activity. It is a business which mixes together many people from a wide range of backgrounds into a creative melting-pot and out at the end of the process there eventually pops a movie. Everyone involved, in that sense, "owns" part of the movie, whether they have acted in it, filmed it, built or dressed the sets, donated or allowed props or locations to be used, or even just given the project their goodwill to proceed.

'We have always been lucky that people have got behind us, as individuals, businesses, local bodies – even central government. Without this ongoing goodwill and willingness to help make things work, we couldn't do half as good a job.

'Maybe it's because the film industry in New Zealand has always been a "roll your sleeves up and get on with it" sort of industry that we get such assistance. Maybe it's because people like helping others who are so blatantly doing what they love doing. Maybe it's because we deal in dreams. Or maybe it's because Wellington is just a better sort of place!'

In the Cannes

'Please bring your Medallion. You will not be permitted to pass security checkpoints without it.' The 'medallion' is, in fact, a cardboard disc, threaded on a piece of string and carrying the words 'The Lord of the Rings ★ Media Event ★ May 13 2001 ★ Cannes', encircled by the Ring-verse. Its face value aside, this medallion is, nevertheless, the only means of access to what is expected to be the coolest party of the 2001 Cannes Film Festival.

Candles flickering in terracotta bowls flank the drive up to the Chateau De Castellaras, which has been transformed by Dan and Chris Hennah of The Lord of the Rings Art Department into a microcosmic representation of Middle-earth. Where better to begin the tour than at Bag End: up the little garden path and duck through the round doorway into a maze of tiny rooms with low, head-banging ceilings and hobbit-scale furnishings; nearby, the façade of 'The Green Dragon' inn conceals ranks of portable lavatories, the cubicles of which are wired for sound to provide the seriously disquieting experience of being in the path of a furious Orc-attack!

Bilbo's 'Happy Birthday' banner flutters bravely across a Party Field dotted with hobbity marquees and stalls serving food: spit-roasted joints, corn-on-the-cob and great hunks of crusty bread.

Gondorian Guards stand sentry duty on the broad steps leading up to the main entrance of the Chateau and through to the courtyard beyond which is decked out with shields and pennants from the fortress city of Minas Tirith.

Inside the Chateau we experience a film-like 'cross-fade' from one Middle-earth culture to another as we enter the throne-room of King Théoden at Edoras: the walls hung with tapestries, the roof-posts decorated with horse-head carvings and everything curiously illuminated by swirling, disco-lights!

Outside, drifting away from the crowds, I come upon Galadriel's swan boat 'parked' in the swimming-pool, and, in a deserted part of the grounds, a pair of black stone gates with curious inscriptions that mysteriously appear and then fade again. These are the Doors of Durin, the fateful entry to the Mines of Moria…

I reflect on the fact that those gates are the way into what will undoubtedly become one of the highlight sequences in *The Fellowship of the Ring*: a sequence which, two days earlier, had been exclusively screened as a 'work-in-progress preview' at Cannes' Olympia Theatre.

Critics attending the daily surfeit of screenings at Cannes are rarely given to displays of approbation, but at the end of the 26-minute compilation, the Olympia erupted with cheers and applause. Any lingering doubts about the project were dispelled. Considerable post-production work has still to be done, but as *Variety* would declare, a day or two later: 'Three "Ring" circus commands attention'.

Back at the party, in a dark corner, I come upon Peter Jackson and Richard Taylor talking together under the shadowing bulk of a huge stone troll looming from between the trees and bathed in a sickly green light. In commenting on the success of the screening and the magnificence of this celebration, I discover that the two men have an infinitely more personal and nostalgic reaction to the event.

'The first time we came to Cannes,' says Peter, 'was in 1992, for *Braindead*. Of course, then we couldn't afford to stay at the posh hotels…'

'And we couldn't afford proper publicity,' adds Richard, 'so we ran up and down the sea-front pinning posters onto the palm trees announcing the *Braindead* screening. As fast as the authorities ripped them down, we pinned up more!'

Peter smiles at the memory. 'And do you know where we showed the film? *The Olympia!*' They laugh. 'You've got to admit, it's all a bit different *this* time around…'

Workshop of Wonders

 A giant paw-print! I am walking along a sleepy road, aware of nothing in particular other than the buzzing of crickets in the gardens of the neat row of bungalows painted in pale pastel-hues of pink and lemon. Then, suddenly, I notice the mark of some great beast, clawed into the concrete pavement! Beside the imprint, an explanatory legend has been inscribed:

'KONG WUZ HAIR'

I have arrived at No. 1, Weka Street, Miramar, home of Weta Workshop. Outside: weather-beaten, sun-blistered buildings and a yard stacked with huge containers. Inside: Middle-earth! The walls are crowded with fantastic drawings and paintings of otherworldly places and creatures, while work-benches are littered with such unlikely objects as Elf-ears and Orc-teeth.

My eye is caught by a large sign (originally made for the film, *Jack Brown Genius*) which reads: 'Regional Centre for the Deeply Disturbed.'

'Did you know that this used to be a mental asylum?' Tall and bespectacled, Richard Taylor has the combined skills of a craftsman and technician, the flair of a showman, the perceptions of a born philosopher and, above all, still retains the irrepressible enthusiasm of a fourteen-year-old passionately in love with comic-books and movie-monsters. Richard Taylor *is* Weta!

'Originally,' Richard informs me, 'this place was an aquatic fun-park with a huge swimming-pool and water-slides. Then, at the turn of the century, it was filled-in and made into a mental institution: an ugly, spartan place with tarmac floors and open beams. During World War II, it became a hospital for G.I.s' families; after which it became, first of all, a factory turning out Exide batteries, then a pharmaceutical factory making Vaseline and talcum-powder. And *then*,' laughs Richard: '*we* bought it, and turned it back into an asylum!'

We walk from room to room, Richard stopping to chat with sculptors, painters and model-makers. Then, unlocking a door, Richard leads me into a room lined with glass cases stuffed with bizarre creatures and strange, sometimes grisly, objects. It brings to mind those collections of grotesqueries found in crumbling Victorian mansions or in the freak-tents that were once an irresistible attraction of American carnivals.

I spot a frog dressed in war-combat gear, a rabid rat-monkey, a demon-possessed rag-doll and a worm with an old man's face. 'These,' says Richard, 'are our past lives!' He sniffs. 'And that smell, is the unmistakable aroma of rotting foam latex!'

More recent exhibits are clearly from the realm of Middle-earth: a large box of 'Sméagol Feet' (big and flat); and another of 'Proudfoot Feet' (large, gnarled and scabrous). 'At the height of filming,' recalls Richard, 'there were thousands of such boxes. We even came up with *these* –' He holds up a pair of hobbit-toed gum-boots. 'Specially made for Sam and Frodo to wear when crossing the Dead Marshes!'

Re-locking the museum – 'Which key is it? Keys, keys – so *many* keys!' – Richard leads the way through the maze of corridors and rooms that comprise Weta's 68,000 square feet of Wonderland.

Towering above me is Treebeard the Ent: a gigantic tree with human features, leafy hair, long, knotty arms and twiggy hands, swathed in plastic sheeting. Nearby are sections of the Watcher in the Water, the Jules Verne-like monster which lurks in a pool outside the Doors of Durin. This is one of the creature maquettes that were built by the Workshop and scanned into the computers so

that the animators of Weta Digital could give life to its sucker-covered tentacles, its fan of spinal horns, its age-rheumed eyes and gaping jaws. Nearby are the horns of the Balrog. Richard Taylor's description of the fearsome denizen from Moria's depths has the ring of a medieval bestiary: 'In form its body is a cross between a bull and a dog with the horns of a ram, the wings of a bat and the tail of a lizard.' Then, as an afterthought, he adds: 'Oh, and its skin is like cold, coagulated lava!'

We pass an exquisite boat – dove-grey with a swan's-head prow – in which, at the very end of the trilogy, the Ring-bearers will take their leave of Middle-earth; I notice a huge pair of cable-controlled spider limbs (used in the horrific encounter with the monstrous Shelob) and pause to watch someone fashioning part of a tower out of blue styrofoam-sheeting: 'Normally that stuff's used for insulating houses…' As I have already begun to discover, very little in Weta Workshop is what you might call 'normal'.

To reach the office, we pass through a wooden door into which a giant insect-shaped hole has been jigsawed. 'That,' Richard informs me, 'is the outline of a weta.'

A native of New Zealand, the weta is an ancient, cricket-like species that is practically indestructible and can grow to be one of the heaviest bugs in the world: 'Yep, it's a cool little beast!' grins Richard. 'And we like to think that the product we produce aspires to the complexity, beauty and, occasionally, even the monstrousness of the weta.'

I confess that I had originally imagined 'Weta' to be an acronym. 'Well,' says Richard, 'we *did* try to work out something along those lines: such as "Wellington Effects and Technical –" and drew a blank! The thing is, it really doesn't matter whether you know what a weta is or not: it's still got a certain ring to it. Ian McKellen turned it into a sort of mantra and chanted "There's no one better than Weta"!'

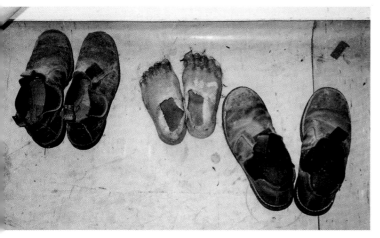

At the foot of the stairs, I notice are two pair of boots and, between them, another pair of those hobbit feet…

The steep staircase is fitted with a lift for transporting Weta's mascot: an elderly Huntaway-Alsatian dog, named Gemma. Though a little long in the tooth, Gemma still can – and *does* – melt your heart with one look of her big, dark, soulful eyes.

The office which Richard shares with his wife and business partner, Tania Rodger (pictured below right with Richard), is a cosy mix of the practical and the outlandish. The no-nonsense necessities involved in running a business efficiently (in-trays stashed with requisitions, order-forms and invoices) are given colour and zest by flashes of surreal fancy: a mishmash of photographs tacked to the walls – giants, fiends, scenes of gore and mayhem – as well as gags and sketches by various "Weta-ers" (as they call them-selves), among them Daniel Falconer, whose highly stylized drawing of Saruman the White and his Uruk-hai creation, Lurtz, (shown overleaf) is wittily captioned 'Saruman and Son'!

A Weta calendar, hanging on one wall, is filled with cartoons by Chris Guise, one of which shows Peter Jackson being confronted by Sam and Frodo wearing absurdly large hobbit ears and feet and asking (not unreasonably) 'What scale are we shooting at here?'

'We are so proud of our involvement in *The Lord of the Rings*,' says Richard, 'there's not more than a handful of scenes in the entire film that don't feature a Weta product.'

Over very English refreshments of tea and Battenburg cake, I discover something of the extraordinary story of how Weta Workshop came to play such a prominent role in this ambitious film project.

Tania and Richard had arrived in Wellington, after completing their studies, with no experience and little understanding of the special-effects business, but with a real passion for creating things. Richard began art-directing television commercials with budgets that were so low that he was required to do more or less everything from design and model-making to make-up: 'Not much money, but an intensely-focused insight into how very exciting this work could be!'

The break-through came with *Public Eye*, a satirical New Zealand television show for which, over a period of two years, they built more than seventy puppets caricaturing leading political figures. Working in a basement flat, on a shoe-string budget, they were producing a puppet every three days, sculpted from industrial margarine by Richard and moulded in rubber by Tania!

separate effects-pieces for a film that has been rated as one of the most gory movies ever made.

Heavenly Creatures, *Forgotten Silver* and *The Frighteners* followed, all with Peter Jackson, as well as the popular television series *Xena, Warrior Princess* and *Hercules*, providing plenty of opportunities for innovative work.

Pooling financial resources with Peter Jackson and Jamie Selkirk (now Supervising Editor and co-producer on *The Lord of the Rings*) and a couple of other associates, Richard and Tania founded Weta Workshop. Convinced that the future for visual effects lay in computer-technology, the company committed itself to a massive loan and purchased its first computer.

Next came – or *nearly* came – *King Kong* (hence the paw-print on Weka Street), a project which involved a huge amount of pre-production work but which ended with the film's collapse. Once again, hope was born out of despair with the first whispers of another – and extraordinarily ambitious – project: 'At first,' says Richard, 'Peter wooed us with the notion of filming *The Hobbit*. But then, of course, he asks: "Why not go for the Big One?" The decision to aim for *The Lord of the Rings* was true Jacksonesque thinking.'

They met and became friends with Peter Jackson when the director had just completed *Bad Taste* and had secured the funding to make *Braindead*. Peter invited Richard and Tania to become part of the model-making team and fired by the excitement of being involved with their first feature-film, they enthusiastically launched into preparatory work for the picture. Then, in what is an all too common film industry scenario, the financing failed and the project was shelved. 'It was,' remembers Richard, 'one of the most miserable days of our professional lives. But early the next morning the phone rang and it was Peter, asking us to join him in making *Meet the Feebles* and we embarked on a highly enjoyable year, working in a run-down railway-shed, making puppets of temperamental hippos, lecherous walruses and disease-ridden rabbits!'

After *Meet the Feebles*, Peter was able to resurrect *Braindead* and, working with a team of nine, Richard and Tania produced the miniatures and over 240

The leap of imagination succeeded and the Hollywood studio Miramax (with whom Peter and Weta had worked on *The Frighteners*) agreed to finance *The Lord of the Rings* as a two-film project. 'At that point,' reflects Richard, 'Peter gave us an incredible gift: he quite simply asked what we would like to do on the project. He didn't *tell* us – he *asked* us.'

Weta's response was – to adapt Richard's earlier words about Peter Jackson – an example of true *Tayloresque* thinking! 'We believed that there needed to be a unity of design on the project like nothing previously undertaken. So, whilst it probably looked incredibly greedy, we wanted to commit Weta Workshop to the highest level of involvement that we could cope with.'

After much discussion and agonizing, Richard and Tania proposed that Weta should take responsibility for the design and fabrication (as well as all the "on-set operation" and post-production work) of the miniatures, armour, weapons, creature-maquettes and animatronics, as well as all prosthetics and special make-up effects – including (as one would expect of the team who had worked on *Braindead*) those involving injuries and gore.

'We wanted the opportunity,' says Richard, 'to paint the world of Middle-earth with a singular creative brush-stroke and to do it to the finest possible level of accomplishment.'

It was, nevertheless, a daunting prospect: '*Scary* is how I'd describe it!' laughs Richard. '*Very* scary. At the time, we were hardly the most highly-experienced effects-technicians and no other workshop in the history of film-making has ever been stupid enough to say that they would do so much.'

We have another cup of tea and another slice of Battenburg and Richard is off again: 'So, my first day at work, after hearing that we're going to be making *The Lord of the Rings*, I'm thinking, "How are we going to start bringing Tolkien's world to life?" There was the text, of course, and, with it, the biggest group of readers in the world, all of whom already had a preconceived idea of what Middle-earth should look like. And there was the director's vision – closely aligned to Tolkien, but still his own, original vision – and then there was *our* vision, because we weren't interested in doing it unless we could give something of ourselves to the look and feel of it all.'

In addition, Peter had come up with the inspired idea of involving two artists, Alan Lee and John Howe, with an international reputation as Tolkien illustrators who could bring to the production a wealth of creative inspiration and authoritative insight.

For Richard and Tania, the challenge was to assemble a team of craftspeople and technicians to realize the cummulative visions of those already involved. 'We had the pick of just about every long-term professional designer in the world,' notes Richard, 'but, instead, we built a team of talented young New Zealanders who were passionate to see the book become a film. They brought to the project a wonderful combination of enthusiasm and willingness: slavishly sticking to Tolkien's word when required; content to stamp the film with Peter's vision, without getting uppity about it; happy to blend my vision into the mix as well; modest and unabashed enough to accept teaching from Alan

Lee and John Howe; and, all the time, adding their own freshness of interpretation.'

Richard recalls the way in which they worked: 'We'd arrive at the Workshop every day at 8.00 a.m., talk about a particular subject and then spend the rest of the day putting ideas down on paper. At 5.00 p.m. Peter would arrive, go over what we'd produced and tell us what he liked. Everything else was culled and the next day we'd start refining the best ideas and developing new ones.'

There followed almost seven hundred days of highly-concentrated design-work: masses of drawings, three-dimensional maquettes of beings, specimen weapons and armoury and the construction of the first scale miniatures of Helm's Deep and Khazad-dûm.

Then came catastrophe! Miramax, alarmed by the way in which projected costs were escalating, decided that the project should be restructured as a single movie. Peter felt that he had no choice but to reject this proposal and *The Lord of the Rings* faltered and collapsed.

'It was a freakish moment,' says Richard, remembering their sense of despair. 'After so much work, so much passion… Riding on the back of the failure of *King Kong*, it was deeply depressing.'

However, Peter was not giving up. He had the option – though it seemed a slim chance at the time – of finding another studio to repay Miramax's investment and take on the project. Having faith in Peter's determination, Weta helped put together an impressive show-reel and an array of pre-production art for the film with which Peter and his producing and scripting partner, Fran Walsh, set off for Hollywood in search of new funding.

Alan Lee and John Howe packed their bags and left for Europe. Richard and Tania kept the rest of the workshop ticking over, while a representative from Miramax supervised the packing of all the artwork, sculptures and dismantled miniatures which, if no alternative deal could be made, would remain the film company's property.

'Then,' says Richard with a satisfying chuckle, 'we got a phone call from Peter: "Unpack everything! Start up the engines! We're back on board!" New Line had caught the spirit of what we were trying to do and had taken on *The Lord of the Rings* not as *two* movies, but as *three*! So, off we went again!' Rather like the weta bug, the Workshop that shares its name seems born and bred to survive.

Richard has to dash off to a meeting, but Tania has arrived with a batch of invoices needing to be processed and I suggest that it will give someone else a chance to say a few words… 'Good idea!' laughs Richard, 'I *do* tend to do all the talking – which is grossly unfair, because at least fifty per cent of Weta's creativity is down to Tania.' He's off, but *still* talking: 'Besides,' he calls back, 'Tania is a *goddess*. First and foremost let's establish that!'

Tania smiles and gives a 'what-would-you-do-with-him?' kind of shrug. The computer on her desk shows a schedule of product-orders, the shelves above are stacked with ranks of box-files: 'Model-making Supplies and Tools', 'Leather', 'Feathers', 'Buttons, Buckles and Trims', 'Crates and Packaging', 'Plastic Polymers and Foams' and 'Fibreglass, Urethane and Silicone'.

'You know,' laughs Tania, recalling their early days in the business, 'we started out as skip-raiders! We had a

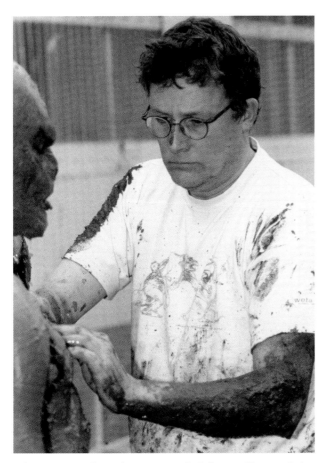

Tania's biggest challenge is to get raw materials, the bulk of which come from suppliers in the United States, ordered and delivered on time. Silicone and foam-latex, which come in 200-kilogram drums, take six weeks to manufacture and another six weeks to be transported, by boat, from America to New Zealand: 'Silicone has a shelf-life of six months, after which results can't be guaranteed; so, by the time it arrives, its life-expectancy is down to *three* months! As a result, we've learned to ensure that we order whatever we need three months before we are actually going to use it.' They have also learned to push the shelf-life of products to the limit: 'After all, you're so pleased to have it once it's here, you'll do anything rather than waste it.'

As with every film – and with *The Lord of the Rings* in particular – shooting schedules change and materials can suddenly be needed sooner than anticipated. 'One of the biggest problems any movie can face,' Tania explains, 'is to have a crew standing around with nothing to do, simply because the materials they need to get on with the job are sitting on a boat or waiting to clear customs.'

white van and, under cover of night, we'd prowl the streets, rummaging through skips and bins and salvaging anything that looked halfway useable. Our first workshop was a sort of permanent junk-fest.'

Those magpie-days taught Tania and Richard the value of lateral thinking: 'You quite often get better results – and a lot more fun – from using your brain to *think* how to do things. We discovered for example that you could make very convincing "innards" from squidging foam latex left-overs into gut-shapes, which were baked in an oven and then dressed with golden syrup and food colouring…'

Weta still uses some of the techniques they learned in times when there was less cash to spend and they have never lost their ability to look at things and see alternative potential uses for them: 'We discovered, for example, that the type of rubber used to make skateboard wheels is so strong and durable that it was perfect for moulding the background swords we made for *The Lord of the Rings*.'

One of the least publicized statistics on the making of *The Lord of the Rings* will be the hundreds of order-books, the reams of fax-paper and the hours of e-mailing time that have gone into keeping the output of Weta Workshop up to the mark. For Tania, the very

ordinariness of some of her daily tasks brings with it an unexpected sense of wonder: 'I order all these materials and they arrive in drums, tubs and boxes: the place looks like a packing-shed but, within weeks, those raw materials have all been transformed into an amazing array of the most wonderful creations. I really love the imagery of things arriving in boringly dull shapes and then going out again in strange, beautiful and magical forms.'

While Tania was handling international supplies, Production Assistant, Tich Rowney, was dealing with local orders and fulfilling all kind of bizarre requests: scouring the countryside for moss and lichen or trying to track down unlikely requirements, such as graphite powder. Normally used for loosening locks, Weta needed to purchase graphite by the kilogram in order to give the Uruk-hai armour a suitably grimed and grubby finish: 'It's filthy, gritty stuff,' recalls Tania, 'and it gets *everywhere*. Once a week, when the staff came to hand in their invoices to accountant Andrew Smith, you could follow their sooty footprints all the way from the workshop, where the armour was being prepared, upstairs and through our offices. We lived with those graphite trails for *months*!'

Getting materials in the necessary quantities was frequently testing. To create the impression that the prosthetic 'skins' of the orc body-suits were shiny with sweat (something which the actors inside had no difficulty in achieving), the on-site Weta technicians would coat the latex with 'KY' lubricating-jelly. After using several hundred tubes of the kind sold in pharmacies, the manufacturer was persuaded to yield the recipe (which is eighty per cent water) and 'Weta-lube' went into production by the drum-load.

There was also the challenge of providing horse-hair plumes for helmets worn by the Rohirrim army. Having arranged to purchase quantities of horse-tails from a pet-food factory near Auckland, Tania was faced with a somewhat unsavoury task: 'Although they were frozen before being sent by an overnight courier, they tended to be somewhat "fresh" by the time they arrived…' Deciding that she couldn't ask anyone else in the Workshop to deal with the horse-tails, Tania personally undertook the task of boiling, disinfecting and clumping the hair: 'Day after day, you'd find me in the back yard in overalls and raincoat boiling away. The trouble was, Gemma got the scent of what was cooking and started haunting the yard…'

I notice a pair of cartoons on the wall (pictured below): T-shirt designs by Johnny Brough, they depict Richard and Tania as 'Papa' and 'M a m a'

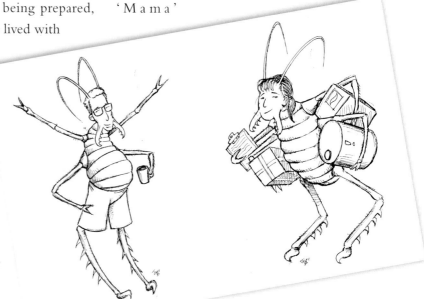

weta-bugs. 'The truth *is*,' says Tania, 'we're really *not* "Mama and Papa Weta". We *never* refer to ourselves as "The Bosses" because people don't work *for* us, they work *with* us!'

At this point, Richard returns: 'Weta Workshop is only as good as the people who've joined us and we've been extremely fortunate that they've not only seized the opportunity to do incredible work, but have taken enormous pride in being part of a team. Their unity of purpose has certainly helped make the task a lot less daunting.'

'I remember,' says Tania, 'someone saying that the greatest thrill about being at Weta, was being able to come to work and enjoy watching other people using their skills. The place has the feeling of a community – we're all working together under one roof; we meet over meals and talk with one another. That's what enabled us to ask people those impossible questions: "Can you work through the night?", "Can you give up your weekend so we can meet this or that deadline?"'

'Of course,' remarks Richard (shown far right, reviewing designs for weaponry with Peter Jackson, Weta designers, John Howe [kneeling centre] and Alan Lee). 'We're constantly juggling concepts: we have got to be a commercial company, and yet we are dealing with all the craziness of the artistic temperament! While somehow managing to fit everyone into what is essentially a "commercial box" we also do everything we can to encourage their intuition and inventiveness.'

'We want people to *want* to come to work,' says Tania. 'If you haven't got that feeling, then you need to find out why. In the middle of production, when everything was at its maddest, I used to love getting up in the morning and coming here.' She pauses and adds – with a genuine sense of it having been a privilege: 'I just couldn't wait to open the front door, knowing that I was going to be stepping right into Middle-earth!'

Back outside, on Weka Street, I find myself scrutinizing the pavement: surely as well as the imprint of King Kong's paw there ought to be – *somewhere* around here – the tracks of a cave troll or, perhaps, even the claw-marks of a Balrog…

The Man Who Builds Trees

'Trees are like people,' observes Greensmaster, Brian Massey (left), 'they grow in much the same way.' Brian heads the sixteen-man Greens Department which is responsible for all the real and artificial environments seen in *The Lord of the Rings*.

We are in the yard at Weta Workshop, the air is rich with the resinous aroma of fresh-cut wood, the ground is littered with sawn-off branches and scattered twigs; everything is covered with a snow-like settling of sawdust.

Brian's skills have helped create the remarkable forest-scapes in Middle-earth, such as the wooded valley of Rivendell and the Elven kingdom of Lothlórien. At the moment, he is on loan to Weta from the Art Department, working on – or, rather, *in* – Fangorn, home of Treebeard, the curious being – part-man-part-tree – who is first encountered by Merry and Pippin in *The Two Towers*. Treebeard is an Ent, one of an ancient race who were once the 'tree-herds' of Middle-earth but who,

over time, grew to become more and more like the trees they looked after.

Brian has a certain kinship with Treebeard: he is a knotty, bushy man and he understands trees. He needs to – he is 'building' sixty-five of them for a miniature set of Fangorn. As with all the 'miniatures' on this film, the word is deceptive – forget any ideas of those green-painted sponge trees found on model-railway layouts, these trees (built to a scale of 1:6) stand almost head-height from root to twig.

'If they remind you of gorse bushes,' says Brian, 'it's because that's what they are!' This particular strain of gorse grows, weed-like, along the wind-battered hills of the North Island coast, some two thousand feet above Cook's Strait. Brian's team has already harvested over an acre's worth, to the delight of local farmers who can scarcely believe that anyone is willing to pay to take it away!

Selecting the best bushes, however, takes an expert eye: 'All the plants have been stunted and contorted into weird configurations by the harsh climate, but we only pick the most interesting shapes – sometimes not more than one or two from an entire hillside – and then we work on them a bit.'

slightly smaller ones which – with the aid of forced perspective – will create the illusion of a sea of trees that reaches way off into the distance.'

The full-size set of Treebeard's domain presented a very different challenge, namely the building of fourteen, hundred-foot high trees – or, at least, as much of their towering trunks as could be accommodated by the limited height of the studio. Basic tree shapes were constructed out of wooden laths around steel armatures. These were then wrapped in hessian and encased in a final covering of rubber tree-bark, moulded from full-size poplars which match well with the gorse bark used for the miniature trees.

'If you're going to build trees,' says Brian, 'then all you need to remember is that they really *are* like people. To begin with, there is the proportion of trunk to height: like humans, trees grow tall and then stop growing *up* and just grow *out*. Then there is the effect of age: like us, the longer trees live, the more bent, gnarled and creaky they become!'

That, of course, is an understatement. To begin with, a couple of main stems will be chosen, spliced and glued together to form a trunk to which other limbs – carefully cut and trimmed – are then added to create tangled roots and interwoven branches. Finally, Brian adds the greenery and covers any tell-tale joints by gluing on pieces of matching bark.

'The struggle,' he says, surveying his mini-plantation, 'is getting the scale right. In close-up, gorse – even at its natural size – already has the look of an old tree about it: dense, tight foliage and weather-beaten bark. So, it's a matter of condensing things down until you have something that might be mistaken for a real tree. That's the secret!'

Except that the *true* secret is that almost imperceptible twist of the limbs which Brian gives the trees of Fangorn in order to make them seem both authentic and fantastical.

When the full complement of trees has been built, Brian and his crew will assemble their miniature forest: 'We'll place the largest and the most intriguingly-shaped trees closest to the camera and surround them with

Locating Middle-earth

It was a familiar sight, yet not quite what one expected. The customs desks at Wellington Airport, manned by four officials in crisp, white, short-sleeved shirts with ties and epaulettes and smiles that were friendly and welcoming yet, necessarily, 'official'. What was odd were the signs over the desks: not the usual 'New Zealand Citizens' and 'Other Passports', but 'Orcs', 'Trolls', 'Wizards' and 'Hobbits'…

This was a full-page newspaper advertisement produced for Wellington City Council to congratulate Peter Jackson on securing the finance to make *The Lord of the Rings*. The caption – 'Welcome to Middle Earth' – told every newspaper reader what the world's cinemagoers were still to discover: that the film version of Tolkien's epic novel was not just being made in New Zealand, but that New Zealand had itself been cast as a leading character – indeed, as the realm of Middle-earth!

'I was horrified!' Jean Johnston Wellington City Council's Film and Television Co-ordinator, is remembering a day's filming on *The Lord of the Rings* that hadn't worked out quite as intended: 'I'd arranged for the use of a disused quarry that had later been turned into a nice, quiet, grassy area. Our Parks and Gardens people, keen to be helpful, had kindly mowed the grass the night before and were intending to further tidy things up by trimming back the trees – all of which was precisely what Peter didn't want for that location! As a result, they had to bring in truckloads of uncut turf to lay on top of the mown grass!'

Everyone, apparently, saw the funny side of this overzealousness by the Parks and Gardens Department; and, if nothing else, it demonstrates the huge civic and national pride which has been generated by Peter Jackson's film trilogy.

'I feel privileged to have had the opportunity to work on this amazing movie!' enthuses Jean. 'It really has been the chance of a lifetime.' It all began for Jean in July 1998: 'Something was in the wind. Peter Jackson's company was looking for a warehouse and, whilst this might simply have been required for storing props, I guessed that it was more likely that they were seeking studio space. People were very tight-lipped about what was going on, so we just had to wait and see. Whatever it was, I knew it was going to be big.'

Big? It could scarcely have been bigger! Towards the end of August, the news broke: Peter Jackson was going to film *The Lord of the Rings*.

Wellington City Council already had a good relationship with the director, having co-operated with him on the filming of *The Frighteners*, but this project was in a different league. At Jean's suggestion Wellington's then Mayor, Mark Blumsky, sent Peter a letter of congratulation – 'That Wellington should be the base for filming one of the greatest stories of all time is fantastic' – together with some celebratory champagne.

'Thank you for your congratulations and your public support,' replied Peter, a few days later. 'I can assure you the champagne was put to its traditional use and am happy to confirm that it was a very fine drop!'

Peter also extended Mayor Blumsky a very particular – and privileged – invitation: 'Whilst many aspects of this production will be veiled in secrecy, please be aware you have an open invitation to visit the studio any time you like. Even if it means sneaking you under the radar-screen!'

For Jean, it was the beginning of a frantically busy time: 'The telephone never stopped. There were councillors ringing for information; there were people from all over the world seeking jobs; there were ex-pats wanting to know whether it was worth coming back to Wellington and, of course, the media wanting news, news, news!'

In addition to dealing with communications, there were numerous practical requirements: Weta Workshop was seeking permission to shoot test-footage at several locations; an old paint factory in Miramar was being turned into a studio which involved consents and raised various issues relating to water, drainage and parking, all of which needed to be resolved before shooting could begin.

By June 1999, Jean was working with the film's Location Managers sourcing various sites for filming in the Wellington region including the woodlands and open spaces of the Town Belt area, which rings much of the city.

Aerial maps were obtained to help *The Lord of the Rings* production company, Three Foot Six, in planning traffic-management and security. But there were also questions relating to Town Belt Legislation and – since roads would need to be closed and certain tracks blocked to public access – consultations were held with interest groups such as the Friends of the Town Belt and Mount Victoria Residents Association.

'Filming agreements,' Jean tells me, 'usually run to no more than two pages, but the document that was eventually drawn up between Wellington City Council and Three Foot Six was all of twelve pages long!'

Film permits, fire permits, building consents: the paperwork proliferated. By the beginning of September 1999, there was a shooting schedule for the Wellington locations, commencing in October: 'Being very aware of the secrecy surrounding the filming,' observes Jean,

'we never mentioned the film by its title, but since there had never been so many crew and vehicles in one area for filming before, people inevitably put two and two together. Suddenly every newspaper, television and radio station were on to it!'

'Welcome to "Wellywood"!' That was the television reporter's opening gambit when, on 11th October 1999, *The Lord of the Rings* commenced shooting in a patch of woodland on Wellington's Mount Victoria that provided the location for the scenes leading up to the hobbits' first encounter with the Black Riders.

I am watching a video-compilation of twelve months' exhaustive television coverage on the project and it is clear that from the outset the excitement was palpable.

Assorted broadcasters scuttled around, trying to give an impression of the vastness of the undertaking, peppering their reports with statistics and, in default of any hard facts, offering a tantalizing dose of speculation. Long-lens cameras managed to sneak a few illicit shots, while anyone who had anything to say – even 'no comment!' secured themselves a few moments of fame!

This was just the beginning. For the next fifteen months the interest, enthusiasm and concerns of the residents of Wellington would soon spread throughout the North and South Islands.

Two of those responsible for coping with the Middle-earthing of New Zealand were Location Administrator Matt Cooper and Supervising Unit Location Manager Richard Sharkey.

'My job,' says Richard, 'was to be the official bearer of bad news!' And, with more than 150 locations spread out across the two islands, there was frequently a fair bit of bad news to be borne.

It was Peter Jackson's visionary decision to shoot as much of the film as possible on location in his native New Zealand. Not just using any locations, but those that were the most visually arresting and, often, the most remote and inaccessible. 'I took one look at some of them,' recalls Richard, 'and shook my head: one of the biggest film crews in the world (over fifty trucks in a single unit) going into places that had gravel roads – if

you were lucky! – it was akin to trying to land a 747 on a dirt track!'

Location scout David Comer, in company with New Zealand's premier landscape photographer, Craig Potton, had flown the islands in a helicopter and located some of the most stunning scenery in the world which might be used to represent Tolkien's Middle-earth. For Richard Sharkey along with Supervising Locations Manager Robin Murphy and her colleagues Jared Connon, Harry Whitehurst and Peter Tonks, it was then a matter of enabling that scenery to be captured on film.

'Our brief,' says Richard, 'was to take the fantasy we were given and turn it into reality in terms of tents, tea, toilets, trash and the transporting of cast and crews from one remote place to another, day in and day out, so that – with luck – our version of reality could then be transformed back into fantasy!'

Joining the project just three weeks before the commencement of filming, Richard realized that he had been handed what he terms 'a seriously hot potato'. Even his previous film experience on three James Bond pictures, *Mission: Impossible* and *Mission to Mars*, didn't make him feel any more secure: 'I was scared, I don't mind telling you! I'd simply never coped with anything

on this scale before – but then, as I very soon realized, nobody else had either!'

One of Richard's first jobs was to see a man about some tents. The meeting took place – outside a scout hall in Auckland…

'These tents,' recalls Richard, 'were so old that the scouts didn't want them any more. Yet, bizarrely, here I was trying to cut a deal to buy them because our multi-million-dollar Hollywood movie *did* want them! Let me tell you, those tents were patched-up and stitched back together more times than anyone could imagine and yet, ironically, before finally giving up the ghost,

they proved to be remarkable survivors. They may have had stakes and guy-ropes and been pretty well knocked-about, but they frequently got us through where the latest, most sophisticated tents with the finest aluminium poles in the Southern hemisphere didn't stand a chance!'

In addition to the scout-tents, Richard would eventually find himself purchasing marquees and floors; over 4000 chairs and 1500 tables as well as lighting and power and provision for one of life's basic necessities: 'We built our own mobile-toilets out of 45-foot long articulated trucks, vehicles that the manufacturers would never have envisaged being put to such a use, let alone driven to the bottom of gorges and half-way up mountains!'

Locations ranged from the easy to the near impossible. In addition to the corner of a park, the edge of a sport's field and a stretch of woodland that was a mere stone's throw from a Wellington housing estate, there were acres of rolling farmland, grassy plains, ancient moss-covered forests, lakes and bogs, sheer-sided river valleys and snow-covered mountain-tops.

Several of the Middle-earth scenes were filmed at more than one location: the sequences of the Fellowship in their boats on the River Anduin were shot on the Rangitikei River, in Kaitoke Regional Park and at Poet's Corner in Upper Hutt; while sequences on the slopes of Amon Hen and the outskirts of Fangorn Forest were filmed at Paradise, Glenorchy and Mavora Lakes, south-west of Queenstown.

There was sometimes a vast distance between places that, in the story, are quite close: the hollow at Weathertop, for example, where the hobbits camp shortly before the attack of the Ringwraiths, was situated at Port Waikato on the North Island, while the surrounding countryside was filmed near Te Anau, in the southern tip of the South Island.

The South Island also provided the locations for Lothlórien Woods, the Misty Mountains, the Plains of Rohan and the road along which the Ringwraiths pursue Arwen and Frodo on their flight to the Ford of Bruinen. The striking hillside of the Dimrill Dale, onto which the Fellowship emerge following their escape from the Mines of Moria, was filmed on the bare, bone-like slopes of Mount Owen, Nelson; while Kepler Mire, near Te Anau, provided the setting for the Dead Marshes, the ancient, waterlogged battlefield through which Gollum leads Frodo and Sam on their way towards Mordor.

The North Island provided most of the sites for Mordor itself, filmed on and around Mount Ngauruhoe and the dormant (but not extinct) volcano, Mount Ruapehu. 'Several of these locations filled me with horror,' admits Richard, 'but it was not my job to veto, simply to facilitate – and, of course to make everyone aware of the possible consequences of what we were going into. I would just put all the statistics and logistics into the pot so as to allow "the grown-ups" to make what I hoped were informed decisions!'

Of the chosen locations, many were beset by all manner of potential problems. The land might be regulated by one of the Maori tribes and, where the natural environments were particularly sensitive, could also be subject to rigorous control by the DoC (Department of Conservation). In several instances, the agreement of a number of interested parties had to be secured by detailed negotiations and the drawing-up of complex legal agreements.

At which point, enter lawyer, Matt Cooper. 'The people of New Zealand, quite rightly, want to protect their environment,' says Matt, 'but, in consequence, doing anything – planting a vineyard, putting in a power station or making a movie – necessitates finding a way through a tangle of red tape.'

For any film-maker wanting to shoot on location in New Zealand, the commitment, in terms of extra budget and personnel, can be considerable: all waste and garbage has to be removed and special permission has to be granted for the use of motorized boats on lakes – other than in exceptional rescue circumstances. There may also be various specific requirements such as a guarantee to avoid areas where particular plants are growing or where birds are roosting.

'I was determined that we were going to do it right!' says Matt with passion. 'Fortunately, I had the total support of Peter and the crew. What you have to remember is that this was a New Zealand production: the Maori and all New Zealanders have a strong respect for the land, an earthy connectedness, so it wasn't difficult to convince people to be careful – to dispose of unwanted litter, to stash a cigarette butt, to leave everything as they found it.'

There was a phrase that became a watchword on the film: 'All that we ever leave behind are the footprints.' Yet quite often, thanks to the painstaking level of post-filming restoration, there weren't even any footprints left behind!

For Matt, there was another reason to respect the natural environments used in the film: 'Tolkien witnessed the devastating effects of industrialization and the way in which it changed – even destroyed – great areas of the previously untouched English countryside that he knew and loved. Because of that, it seemed especially fitting that we show our respect for this landscape and acknowledge that it was far more than just a series of fabulous movie sets.'

A devoted fan of *The Lord of the Rings*, Matt had read *The Hobbit* at the age of eight and the trilogy three years later. 'The moment I heard that Peter Jackson was planning to film *The Lord of the Rings*,' recalls Matt, 'I knew that I had to be involved.' Learning that locations were being scouted, he sent a letter to Three Foot Six, telling them that he knew Tolkien's books, was an environmental lawyer and asking whether they needed anyone to work on the obtaining of permissions. He added that he just happened to be coming to Wellington on business and that he would call and see them.

'The last part,' admits Matt, 'was a complete fib! I went to Wellington solely to get a job on the film! I turned up on their doorstep at a point when they happened to need someone to do work on health-and-safety issues and told them: "I'm your man!" I quit my job in Auckland, packed my bags and set off for Wellington with my cat, Sméagol. I started work on the very day on which New Line gave the project the green light. From then on, the job snowballed. It was an exponential learning curve and there were many days when I wondered just what I'd got myself into!'

So, too, did Richard Sharkey on his arrival from England: 'I kept asking, "Why am I here? Why are we doing this?" But, of course, nothing in life that's worth doing comes easy. That was the biggest lesson I learnt.'

Some locations, such as the mountain range known as the Remarkables, outside Queenstown on the South Island, which were used for the scenes of the Fellowship on the snowy slopes of Caradhras, were so isolated that they could be reached only by helicopter. Others were less remote, but no less fraught with difficulty.

The fact that the Helm's Deep sequences were to be shot in a quarry not far from Wellington (a location that would later double for Minas Tirith) didn't prevent Richard from having several sleepless nights: 'The set was seriously limited by the quarry walls. We did a bit of digging and blasting, but we were effectively working in a hole which didn't give us sufficient room for several hundred Elf and Uruk-hai extras to get into costume and make-up, let alone have breakfast.'

The quarry was situated on a busy main road and, since the nearest place to locate a base was on the opposite side of the road, the cast had to be transported to the quarry in fleets of buses that were forced to make hair-raising dashes across the relentless flow of traffic.

'Unfortunately,' says Richard, 'this added considerably to the time between someone finishing their bacon roll and arriving on set. However, once the immediate disgruntlement had been got over (it was, apparently, my fault that the road had been built there in the first place!), everyone made the best of it; which is something that was true of whole film: we always made the best of what was there – places and people.'

It is an attitude that New Zealander, Matt Cooper, recognizes: 'Pitching in. Getting the job done! That's the New Zealand way.' He has particular memories of filming on DoC land at Mount Ruapehu. A location had been selected: on the upper slopes, Elijah and Sean were to be shooting Frodo and Sam's ascent of Mount Doom; further down, an army of 500 extras would be filming scenes for the Prologue of the Last Alliance of Elves and Men in their conflict with Sauron. All the applications had been made and approvals secured, but when Peter Jackson arrived on set, he decided that he wanted to film at another site, two valleys away: 'Immediately, I was on the mobile phone, calling the conservation authorities, asking them to come and discuss the new site, tapping away on the laptop into the small hours of the morning, making endless changes to documentation.'

'Most people,' says Richard Sharkey, 'understand that location managers are at the mercy of the weather. But we are also at the mercy of the director and his changes of mind – which are sometimes worse than a change in the weather! Naturally, there were times when we muttered and moaned, but so what? If Peter made our lives difficult in the interests of making this the best

picture possible, then we owed it to him to help him get it right!'

Further difficulties were to emerge when filming eventually began at Ruapehu, since the area is noted for a particularly ancient growth of moss and the agreements with the DoC included undertakings for its protection. 'We laid boardwalks for cast and crew,' remembers Matt, 'but there was far too much trampling going on. So in desperation we used carpet!'

Locations Co-ordinator Alicia Williams found an office that was being refurbished but which had not yet disposed of its old carpeting. 'It sounds bizarre,' laughs Matt, 'but we shipped five tons of the stuff and carpeted the mountainside! It's not something I'd like to go through again: watching people laying it for rehearsals, taking it up for a shot and then relaying it, particularly when the weather turned bad and the carpet became totally bogged down with wet snow. However, we protected the moss and the expense of doing it in the right way was minimal within the scheme of the whole budget.'

'I have to say,' comments Richard, 'I thought we were throwing away good money on a lost cause. You can't make an omelette without breaking eggs, and I would probably have argued that if anyone agrees to 500 people acting out a battle on the side of a mountain, then they've got to expect some moss to get trampled.

But Matt and the local DoC set their sights higher than that and I now believe they were absolutely right.'

For both Richard Sharkey and Matt Cooper the most demanding location was undoubtedly, Mount Potts Station in the Rangitata Valley on the South Island. An impressive hulk of mesa, known as Mount Sunday, rising from a plain and ringed by mountains, it was to be the site for the Rohan city of Edoras.

'The first thing that struck me,' remembers Matt, 'was that, even without any buildings there, it was exactly like Alan Lee's painting of Edoras. It was a place of contrasts: I saw it on my first day in brilliant sunshine and couldn't imagine anywhere more beautiful in the world; the next time I went, there were gale-force winds and driving snow and, suddenly, it was hardest place in the world. The decision to film there was a tough one to make.'

Richard concurs: 'Consider the facts. There are no roads, to speak of, in or out of the actual location; it's a two-hour journey (four-wheel drive vehicles only) from the nearest town, where they've already told us they don't have sufficient hotel accommodation. And yet this is where we're going to be filming with upwards of 300 extras a day. Not only that, but I'm working with

a director who wants to be able to film a full 360 degrees from the highest point and, somehow, I've got to locate three acres of marquees, two acres of trucks and stabling for 200 horses without their getting into any shots! Eventually, Supervising Art Director Dan Hennah made us a large "rock" with which he created a sort of hidden corridor in which all the vehicles could be parked, unseen. But, at the time, it felt as if there were infinitely more questions than answers.

'Ultimately, the biggest question was: "Yes, it looks fantastic, but do we really have to make life quite so difficult for ourselves?" The answer, however, was beyond all argument: it was perfect!'

Mount Potts lies within what is called a South Island Statuary Acknowledgement Area, so Matt began consultations with the local authorities: the regional council and representatives of the Iwi and Ngai Tahu peoples. Since salmon rivers run across the land, it was also necessary to talk with the government department responsible for fish and game. In all, five separate applications had to be completed and negotiated.

'Any film unit is like a small army,' notes Richard, 'which is why everything requires the strategy and precision planning of a military campaign!'

To begin with, two roads needed to be built: an access road for the fleets of trucks getting to the site (the last part of which needed to look like nothing much more than a horse-track meandering past a series of burial mounds which the greens department would add to the landscape); and a service road that ran to the top of Mount Sunday by a back route that would not be seen on camera.

The five kilometres of road alone took a local contractor three months to build: the grass and top-soil were carefully lifted and preserved; the road-surfacing was laid, using gravel dredged from the local rivers. At the conclusion of filming, all the gravel would then be scraped up and deposited back into the rivers, the original earth re-laid and the tussocks of grass re-planted. As with all the locations used in the film, there was the weighty knowledge that whatever extraordinary transformations a place might undergo, as much effort, time and money would be required, afterwards, in order to return the location to its natural state.

Two bridges were built – using converted flat-bed railway cars – designed so as to ensure that there was no disturbance to the flow of the rivers or interference with the resident salmon.

A main unit-base was set up at the bottom of Mount Sunday, comprising a shingle bed onto which tents could be erected to accommodate costumes, make-up and catering; while another base was established towards the top where a few trucks could be parked before access dwindled to a last, winding road, suitable only for smaller vehicles, leading to the summit where, over a six month period, the Art Department constructed the sets for Edoras with its stockade, stables, out-buildings and the great Golden Hall of King Théoden.

'It was a mind-boggling achievement,' says Richard. 'Construction crews building sets with steel girders (instead of the usual timber); unable to use cranes because of the 140-knot winds; spending an inordinate amount of time trying to drill a single bolt into the hardest rock they'd ever come across; and in weather conditions that were so horrendous that our new-built road became impassable and the diesel froze in the vehicles!'

Matt endorses Richard's view: 'A phenomenal effort. Twelve months preparation, and for what?' He laughs and shakes his head in acknowledgement of the amazing fact he is about to share: 'For three weeks' filming!'

'Despite all the problems and headaches,' adds Richard, 'one thing is certain: it is the best and most appropriate location on the entire three films. It was made for the job.'

'Of course,' grins Matt, 'when audiences see it on film, they probably won't believe it's a real place at all! They'll think it's just another great effects shot! But I know, because I was up there; the wind was whistling, snow was falling out of a dark sky and a hawk was hovering,

wings outstretched, high above the Golden Hall. That day, I was in Edoras!'

Both men are acutely aware of what they gained from the often testing experience of creating Middle-earth on film.

'I savour all the little victories,' smiles Richard. 'At the end of every day on which we achieved what we set out to achieve having got people safely in and out and without any undue waste of time and money. I was usually the last person to leave the set at night and as I drove away, I'd feel so much joy and excitement that tears would come to my eyes. *Yes! We've done it! We've got it! And we haven't let the side down!* They were often short-lived little victories, because I was usually on my way to sort out some other problem and tomorrow is always another day!'

And for Matt? 'It was an extraordinary and remarkable experience: to go from wearing a suit in a law office to finding myself a part of this amazing venture – working flat out, round the clock, in extreme conditions and then, in the midst of all the exhaustion, to be watching dawn come up on the plains of Rohan or the sun setting on Mount Doom.'

A Hall Fit for a King

'The effect I wanted to create was of a building that was solid and highly-decorated: made of timber, but girded and held together by heavily-wrought pieces of bronze, iron and gold used both to embellish and to strengthen.'

Alan Lee is talking about his conceptual art for Edoras, the stronghold of the horsemen of Rohan. The creative process began in a very particular way: 'A lot of my drawings start as a kind of exploration. I imagine myself entering a place, walking around and visualizing what I might see at any point.'

As with all his explorations, Alan's guide-book is Tolkien's original narrative which contains several tantalizingly brief descriptions of Edoras. We are told that Meduseld, the Golden Hall, has the appearance of having been 'thatched with gold'; while within it is long and wide, high-roofed and many-pillared. A place of half-light and shadows, the gloom accentuated by the smoke from the open fire and the ancient tapestries hung upon the walls.

'The Golden Hall of King Théoden,' says Alan, 'had to be regal and majestic. The intention of the original builder would have been to direct the visitor's gaze – via an avenue of ornately carved pillars – to the king's throne on its raised dais at the far end of the hall. So we designed capitals for those pillars that used emblems appropriate to a semi-nomadic, hunting people like the Rohirrim: sun-bursts, hounds and hawks, boars' heads and rams' skulls.'

Above all, there was the recurrent horse motif: from the finials on the rooftops (cutting dramatic silhouettes on the skyline) to carved pillars and

embroidered banners. The many and varied uses of the equine form are highly stylized, accentuating the sinewy strength of the animal on which the culture of Rohan was so dependent.

In drawing the great doors to the Golden Hall, Alan adorned them with a dragon. This seemingly fanciful addition was, in fact, inspired by a passing reference in one of Tolkien's appendices to *The Lord of the Rings* which told of the slaying of the dragon, Scatha, by the mighty Rohan hero, Fram. The same source also provided the story of

Léod, the tamer of wild horses, who was thrown by a white foal and died from striking his head against a rock – a tragic event graphically commemorated on one of the hangings in the Great Hall.

However important the decoration, it was also essential that the structures should be functional: so that the exteriors of the buildings could be constructed on location, while the interior sets (despite employing the various tricks and cheats of the studio set-builder) would look equally authentic.

'Much of the historical reference for this period of architecture,' explains Alan, 'is based on supposition, because early wooden structures simply haven't survived, so the starting point for the Golden Hall of Edoras was

Heorot, the hall in *Beowulf*, together with Beorn's Hall, which Tolkien describes and depicts in *The Hobbit*, and structural hints from historic wooden buildings from other cultures such as those of Norway and Japan.'

Alan and Helen Stevens, the draughtsperson assigned to the job, estimated the load-bearing ability of the timbers and applied that information to a scale model: 'We needed to understand, and convey, a sense of the weight and strain that these highly decorated pillars would have had to carry. It was essential that – inside and out – the Golden Hall should look as if it were a real, as opposed to an imagined, building.'

Drawing his inspiration from a reference in the book to the heavy, double-barred doors to the hall, Alan devised a complex locking system with two sliding, pivoting beams that could, in turn, be lowered and secured in place. Although, in the film, they are never seen being used, they were, nevertheless, designed and built to work.

'For all its magnificence,' says Alan, 'the Golden Hall is *old* – indeed, it was old even before Théoden's time!' It was important, therefore, to create a feeling of age: wall-hangings with their scenes from Rohan history and mythology were carefully worn down, so that the once-vibrant colours had the faded look of cloth dulled by age and dust. 'The effect of ageing,' notes Alan, 'is very subtle; it needs to be unobtrusive, almost subliminal. And yet, when Gandalf, Aragorn and the others first enter Meduseld it should feel to them as it might feel to us were we to enter a building from the Elizabethan era.'

For all its antiquity, the Golden Hall has sophistication that some might find surprising. Alan Lee is unrepentant: 'There is a tendency – because all the evidence isn't there – for us to look back at the Dark Ages and see them only in a muddy way that assumes that life was rough and unrefined. But consider the artefacts that remain – jewellery, metalwork, weapons – they are so exquisite that it is surely quite unreasonable to believe that these people had such beautiful possessions and yet lived in rough-hewn places devoid of similar finesse. *That* is my justification for proposing a building that is as magnificent as King Théoden's Golden Hall.'

Setting the Scene

 'Go in and take a look around,' says Dan. I hesitate. I am standing in front of one of the most famous doors in literature – round and green with a door-knob in the exact middle.

It is a moment of pure magic: I forget the fact that I am in a vast, somewhat dingy cavern of a sound-stage. I forget the other curious and intriguing sights that, only seconds before, were holding my fascinated gaze: bundles of fire-proof faggots for the funeral pyre in the Stewards' Tombs; stalls from the stables at Edoras, decorated with a gilded frieze of running horses. Instead, I am now drawn, inexorably, towards that green door…

After all, it was from this very door that the road began that carried first Bilbo and then Frodo away on their adventures. The road that led to Rivendell, the Misty Mountains, Lothlórien and, beyond, to the Land of Shadow. The road that goes ever on and on…

My guide is Dan Hennah, Supervising Art Director, Set Decorator and as exuberant a companion as you could wish for when travelling in Middle-earth. Bearded and with a mane of wild grey hair, Dan would (were he considerably shorter) make a rather splendid dwarf. Once again, he invites me to go in. I knock – an absurd whimsy! – and push open the door.

No sign of Bilbo. No sign, either, of the Ring lying on the tiled floor of the hallway, waiting for Frodo to pick it up. Instead, there's a sudden glare of fluorescent lights and a sound of whining drills and thudding hammers.

Dan follows me in, pointing out the elaborate hinge, swirling over the inside of the door with fernlike tracery. 'Hand-beaten steel,' he says, 'antiqued to look like wrought-iron.'

I remark on the impressive detailing and Dan chuckles. 'Yes! You wouldn't believe the discussions that went on about this place! There must have been several hours of serious debate on the subject of doorknobs alone!'

The fastidiousness shows: in the decorative carvings of oak-leaves and acorns and the round, leaded-light windows; in everything from the lovingly-polished tree-roots, pushing their way into the hobbit-hole, to the fresh-scrubbed, terracotta floor-tiles. 'Fibreboard,' reveals Dan, pleased that I am fooled, 'painted and hard-coated.'

The hall leads, via a small vestibule, to the living-room with its semi-circular fireplace ornamented with a

cramped that Ian McKellen's Gandalf would be forever banging his head against the beams.

Leaving Bag End, we head for the offices of the Art Department. As we walk, Dan tells me about his approach to the project: 'Having read *The Lord of the Rings* at least six times over the years, I saw our job as being to create the living detail of Tolkien's world. That's why we were forever going back to the book: we'd read the script to find out *what* was happening, but we'd always consult the book to find out *why*!'

It has been a phenomenal undertaking: four hundred artists and craftsmen designing and building a total of three hundred sets on a relentlessly demanding cycle. At any given time there were three sets in construction, three being used for filming and three in the process of being demolished! 'The only way to cope' says Dan, 'was to take the date on which filming on a particular sequence was scheduled to begin, and chart everything *backwards*: if a set was likely to take three days to dress, four days to paint and three weeks to build, then we'd know that we *had* to start construction on a certain date and no later.'

Not that everything always went according to plan – especially, as Dan vividly recalls, towards the end of principle filming: 'There were five units, all shooting at the same time, so we had to have shifts of workers constructing

carved garland of bulrushes. Here set-builders and finishers are busily painting the walls and varnishing the simulated wooden door-surrounds, readying the set for the filming of various 'pick-up shots' needed for *The Fellowship of the Ring*.

The tunnel-like passageway is not only curved, but also twists to one side: 'It's called a compound curve,' Dan explains, 'probably the most difficult bit of construction in Bag End and one that we had to get right at two different scales on two different sets.'

This is the full-size set, designed so that Elijah Wood would be in perfect scale with his hobbit surroundings. Outside, round the back, is another, small-scale set, designed to be so

sets twenty-four hours a day, non-stop! Keeping all that rolling was…' he hesitates, smiles and shrugs, 'well, let's just say it was fairly demanding…'

Anything – but usually something totally unforeseen – could threaten a snarl-up in the schedule: 'You build an idyllic forest set with an artificial river,' says Dan, as we make our way upstairs, 'and, for some bizarre reason, instead of running clear and sparkling, the water looks as if come from a scummy sewage pond.'

Inevitably, there was a good deal of brinkmanship: 'We often finished a set only an hour or two before the start of filming. I'll never forget the Glittering Caves: we'd worked through the night to achieve a very particular look and we were still painting as the crew walked in the door. There we were, frantically throwing handfuls of party-glitter onto the wet paint as the cameramen finished off their cups of tea and started setting up. Making magic happen is never easy.'

At the head of the stairs is a large drawing of Saruman, posed in a pastiche of those famous American war-time recruitment posters: 'Uncle Saruman needs YOU!'

Walking through the corridor of the Art Department is like strolling through the pages of an illustrated edition of *The Lord of the Rings*. Pinned along the walls are drawings, paintings and inspirational photographs for each of the many and varied locations in the story. The artwork is predominantly by Alan Lee and John Howe, interspersed with vivid, impressionistic colour renderings by Paul Lasaine (below), who passed through the Art Department on his way to become an Art Director on Visual Effects. There are even examples of Tolkien's own visualizations.

'Our aim,' says Dan, looking at one of the author's original sketches, 'has been to stay true to Tolkien's vision and to the accepted versions of that vision.'

There we see the gruesome torture-chamber in Barad-dûr; here, the serene elegance of Celeborn's chamber in Lothlórien, which Dan disarmingly describes as 'an ethereal, art nouveau tree-hut'!

Images from all three films crowd in upon the eye: Weathertop; Amon Hen; The Black Gates and Shelob's Lair: a labyrinth of tunnels, like upside-down arches with acid-pitted rock above and smooth spider-patinaed surfaces below.

Building so many exotic locales required all manner of engineering skills and industrial equipment, such as the giant pumps used to circulate the several thousand gallons of water essential to create the shimmering waterfall curtain for the Window on the West.

The Art Department also engaged in a good deal of lateral thinking. The problem, for example, of creating the *ithildin* lettering on the Doors of Durin (which can only be read by moon or starlight) was eventually resolved using the reflective material normally utilized for 'cat's-eye' motorway markings.

Finding the right materials in sufficient quantities was always challenging. Since real trees on set have a maximum 'leaf-life' of five days (due to the intense heat of the studio lights), millions of *silk* leaves had to be

'Normally,' says Dan, 'if a miniature set is required, it's built afterwards – scaled down from the full-size set. But not with Helm's Deep! Weta Workshop had built the miniature long before, in the earliest days of the project, so we had the somewhat anxious-making task of scaling-up and building our set based upon the model.'

At the end of the corridor is the office of Production Designer Grant Major, the man imported from China to help foliate the woods of Middle-earth.

ultimately responsible for resolving many such dilemmas. 'This film,' he tells me, 'has been epic in every sense of the word.'

In contrast, the buildings at Edoras were roofed with authentic thatching: 'We bought a ten acre field of wheat,' remembers Dan, 'harvested and stooked it in the traditional way, stored it in a rodent-proof shed and transported it to the Edoras location by the truckload.'

Grant, who was designer on Peter Jackson's *The Frighteners* and *Heavenly Creatures*, believes that the commitment required by *The Lord of the Rings* was essentially the same as that on any other movie: 'Every film, if you do your job well, demands that you get into it body and soul. The only difference here was one of scale: it was the same dedication – but to the power of three!'

Six full-time thatchers were on hand throughout construction. All self-taught (thatching is not an established craft in New Zealand), they secured the bundles of thatch with plastic stripping and used brad-guns to fix it to the plywood roofs. It worked, as Dan proudly points out: 'Not only did it *look* right but, despite being subjected to 140 kilometre-an-hour winds, every bit of thatching was still in place when we finished.'

The office walls are covered with more sketches and drawings as well as with charts and schedules.

'We have created everything from richly-decorated palaces to crudely-hewn caves and each environment has offered a different challenge; but our work is always geared towards one thing: creating an environment in which a dramatic scene takes place that tells the story.'

We stop beside a series of sketches of Helm's Deep. The Art Department constructed whole sections of the ancient stronghold in a quarry near Wellington, including the causeway, the courtyard, the tops of two walls, and, at full height, the massive Deeping Wall which Tolkien describes as being wide enough for four men to walk abreast.

Consider the interior of Orthanc: on one level there was the task of constructing an edifice that has supposedly been carved from obsidian rock. In set-building terms, this involved chipping and shaping walls out of polystyrene, plastering and then painting them with black lacquer and finally, to give the surface an impression of depth, applying a coating of wax. There was also the requirement, as Grant explains, to make it the right setting in which to confront Saruman: 'It was vital that Orthanc suited the dark, fractured, psychological personality of Saruman, because believing in a setting helps us believe in a character.'

Like many others working on the film, Grant frequently refers to the need for places, creatures and things – however fantastic – to look *real*: 'Audiences need to be helped towards suspending their disbelief. We have to enable them to believe that a hobbit or a Balrog might actually exist!'

Grant is also utterly pragmatic as to how this has been achieved. 'It was,' he says, 'all down to three things: budgeting, budgeting – and *budgeting!* We began, naïvely with many unanswered questions. When in doubt, the general principle was: "Do something else for now and we'll work it out later!" But, eventually, "later" came, and we began to realize exactly what we had taken on.'

More and bigger sets were being called for and all of them were being required for longer than had been originally estimated: 'I saw my role as not merely delivering what was wanted on time and to budget but also protecting the quality of what was being produced.'

Attempting to work wonders and make marvels on a day-to-day basis was its own reward: 'It was immensely fulfilling to work on such a big canvas – to be able to spend so much money to create such a big world. But it had to be done as a partnership of many talents.'

Key figures in that partnership were Conceptual Artists Alan Lee and John Howe (shown above sketching before the party at Cannes), who, between them, were to shape much of the look of the film. The two illustrators, whose careers had already taken them deep into Middle-earth, brought an individual and combined vision to the project that would carry through from drawing-board to screen. 'It always began with Alan and John's pictures,' reflects Grant, 'even before they both arrived in New Zealand, Peter Jackson would be talking about a setting or a scene and he'd reach for one of their paintings and say: "It's got to look like this!" When they joined the project, I simply wanted to harness their extraordinary talents and facilitate the creation of the world they envisaged.'

Each artist brought a particular, and quite different, approach to the project: Alan Lee, living on Dartmoor, England, contributed a strong sense of the natural, elemental world and what can only be described as a quintessential 'Englishness' to the film. In contrast, the gift of John Howe – born in Canada, living in Switzerland and resolutely drawn towards the gothic and outlandish – was one of fire and darkness and the shadowy forms of monstrous creatures.

John Howe is now back home in Switzerland, after eighteen months of working on the project, but Alan Lee is in the next office and still at the drawing-board!

'I draw in a very unconscious way,' says Alan (pictured below, imagining Hobbiton), sketching as he talks, 'I don't actually sit down and think up an image and then draw it. I'll start off with almost nothing more than a feeling and maybe some sense of shape and movement and then just put the pencil on the paper and see what it wants to do that day.'

He is working on a drawing for the design of the Grey Havens in one of the final scenes in the third movie. Having a conversation with Alan Lee is a little like sketching: it is sometimes direct and to the point, sometimes meandering and discursive; it is sometimes a slow, thoughtful process, sometimes one in which the ideas, like pencil lines on paper, come quick, thick and fast.

'The way I have always worked previously,' explains Alan, 'is in making

sketches that eventually lead to a finished picture. On this project, it is *all* about sketching. There's nothing between your mind and the image – no colour and very little composition – so it takes a number of stages out of the equation. I find that very exciting, because it is still heading towards a finished picture, with the one difference that it will be a *moving* picture!'

Working on large sheets of acid-free backing paper ('it's very heavy with a great texture') and using either charcoal or pencil ('anything from a "B" to a "5B"'), Alan has produced more than a thousand sketches – and the work is not finished yet!

There are upwards of another two thousand drawings in dozens of sketchbooks, large and small. 'I am an inveterate doodler: if I've got a surface within reach and a pencil in my hand then it invariably gets covered with drawings!'

Alan leafs through a couple of sketchbooks filled with emblematic designs of birds and horse-heads; lamp-stands for Saruman's chamber; a statue in Rivendell; an icon for Minas Tirith or ideas for Gandalf's three staffs – all of which are based on or incorporate the 'G' rune. On one page there's a detailed drawing of a hobbit-hole, complete with tethered goat and beehive, on another a preliminary sketch for the Witch King…

'I've probably done more drawings for this project,' speculates Alan, 'than in the whole of the rest of my illustrating career! After years of working on my own, it's been particularly stimulating to be part of a team, sharing in everyone's energy and enthusiasm.'

At the head of that team is Peter Jackson. 'Peter is the *real* artist,' says Alan modestly, 'the rest of us are merely

attempting to help realize his vision. Most of the time we seem to get it right, but every now and again, we've had to throw ideas out and start again. Personally, I've found it stimulating to be told to try something different or to be more exciting: as an established illustrator, I've not been told that for a very long time!'

That is how it begins: with Peter's initial vision translated into concepts by Alan Lee and John Howe, which are then rationalized and budgeted by Grant and Dan. Next, draughtspersons and model-makers take the sketches and designs and work out ways to turn them into places that could actually be built. After which, under the watchful eye of Dan Hennah and a group of supervisors – Ed Mulholland (Construction), Kerry Dunn (Set Finisher), Sam Genet (Sculptor), Matt Wratten (Engineering) and Brian Massey (Greensmaster) – an army of workers transform the final, cumulative vision into three-dimensional reality.

'Of course,' says Alan, 'no one person can fully claim the authorship of the project. I feel more like an

of Khazad-dûm.

'For Moria,' Alan tells me, 'we wanted to evoke a feeling of somewhere that, whilst having been hacked from the mountain's roots, was sophisticated and refined. The inspiration came from the straight lines of Dwarvish runes and gave a look that was geometric and crystalline.'

There are several plans mapping the different areas in the mines and an elaborate (and unused) suite of sketches showing the convoluted route – involving gantries, walkways, planks and a bucket on a rope – by which Gollum may have tracked the Fellowship through the mines.

A vast amount of thought went into creating settings for the journey through Moria, a pivotal sequence in *The Fellowship of the Ring*. Alan speculates, for example, on the enormous size of the Dwarrowdelf chamber: 'There is no logical reason for the pillars to be so tall or, indeed, for anything in Moria to have been built on such a large scale, and yet it doesn't feel odd, suggesting as it does the scale of the Dwarves' craft and imagination.'

There is also the fateful Bridge: 'Tolkien's description is clear enough – slender, lacking kerb or rail, spanning the chasm with one curving spring of fifty feet. Some artists have drawn it as thin as a knife-blade but it needed to look like a bridge that real people could run across. In our conception of Moria it is the one thing that is curved and is, perhaps, all the more powerful as an image because a curve is part of a ring…'

architect: initiating a process and following it through as far as possible, while learning to let go and accept that others have to take what I've drawn and make it tangible.'

For an hour or more we flip through stack after stack of drawings (some of which run across more than one sheet of paper) with Alan occasionally commenting on a particular look or effect: 'Orthanc had to be striking; angular, sharp and fang-like…' or 'Caras Galadhon, the Elves' City of the Trees, needed buildings that were graceful, flower-like and slightly other-worldly.'

A sketch of Moria in the glory-days before its ruination by Orcs leads to several hundred more, tracing the Fellowship's journey from Moria Gate via Balin's Tomb and the great hall of Dwarrowdelf to the Bridge

Alan also produced many concepts for a possible sequence depicting the struggle between Gandalf and the Balrog: their fall, deep into the abyss beneath Khazad-dûm and, deeper still, through fire and water, to the uttermost foundations of stone; then their long, wearisome climb, by secret ways and the many thousand steps of the Endless Stair, to the highest peak of the Misty Mountains and a final, cataclysmic confrontation. He sifts through his sketches of the Endless Stair which twists and turns in a maze of Escher-like illusions: 'I wanted to convey a feeling that they are struggling in an unreal space – somewhere between life and death – Gandalf pursuing the Balrog up, down and around; now coming towards you; now rushing away; a roller-coaster of a tracking-shot, during which the whole axis might turn, creating the vertiginous feeling of not knowing which way up you are!'

From the Endless Stair, we move on to Fangorn, the Ruins of Osgiliath and the Paths of the Dead. Our conversation could continue for as long as there are drawings to look at, but Alan needs to return to his sketch of the Grey Havens, since John Baster and several other model-makers are waiting to start work on the miniature set. As Alan takes up his pencil again, Dan Hennah returns and whisks me off to visit some more sets.

A born storyteller, Dan has dozens of tales about the unexpected problems of recreating Middle-earth on various tracts of New Zealand countryside and, even, in the reasonably controlled environment of the studio. 'Everybody will tell you about the weather,' he laughs, 'floods and freeze-ups; days when we were snowed in and others when we were rained out. We built an entire set beside a river in Queenstown for the Fellowship's landing at Parth Galen and, before the film crew could arrive, the river rose fifteen metres and washed the whole thing away!'

Dry spells were also problematic. Built on farmland near Hamilton, the location sets for Hobbiton were established a full year before filming began to allow the

landscaping to have settled into a natural look in time for a spring shoot. Then, however, the Hobbiton scenes were rescheduled for mid-summer: 'To our horror,' says Dan, 'the rolling green hills turned into rolling *brown* hills, so we found ourselves having to set up an entire irrigation system in order to get the grass green again!'

Ironically, a later location – for the Battle of the Pelennor Fields – was found to be rather *too* verdant, a problem solved by the Greens Department which concocted a solution derived from the natural fatty-acids found in coconuts. 'We sprayed it onto twenty acres of grassland, which miraculously turned brown over night and stayed that way for ten days before returning, completely unharmed, to its natural colour.'

Grass, it seems, is a constant challenge – especially on studio sets where it needs to look real, but not as neat and tidy as the uniform turfs obtainable from the average garden-centre. The answer is to negotiate with a turf company to 'grow on' some of their grass to a length of six inches which can then be, literally, combed and trimmed to shape on set.

We arrive at Studio A: part of a former paint factory, it is fifty metres long by twenty-five metres wide and nine metres high, and has formerly been Galadriel's glade, Elrond's chamber at Rivendell and the interior of Orthanc. It is now being prepared for pick-up shots in the Golden Wood of Lothlórien.

'I have to say,' remarks Dan, with some pride, 'we are rather good with trees!' That is true; of the trees we are standing among, it is not immediately obvious which are real and which are artificial.

'We've even infiltrated them into genuine forest locations,' Dan continues. 'We were in a beech forest and had added several huge tree trunks of our own – nine metres each of wood and steel! When the crew arrived, a number of people stared in amazement and asked how on earth we'd managed to find this incredible forest with all these enormous trees – until, of course, they looked up and saw that the trees suddenly stopped at mid-height!'

At the other end of the studio is the fire-charred interior of one of the caverns beneath Isengard. Putting his shoulder to a huge panel of smoke-stained rock (conveniently fitted with casters), Dan swings it into place, creating a craggy, claustrophobic hollow that will be used to film a scene in which Saruman's fighting Uruk-hai mark one another with the sign of the White Hand.

The cavern walls are made out of polyurethane foam, using moulds taken from casts of genuine rock-forms. Supported on a wooden framework, the rocks are 'pinned' together – using kebab sticks! – and given a coating of spray-foam which, simultaneously, bonds them and fills any gaps. Paint and texturing are then applied, set dressing is added (in this case, pit-props, ropes and pulley-wheels) along with suitable effects (flame-bars and smoke-machines) and the desired look – hot and hellish – is spectacularly achieved.

I look from one end of the studio to the other: here, great

banks of flame-seared rock; over there, the greens and golds of a forest glade. The juxtaposition of two film sets, two vastly different realms – one a nightmare of oppressive darkness; one a dream of radiant light. It is impossible not to be awed by the magic of the film-makers' craft.

'Of course,' says Dan Hennah, 'on film you will see perhaps fifty per cent of what you see here. And, of what *is* seen by an audience, much will go unnoticed because these are just the settings for the drama – not the drama itself.'

Passing through the studio doors, we find ourselves back in what we confidently refer to as the *real* world. 'In our business,' reflects Dan, 'people only notice what we do when we get it wrong!' He thinks for a moment, then adds: 'It's not much good if it's an ego-trip you're after; but it's how it has to be: do it well, do it right - *and nobody will notice!*'

From Bag End to Barad-dûr

'Bag End is *our* Bag End, you know!' John Howe (shown right, exploring some questions of scale on the hobbit-sized set) is being playful, though I am almost fooled by the serious look which he gives me and the thoughtful way in which he strokes his beard.

'*Our*' Bag End is really *John's* Bag End: a painting which he made for a map-book on which the two of us collaborated in 1995. Reproduced on the cover of *There and Back Again: The Map of The Hobbit*, it shows the hallway of Mr Baggins' home with the front door standing open onto a beckoning landscape of fields and woods and distant, misty hills.

'That was precisely what Peter wanted: to be able to walk into the cover of the map. So, that's where I started.'

It was, however, a limited view of Bag End: the carved decoration on the beams and panelling, the settle, chest and chandelier, the distinctive round windows, the tiled floor, the door…

As John designed the other rooms in Bag End, it became clear that this hobbit hole was going to look significantly different from other dwellings in Hobbiton. 'To me,' says the Canadian-born artist, 'Hobbiton felt like what England felt like what England

would be – if you had never *seen* England! And since Mr Baggins is viewed rather like the local squire, I wanted Bag End to be the English manor-house, more luxurious and refined than the homes of his rustic neighbours, but still totally "Olde Worlde" – with the *e*'s on the end, of course!'

Since the artist now lives in Switzerland, it is not too surprising that there is also a strong continental bias to the design, such as the addition of wooden shutters on the *inside* of the windows.

'Perhaps,' says John, 'it can best be described as a continental foray into fantasy England!' Art nouveau is a specific influence but in a somewhat unusual manifestation: 'Art nouveau architecture can look stupendous – I love the curves and the use of natural forms – but it is always so *rigid!*' John's vision of Bag End is a direct reaction to that rigidity: 'I've always dreamed of creating a sort of *humanized* art nouveau that would have the same elegance, but with room to move and breathe – and even, to hang a few pictures on the wall!'

There were many other challenges awaiting John beyond Bag End, such as the Dark Tower of Barad-dûr: 'Once again, at Peter's request, I started with one of my own images, but each time I worked on it, I'd find myself becoming more and more extravagant, going deeper, going higher!'

Indeed, for the first time in many years of depicting places in Middle-earth, John went to the topmost pinnacle of Barad-dûr. 'I'd always avoided drawing the top – the place from where the Eye of Sauron looks out across Mordor, searching for the Ring. I didn't know how to illustrate it. Now, I had to go all the way – three thousand feet up – to discover exactly what it looked like – and then draw it!'

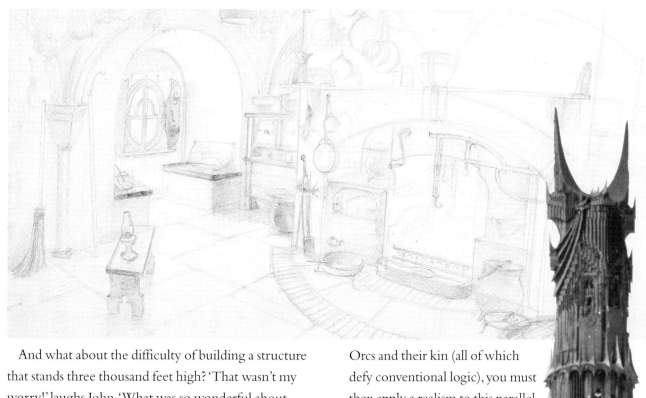

And what about the difficulty of building a structure that stands three thousand feet high? 'That wasn't my worry!' laughs John. 'What was so wonderful about working on this film was that nobody ever said: "How are we supposed to build a tower that tall?" Just as nobody said: "How do you think a single hinge is going to carry such a large, heavy, round door?" Nevertheless, despite –

or perhaps *because* of that – we attached great importance to a notion of historical reality in a fantasy universe.'

In such a universe, John argues, it is necessary to accept such fantastical elements: 'Having conceded the possibility of absurdly tall towers that are a physical manifestation of the owner's persona, or the existence of Balrogs, fell-beasts,

Orcs and their kin (all of which defy conventional logic), you must then apply a realism to this parallel "reality". Of course it's incredibly empirical, but I *did* pay attention to Bilbo's front door and how to hang it! Honest!'

As John Howe recalls, they were confronted, from the very beginning, by both the extraordinariness of the task and the freedom with which to accomplish it: 'On the day we arrived, Peter told us: "If you guys can draw it, we can build it!" Well, we *did*, and they *have*!'

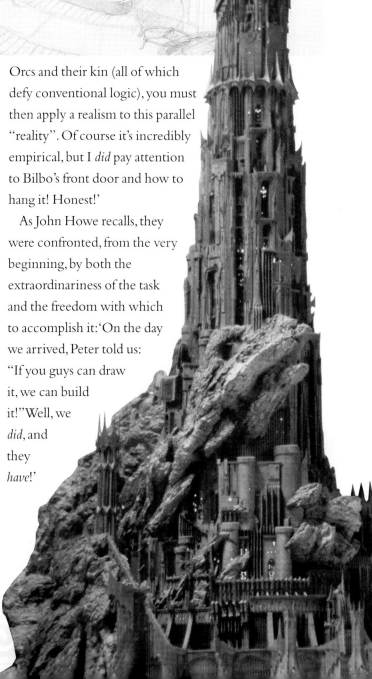

It's a Small World

Night. Silence. We move from a large stony outcrop across a barren deserted plain towards the stronghold of Helm's Deep where the beleaguered people of Rohan will soon face a terrifying attack from Saruman's Uruk-hai.

At the feet of the mountains, a great fold in the rocks forms the Deep, an ancient refuge protected by the mighty Deeping Wall. A steep ramp leads up to Helm's Gate and, rising high above into the darkness, is the tower known as the Hornburg. From a culvert beneath the wall, the Deeping-stream – gleaming a curious, luminous green in the moonlight – runs out across the plain, widening, at one point, into a small green pool.

The silence is broken by a voice in the dark: 'Nice puddle!'

It is 8.30 a.m. and we are in Peter Jackson's viewing theatre watching the 'rushes' of the previous day's filming on the miniature set of Helm's Deep.

The green 'puddle' has been created by the use of fluorescent paint and ultraviolet light and will, eventually, be replaced by digital water. As the shot is re-run again and again and discussed by various voices in the darkness Richard Taylor, head of Weta Workshop, whispers an explanation: 'Since there'll be ten thousand digitally-created Uruk-hai crossing that plain, the guys in "Digi" need to know exactly where that puddle is, so they can create a "splash" if any of the Uruk-hai happen to march through it.'

I am about to ask what is probably a rhetorical question: why add such a seemingly trivial detail that must involve a multiplicity of costly, time-consuming tasks? Before I can do so, however, the lights in the theatre come up and Visual Effects Director of Photography Alex Funke and his team are off to grab a bite of breakfast before grappling with the complexities of another day's filming in their miniature version of Middle-earth.

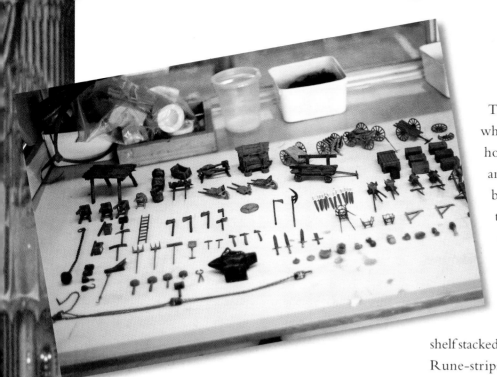

The first thing to catch my eye is an array of what might be described as medieval doll's-house furnishings: wooden stools, benches and buckets, grindstones, wheelbarrows brooms and braziers. On a nearby table are trays of moss, ferns and pieces of bark; and a collection of pots containing gravel and pebbles, carefully graded according to size.

There are cans of lighter-fuel, bottles of turpentine and baby-oil, a paint-pot labelled 'Rivendell Green' and shelf upon shelf stacked with tins and boxes marked: 'Khazad-dûm Rune-strips', 'Isengard Machinery' and 'Moria Cemetery Stairs'.

I express my amazement at how real the miniature version of Helm's Deep looks on film. 'That,' says Richard Taylor, 'is in no small part down to Alan Lee's superb architectural designs. I sometimes think Alan should have been around nine hundred years ago and in charge of defending Britain!'

There is a choice of exits from the theatre: one door leads into Weta Digital, the other takes you to Weta Workshop. We take the Workshop route and immediately I am Gulliver in Lilliput…

I pick up a minute figure of a bowman in silver plastic and Richard laughs: 'One of the first jobs we ever did on this film was scouring the world in search of 35th and 72nd scale plastic medieval soldiers! We found and bought 75,000 of them – very probably the entire world's stock! We had teams of people sticking them onto boards to create blocks of armies, so that Peter could start choreographing the battles.'

There are more boxes: 'Ping-Pong Balls', 'Paper

Looking up, I suddenly realize that Gulliver is now in Brobdingnag! Built to a mind-numbing 76th scale and soaring thirty feet above me, to within inches of the roof, is the Dark Tower of Barad-dûr, Sauron's grim bastion in the Land of Mordor. Fang-like and forbidding, encrusted with fortifications, pock-marked with windows like thousands of tiny, lidless eyes, it is a three-dimensional realization of an illustration by John Howe.

It is, I suggest to Richard Taylor, preposterous to refer to such a structure as a 'miniature'! 'True!' he agrees, 'which is why we've taken to calling them "bigatures" or "megatures"!'

Like so many aspects of filming *The Lord of the Rings*, it is all comes down to matters of scale. 'What we always have to remember,' says Richard, 'is that these great edifices are actually *populated* by beings of some kind, so whatever size within the picture Alan Lee or John Howe draws an average five-foot-six high creature, determines the scale of the miniature. With every new drawing, I am frantically searching for that figure! Sometimes, it seems little more than a dot on the structure and then I know that we're in for another colossal miniature!'

In truth, Richard loves confronting the challenges of his miniature kingdom and recreating the places imagined by the two artists: 'Our aim has been, quite simply, to facilitate Alan and John's combined vision, because we knew that it was going to be the *best* vision possible.'

Doilies' and 'Spiced Tea-bag Flocking'. My puzzlement at these items is answered by Miniatures Builder Mary Maclachlan (pictured above with John Baster), who is working nearby: 'Ping-Pong balls,' she tells me, 'are really useful: cut in half they make perfect bowls or – the other way up – small domes for buildings. As for the doilies, we use those for ornamental trims – you simply cut off part of the frilly bit, stick it onto a fascia, blend it in with filler and you have wonderful architectural detailing!'

And 'Spiced Tea-bag Flocking'? 'Well,' explains Mary, 'one day, when I was making a cup of herbal-tea, the tea-bag broke and the stuff inside looked jolly interesting! I discovered that it makes perfect peat-litter for miniature forest floors! It's pure serendipity, of course, but now, whenever I have any new tea-bags, I always pull one apart to see what's inside! The great thing about *spiced* tea-bags is that they're not only useful – they smell nice, too!'

Not that it isn't sometimes a scary prospect, as Mary Maclachlan confides: 'I tell you, it's a model-maker's nightmare! You've two weeks to build the model but "Don't worry," they tell you, "it'll only be used in a long shot to create a broad brush-stroke for a setting." Then they get it on set and there's the camera going in really close, shooting perhaps as little as two inches from the surface! It gives you heart-attacks!'

Building Barad-dûr was particularly demanding. It began early, in 1999, with John Howe's drawing and was then constructed as a two-metre high maquette. 'On most productions,' observes Richard, 'miniature work doesn't kick-start until a project is well into production. From the outset of *The Lord of the Rings*, however, Peter wanted to see Tolkien's world as fully visualized as possible. So we made elaborate architectural maquettes which enabled Peter to view them in great detail with a "lipstick camera", an incredibly small device that allows

you to "enter" a miniature, as if you were walking around on a full-sized set.'

Several of these maquettes – including Barad-dûr – were also filmed as wide-shots, but, eventually, larger scale versions had to be built. 'This was obviously going to be big,' remembers Mary, 'and there was a tightish time-limit on the job. After a huge amount of work, it was finished and Peter came and took a look at it. *Disaster!* He felt that it somehow wasn't capturing what *he* saw in his mind's eye: yes, it was true to John's drawing, but it wasn't quite *his* Barad-dûr... I went for a very long walk, sobbing in despair: how could I find that "X-factor" that Peter was looking for?'

Time was running out, but with assistance from Weta sculptor Ben Wootten, Mary started re-working the miniature: 'The atmosphere was electric! We were within an inch of what Peter wanted! The clock was ticking and we were sculpting like crazy! Then, somehow, we *got* it! Peter saw it and just said: "That's lovely..." And we collapsed!'

Mary smiles, remembering, and then adds: 'You always know when there's something extra in your craft that wants to come out – if only you can find it and set it free! And if there's ever been a film that can drag a little bit extra out of people, then this is it!'

The evidence of that is all around: the Stone Trolls (standing four and a half metres high), the giant figures of the Argonath, beneath which the Fellowship sail after leaving Lothlórien (not the sky-scraper size that they appear in the film, but larger than the average public statue); the great, many-columned hall of Dwarrowdelf in Moria and an incredible scale version of one of the Corsair ships from the third movie. Built exclusively by John Baster, Weta's Senior Miniatures Technician, the ship has capstans, coiled ropes, cross-bows, stacks of bolts, vicious implements on the side of ship for cutting the rigging of enemy vessels and even a 'dunny' (an antipodean word for lavatory) poised perilously over the back of the ship!

Next, we come across the Hobbiton factory, a vision of which Frodo sees in Galadriel's mirror. The once-picturesque water-mill, now corrupted into a darkly sinister symbol of urban industrialization, was based on another John Howe design. The attention to detail is mesmeric: the decaying roof that is bodged and patched; the rusting pipes, flues, brackets and ladders.

'I love this building!,' enthuses Richard. 'It has the crackpot appearance of a building drawn by William Heath Robinson or Dr Seuss, but with an overpowering sense of menace – *and* a terrible beauty.' He indicates the swooping line to the roof: 'That is the sweep of John Howe's pencil. It is like the wing of a raven!'

Among the miniatures still to be filmed is Grond (shown above), the mighty battering-ram used by the Orc-army to attack the gates of Minas Tirith. The work of Miniatures Builder David Tremont it takes the form of a huge, snarling wolf – its hide, of beaten metal, inscribed with Black Speech – chained up within a great cage on wheels.

'The plan,' explains Richard, 'is for it to be pushed by trolls; Orc-archers will be riding on the top and there will be burning braziers discharging blinding clouds of black, oily smoke. As Grond swings to and fro and smashes at the gates, it will almost be as though the creature were desperately trying to break free from its shackles.'

Nearby are the gates, constructed out of polystyrene and balsa wood so they will be able to break and splinter, and with lead hinges that will easily distort under the gruelling onslaught of Grond.

'Time to go on,' says Richard, 'time to take the Paths of the Dead!' And we are passing between sculpted rock walls in black styrofoam carved with a riot of ruined buildings – steps, doorways, towers and turrets – all this way and that and each numbered with a small yellow sticker and painted a luminous green for the purposes of digital camera-work.

The sequence in *The Return of the King* is, as Richard explains, a good example of Weta ingenuity: 'It would be hugely expensive to build these as one-off miniature sets. So we try to find parts of any setting that can be built as units. Our technique is to take polystyrene board and crush various architectural detailing into it, then we use those for making moulds that will enable us to produce component pieces that can be "cookie-cut" and assembled into vast environments. Much of this work has been done by young people who may not have had much experience to offer but who've brought to the project masses of unflagging enthusiasm.'

At the end of the Paths of the Dead we find John Baster. Pinned to the wall behind his drawing board is a child's painting of a smiling girl on a bright green hill under a huge yellow sun. Right next to it is John Howe's brooding illustration of the Nazgûl fell-beast swooping past Barad-dûr…

'We've been through so many different styles,' says John, 'and it is all down to John Howe and Alan Lee. These two incredible illustrators have given us the vision to create these extraordinary places in with such incredible richness and so much depth of design.'

John is currently working on the miniature set for the Grey Havens in the final film: 'We will be creating an Elven style of architecture for the Havens that will use many of the same design motifs found in Rivendell, but which we will be adapting to suit structures built from stone rather than wood.'

Working on a sheet of tracing paper laid over one of Alan Lee's drawings, John is using different-coloured pencils to indicate the various component parts to the set: 'Neither Alan or John ever give us scale drawings, but their ability to visualize things in three-dimensions is so good that when they hand us a folder of drawings, they are as good as plans!'

'Originally,' adds Richard Taylor, 'the draughtspersons who made all the excellent scale plans for full-size sets were also drawing up plans for the miniatures, but Peter put a stop to that, preferring our builders to work directly from the original sketches, so as not to lose anything of Alan and John's artistic interpretation.'

'There's always so much to work from,' says John Baster, 'my job is simply to take what they visualized and realize it. The information is so clear that I can build it exactly as they drew it!'

Despite the modesty of Weta's miniature builders, their skill in recreating the conceptual designs with such authenticity of detail and on such a small scale is astounding. They have also to work out how the sets can be taken apart, not only to allow lighting technicians and camera operators access to these miniature worlds, but also in order to be able to transport the largest models from the workshop down a few hundred yards of Camperdown Street to the studio.

'There have been times,' remembers Richard, 'even when we've broken the sets down into transportable pieces that we've had to lift the overhead electricity cables to get them through! You'd see some huge tower on the back of a truck and us with long poles gingerly raising the cables! Just to be on the safe side, we'd wear rubber-soled boots and those pink rubber gloves you use to do the washing-up!'

The studio, where miniature sets are still being filmed, is our next stop after a short detour to the ruins of Isengard, which have been erected in a car park behind one of the buildings.

Construction of this particular miniature set began with the laying of a concrete ring (twenty metres in diameter), to carry the walls of Isengard, with a pad of concrete in the centre supporting the scale model of the Tower of Orthanc. In the background looms a polyurethane mountain range, weighed down by great piles of earth. 'We get a lot of wind here,' explains Richard, 'so we've got to make quite sure the mountains don't suddenly get blown away!'

Stepping over the outer wall (fifteen to twenty centimetres in height), we walk like giants around the ruined remains of Saruman's domain. The fire-scarred ground is dotted with the sooty domes of brick furnaces; while yawning caverns contain an intricate labyrinth of gantries and walkways reached by tiny ladders. There are miniature cranes, hoists and lifting-gear, all unattended, yet all turning, raising and lowering; and, deeper still, are the minute flickering lights of fires and forges.

Each 'pit' together with its tiny content was, I discover, built as a miniature set and then sunk into holes dug in the ground along with a network of pipes carrying the required fire and smoke effects and the electricity needed to power the lights and turn the wheels and gears. The armies of Orcs slaving away in the hot, smoky depths will be added digitally later.

Suddenly, I trip and almost stumble. Looking down from my lofty height, I realize that I have caught my toe on the blackened stump of a sawn-down tree and uprooted it! I am amazed and mortified. 'Don't worry,' laughs Richard, 'the place is *supposed* to be in ruins and we've only one more shot to film and then we're going to flood it!'

We continue with our tour and, on entering the studio, I am brought up short by the staggering set for Minas Tirith, the

great city of Gondor, glimpsed first in *The Fellowship of the Ring* when Gandalf is seeking knowledge of the One Ring, and a key location in *The Return of the King*.

Tipped forward at an angle (in order to film an aerial shot in the third film) it looks utterly surreal: a cross between some medieval municipality and a spaceship in a science fiction movie…

The detailing is so intricate that for a second I forget that I am looking at a model and fancy that I am flying over a real city!

Seated upon a rocky prominence thrust out from Mount Mindolluin, the City of the Kings is an extraordinary citadel, built upon seven concentric levels culminating in the High Court and the lofty Tower of Ecthelion (the White Tower) rising fifty fathoms from base to pinnacle.

The detailing on the miniature is astonishing: each level is a jostling crowd of buildings with parapets and domes – made from half ping-pong balls, no doubt! There are formal squares with trees, shrubs and heroic statues; courtyards with pumps and wells; tangled mazes of winding streets; and houses with minute lines of washing blowing on their roofs and tubs and barrels in their back-yards.

Here, Richard Taylor leaves me with Alex Funke, the Visual Effects Director of Photography (pictured below) whose illustrious career includes work on such films as *The Abyss, Total Recall, Starship Troopers* and *Mighty Joe Young.*

'Nowadays in Los Angeles,' says Alex, 'we just go and rent whatever we need; in New Zealand, we solve problems by inventiveness! It's what they refer to here as "No. 8 Wire Technology" – give a New Zealander a piece of No. 8 fence-wire, and he'll build you pretty much anything!' It is an attitude with which Alex readily identifies: 'It's what we do in Effects all the time: invention and improvization, creating one thing out of something else!'

It is also a reminder of how things once were in the special effects industry. 'There was a time,' recalls Alex, 'when every effects house had its own designers and machinists and built all their own rigs, but those days have more or less gone – except here! So, for me, it was a wonderful opportunity to reinvent the wheel all over again!'

While still in Los Angeles, Alex began assessing the requirements for establishing a miniatures unit and Weta Digital's VFX Cinematographer, Brian Van't Hul (whose film credits include *Contact* and *Forrest Gump*), began custom-building two motion-control rigs. 'Brian's rigs,' says Alex, 'were the result of an evolutionary process and are wonderfully elegant and efficient.'

Operated by computers that calculate true Cartesian axes, the motion control (or 'mo-con') rigs have the ability to replicate any move many times over and are known around the studio as 'The Crucifix' and 'The Big Boom', which has an arm-reach of ten metres, the longest of its kind ever built and a necessity for filming the huge miniatures on *The Lord of the Rings.*

Pausing at an area of the studio carrying a sign with a red skull and crossbones and the warning: 'Do Not Touch ANYTHING!', Alex introduces me to Moritz Wassmann, a mechanical engineer – not to mention gunsmith and diving instructor! The floor is littered with gleaming silver curls of milled metal and Moritz is surrounded by lathes, drills and stacks of drawers filled with nuts and bolts, screws and rivets.

'It is a real luxury,' says Alex, 'to have an in-house engineer, let alone one as eclectic as Moritz: give him an idea on the back of an envelope and in a couple of hours he's brought you exactly what you wanted – only twice as good as you thought it could be!'

From the prototype parts from the two mo-con rigs, Moritz has built a third rig which is currently being used to film the miniature set of the Cracks of Doom. Appropriately, it has a plate bolted to the side of the arm carrying the name 'Frankenstein'!

'This film,' laughs Alex, 'is nothing but wall-to-wall fires! Khazad-dûm, the pits of Isengard and now the Cracks of Doom – all full of fire and lava, which are amongst the most challenging stuff to film!'

Built to 1/14th scale, this is more than just the rocky interior of a mountain. There are spouts from which molten lava will pour, carved pillars and a jutting promontory reached by an arched brick bridge. The architecture, though clearly ancient and incomplete, conveys a sense of power and authority and serves as an indication of a will that can harness and control the forces of nature. It is to this place that Isildur came and failed to destroy the Ring and it is here that Frodo must also come at the very end of his quest.

Hellish images by Bosch and Doré come to mind, even before the addition of special effects such as billowing steam and cascading lava which is currently represented on set by strips of orange reflective fabric of the kind normally used in making safety-jerkins!

'Whatever the setting,' says Alex, 'it comes down to the same thing: in miniature, everything is magnified, so we are always dealing with very subtle variations – the tiniest turn of a light will make the difference between something too bright or too dark. So, we have forests of stands holding little bits cardboard and endless pieces of netting supported by wires: anything to reflect light in or deflect light out.'

And all that paraphernalia on set brings its own problems: 'Everything has to be rigged in such a way that it won't shift or sag, because it's got to remain wherever we put it for maybe a week while we film a shot. At the same time, there are probably people still putting in finishing touches to the set and, inevitably, the place where we want to put a light is precisely where they need to be working. But that's how it is!'

In addition to the miniature sets various effects-shots are being collected. One team are currently smashing pieces of rubble with hammers and filming the process as a reference for the technicians in Weta Digital who will be adding puffs of dust particles to the scene in which the cave troll is crashing about with his mace.

On the other side of a black curtain, another team is filming a flaming torch turning on a spindle which will be digitally added to a shot of Boromir almost losing his balance on the broken staircase in Khazad-dûm and dropping his torch which will – thanks to the work of the Miniatures Unit – be seen spiralling away into the abyss.

Nearby slurping noises entice me to peep behind another curtain where, I discover, they are busily filming lava flows. The lava (made from the same thickening-agent that burger stores use in making hot apple-pies) is poured at different speeds and varying consistencies – from quite watery to rather lumpy. The splattering results are captured on camera and will be used to digitally replace those luminous strips of material on the miniature set…

creature – and now we're putting the eyeballs back in!'

Had they told Peter that the model hadn't been built to do either of those things, I ask? 'No!' chuckles Richard. 'If it isn't going to hold up filming there is no need to worry Pete by telling him there's a problem. We remained cool, rode it out and have now spent half an hour making it happen! Opening the mouth is going to be tricky. But we'll do it! Peter will be none the wiser, and hopefully, happy with the results.'

'Yes,' says Alex Funke, 'it's all very finicky, very frustrating and immensely tiring and it's certainly not a job for anyone who isn't naturally calm!'

The truth of this is borne out the very next day when I am supposed to watch Miniatures Director of Photography Richard Bluck filming the flooding of Isengard. Outside, the wind is blowing and stormy clouds are piling up behind the hills. Inside, Richard is having to reschedule his day: 'Far too windy,' he tells me. 'Not only is it whipping up the waters around Orthanc into waves that will never look convincing in miniature, but the large blue-screen against which we needed to shoot the set was billowing like the sails on a yacht in the Americas Cup! The weather report's not good, so we've decided to investigate Grond instead.'

This is greeted by a roar of laughter from Richard Taylor, who emerges from behind the model of the battering-ram, screwdriver in hand: 'We just had a meeting with Peter,' he tells me, 'and it seems that he really wants Grond's eyes to glow and its mouth to open. The trouble is,' laughs Richard, 'our model doesn't do either! Anyway, we've dug holes into the head, lined them with lead and tin-foil, fitted bulbs – the cable for which is having to be fed down the entire length of the

As Richard Taylor leads me back through the studio, we stop by the miniature of Helm's Deep (seen above right, receiving some last-minute attention from Miniatures Technician, Verena Jonker) which I had seen on film the day before: A model it may be, but it is hugely (or, maybe I *should* say, *minutely!*) impressive: the craggy slopes of the mountain, the great walls, Helm's Gate, the Hornburg and, before them, the wide plain with its rocks, boulders and tussocks of grass, between which the Deeping-stream snakes its way.

Constructed to 35th scale, it stands four metres high by five metres across and is filmed using a 'snorkel camera' which skims across the model only a few centimetres from its surface, but which, on screen, appears to be moving at about human – or Orc – head-height!

'Helm's Deep is one of the last miniatures to be shot,' comments Richard, 'but it was the first model that we built. We agonized for a long time over how we were going to make these vast walls look as if they had been built out of real stone.' The solution was a 'brick-tool device' (referred to at Weta as the 'Fred Flintstone Roller') which comprises a small roller, the surface of which is covered with random texture created using car-filler! When rolled over the surface of the scaled-down styrofoam building blocks, it effectively creates the look of time-worn stonework.

As with so much in this miniature world: the answer to a problem is often unlikely but, surprisingly simple: the scale-tussocks of grass, for example, are actually tufts of goat's hair.

'I really don't think,' says Richard, 'that any other effects company would have been as audacious as we have in building miniatures to such a small scale, because, frankly, to do so is to walk on the edge of failure. Building miniatures is like sitting a math exam: if you do the equations correctly, you'll get 100%. Get them wrong and you'll fail.'

There is, I can't help thinking, little doubt that Weta will pass the exam!

Miniature Myths

Sooner or later, every model-maker in Weta Workshop's Miniature Department learned a hard lesson: 'Never believe *anything* that *anyone* tells you about the model you are making!' Miniatures Builder, Mary Maclachlan drew up a list of some of the most commonly (and confidently) expressed items of total misinformation:

'I know it's only 1/166th scale, but the camera will never get that close...'

'Don't bother to detail that side of the model, you'll never see it...'

'They won't put lights in that, you can make it in polystyrene...'

'You don't need to reinforce that bit, no one will stand there...'

'It's a wide-shot model, you'll never see the join...'

'We won't put motors in those, you can glue them down...'

'Make that section removable, we promise not to lose it...'

Famous last words!

Lost in Lothlórien

There is an autumn-like flutter of leaves, as a lighting technician on the raised platform of a cherry-picker gingerly reaches between the branches of the tree to adjust the angle of a lamp. Then the platform starts its noisy descent and more leaves cascade to the floor. I stoop to pick one up: a sprig of small, green plastic foliage that has been carefully spray-painted yellow on one side.

This is Caras Galadhon, the Elven City of the Trees in Lothlórien, which Tolkien describes as soaring like living towers to a height that can scarcely be guessed. Even though built to 1:12 scale, the miniature set still cannot be accommodated as a single piece within the confines of the studio.

In consequence, Caras Galadhon comes in two parts: top and bottom! At one end of the sound-stage are the gigantic tree trunks, rising twenty feet or more from a tangle of giant roots and a carpet of moss and fallen leaves, before stopping abruptly, lopped off in their prime. At the *other* end of the stage are the *tops* of the trees, soaring high above my head, their silver bark creating misty patterns in the soft blue-grey electrically-created twilight.

In something approaching a reverie, I notice hundreds of little houses, with graceful tracery walls, perched high among the branches and reached by slatted stairs that spiral round the boles of the trees under tiny cloisters with intricately carved pillars.

A voice suddenly brings me back to reality: 'We call those "caterpillars"!' Miniatures sculptor Jon Ewan is keen for me to know as much as possible about the mysteries of Caras Galadhon.

Apparently, the fascia of each arch on the caterpillars has a swirling art-nouveau design moulded from a minute carving in wax; the roof of each house comprises five different elements; the tracery screens are made from acid-etched tin that can be bent to fit into the various openings of windows and doors; all the variously shaped and sized buildings have names around the studio such as the oriental-looking 'Chinese Temple' or 'Madonna's House', which is topped off with two large domes!

I notice that the windows are lined with a translucent greeny-gold material creating a pale, iridescent shimmer. 'Polyester lamé,' John informs me, 'cheap Mardi Gras stuff, called "Glamé", but which we call "dragonfly-wing fabric".' Then he points out the several hundred blue and white fairy-lights strung up amongst the branches and across the branch-bridges between houses: 'Elf street-lights! In miniature, of course, you won't see the cables, only a mist of tiny lights.' It is a look inspired by Visual Effects Art Director, Paul Lasaine, whose conceptual paintings of Caras Galadhon were studded with vibrant pinpoints of blue light.

Lighting the City of the Trees has not been easy, as Miniatures Director of Photography, David Hardberger, confirms when he joins me on set: 'Ideally, you'd set up one big light representing the sun at the opposite end of the studio from the miniature, but because of the scale of the trees there's simply not the space. So we ended up using nine different suns all from the same direction, but being very careful not to get multiple over-lapping shadows, because that's one thing you never get with sunlight!'

David Harberger, whose recent assignments include work on *Dante's Peak* and *Dinosaur*, learned his craft working with the legendary special-effects wizard Douglas Trumbull on *Close Encounters of the Third Kind* and *Star Trek: The Motion Picture*. He is acutely aware of the problems of working in miniature: 'Film normally runs at twenty-four frames per second, but we only shoot one frame of film every five seconds! At that speed it is a challenge to get enough light and keep everything in focus, especially on the night shots in Lothlórien. Peter Jackson wanted a look that recalled the engravings of Albrecht Dürer, so we've got a foreground that is almost black, contrasted with fractionally lighter mid- and background vistas that recede away into misty depths.'

Above all, the end result must be believable: 'How many people have seen a spaceship?' asks David. 'Apart from a couple of people in Mississippi who see them all the time, none of us! But everybody's seen a forest or a picture of a forest. People know what a forest looks like. The skill is in taking things that people have seen all their lives, recreating them in a miniature scale and making them believable!'

Creating the believable often involves the totally unexpected: as we are leaving Lothlórien, Jon Ewan points to the grass between the tree roots: 'Desiccated coconut,' he explains, 'sprayed green.' Coconut? 'Yes, but only the fine type; not the coarse stuff!'

High above, another lamp is being adjusted and there is another fall of leaves. I am pondering how many thousands of these leaves have had to be painstakingly painted green-turning-yellow, when I notice a crew member wearing a T-shirt with a slogan that says it all: 'This isn't ART – it's endurance'!

Light on Rivendell

"God-rays", we call them!' Miniatures Director of Photography Chuck Schuman (shown below) is referring to fingers of brilliant light, reaching over the gabled roofs and between the towers of Rivendell to touch a balcony here, a balustrade there…

Chuck has an illustrator's eye: 'It's all about the play of light and shadow,' he says, 'and this is dawn over Rivendell: deep, saturated colours; the first rays of early sunlight gilding the towers, kissing the sides of the buildings with white silver; with just a trace of morning mist and dew.'

Pinned onto the wall of Chuck's office is a stunning series of photographs of lighting experiments for the miniature model of Rivendell – as it might look in the pale colours of pre-dawn, at the dazzling moment of an orange-red sunrise, through the fierce blue and yellow intensity of mid-day, to the subtle golds of late afternoon and the violet shades of evening.

Looking at the photographs, I am reminded of the paintings of the twentieth-century American artist and illustrator, Maxfield Parrish. I mention this somewhat hesitantly, but Chuck smiles delightedly: 'That's the man!' Seizing a large volume of Parrish's paintings from beside his desk, he begins flicking through its pages. 'These extraordinary, breathtaking "dream-scapes" were among my inspirations!'

Today, Chuck Schuman happens to be celebrating his first year on *The Lord of the Rings*: 'My excitement for this project began with Alan Lee and John Howe's vision of Middle-earth which is magnificent, yet intimate. There are incredible scenic vistas, but when you get down to the earth itself, every path has a destination, every rock has a history, every tree deserves the name that it has. Look as hard as you like, more and more detail is always opening up – there's the macro in the micro…'

Finding a way of creating that look in three-dimensional miniatures employs many of the Academy Award-winning visual-effects skills which Chuck demonstrated on *The Abyss*, *Total Recall* and *Terminator 2: Judgment Day*: 'Our aim is to create convincing atmospherics, sometimes only the smallest of touches, that will connect an effect to reality and help an audience to accept it as a complete illusion. We use a variety of techniques to do this – in fact, just about every kind of "smoke-and-mirrors" deception you can think of!'

The reference to smoke is an apposite one: 'Add a little smoke and it dissipates the light and creates an impression of great depth; this miniature set isn't more than twelve feet deep, but smoke takes on so many layers that the buildings appear to reach away into the distance for half a mile or more.'

any smoke pumped onto the set would begin to drift and disperse, creating a bizarre pulsating effect on film.

'As with any problem,' laughs Chuck, 'we always manage to pull something out of our bag of tricks! One of our technicians, Chris Davison (who calls himself the Motion Control Boffin), devised what I refer to as my "smoke-sniffer"! A highly sophisticated smoke-sensor, it uses an infra-red beam to detect and regulate the precise level of smoke being added to a miniature set.'

The filming of Rivendell is now complete and Chuck is working on a miniature set for the interior of the Cracks of Doom in *The Return of the King*: 'There's going to be plenty of opportunities to experiment with colour there! It's Hades; the throat of Hell; Dante's *Inferno*; any and every image you can call to mind of hell-fire and damnation: explosions of lava, eruptions of fireballs; smoke, steam and noxious fumes, ending in a cataclysmic earthquake and "shake-rattle-and-roll" time!'

He pauses and takes another, wistful, look at his tranquil pictures of the Last Homely House: 'Rivendell is something of a theatrical departure from the rest of the film. For much of the movie, the hobbits find themselves in the wild, in the dark, with fear all around them. Amongst so many inhospitable places, I wanted Rivendell to be a safe-haven, an oasis of beauty and calm.'

Smoke can also transform a spotlight into a sun: 'We could put the light right into the shot so that the buildings play in silhouette, and, by simply adding the right level of smoke, the physical presence of the lamp becomes magically masked within its own bloom of light.'

The challenge, however, is to keep the flow of smoke evenly dispersed across the set throughout the long, slow process of filming. Since, in order to shoot a single frame of film, the camera lens will be open for anything up to two seconds and then closed for the same period of time,

Department Store for Middle-earth

 Dead horses! It is a bizarre and alarming sight and certainly not something I had expected to confront when Art Department Manager Chris Hennah (shown below) offered to give me a tour of *The Lord of the Rings* prop store. But these equine corpses – regimentally stacked on shelves, their limbs stiff with rigor mortis – are just that: props.

'Oh, dear,' says Chris, suddenly noticing that a couple of horses have slipped off the stacks and that a white one, buried underneath, looks decidedly squashed. 'That one really looks a bit sick! Still, it *is* meant to be dead!'

I have to ask, why all the dead horses? Chris explains: 'Peter had been looking at old engravings of the Napoleonic Wars showing battlefields that were a tangle of bodies – living, dead and dying. He felt strongly that battle scenes in movies hardly ever showed a true picture of the human and animal debris involved, so he wanted the battlegrounds in the movie to be full of dead people – and horses. Well, you can get actors to lie still for a shot, but it's harder with horses – so we just made them!'

Forty of them… Being asked to make forty dead horses might sound a little unusual, but for the Art Department it was only one of hundreds of curious requests and a lot less demanding than many. 'After all,' says Chris, 'at least we all knew what a dead horse should look like – we were more challenged by the need for Elven glassware and hobbit pottery!'

On films with a contemporary setting, the props (or 'properties') can simply be bought or borrowed, while on a period picture, it is often possible to get historic items on loan from museums and collections. However, filming a story set in the imaginary world of Middle-earth meant that virtually every single item had to be custom-made. After all, you can't pop down to the nearest convenience store and pick up a palantír when you need one.

As it happens – and maybe not too surprisingly, since a 'seeing stone' is a relatively uncommon objet d'art – Saruman's palantír turned out to be a tricky prop to make. Described by Tolkien as a crystal globe, the Art Department experimented with a number of versions made in glass (some containing mysterious milky swirls) before eventually settling on a heavily-lacquered wooden ball with an added touch of computer effects wizardry.

As well as occasional rarities such as the palantír, there were hundreds of bespoke items of a more common-or-garden nature: buckets, baskets, brooms and brushes; and a collection of ladders, carefully labelled: 'General Hobbiton Ladders' and 'Orc Siege Ladders', the latter having a rather more rough-and-ready look, their rungs lashed on with ropes rather than secured with nails.

For any fan of *The Lord of the Rings*, this is a veritable Aladdin's Cave: crates and chests from Balin's Tomb (as ransacked by goblins) and the forge-bellows and anvil used by the Elves in re-forging Narsil, Aragorn's broken sword.

Every box begs to be opened: 'Grappling Hooks (Helm's Deep)'; 'Chains (lots of)'; 'Skulls (generic)' and what on Middle-earth are 'Mordor pot-holders'?

A large box of 'Books (spines only)' prompts an explanation from Chris: 'We needed *shelf-loads* of books, so we took casts of a variety of genuine book-spines, made moulds and then produced as many as we needed. Some spray-paint and a few decorative touches and you've got a library!' There were also a lot of authentic books and hundreds of scrolls that had been hand-written on hand-made paper. 'Since the actors had to be able to unroll the scrolls and open the books,' explains Chris, 'these particular props were a continuity nightmare! There were notes and scraps of paper poking out of some volumes and lots more scattered over the table at Bag End or in the library

at Minas Tirith. Since many of them were written in Elvish, someone not only had to remember where all these bits and pieces were positioned on set, but also which way up they went!'

Noticing a box of 'Bilbo's Party Invitations' (what collector's items those would make!), I ask Chris the obvious question: how did they set about putting together this extraordinary horde of things – some as singular as the Mirror of Galadriel, others as work-a-day as the Bag End kitchen kettle?

'To begin with,' she replies, 'you need a confident and unflappable Props Master.'

That person proved to be Nick Weir, an experienced art director who – aided by Props Buyer, Nick Riera – undertook the massive task of finding and commissioning the many and varied artisans whose combined talents would supply the essentials of daily life in Middle-earth.

'After that,' adds Chris, 'you need lists. Lots of lists, all double and triple-checked!'

The starting point had to be the scripts: preliminary 'read-throughs' were undertaken by Chris and Nick as well as by Dan Hennah, Chris's husband and Supervising Art Director on the film. As each of them read, they noted carefully every reference to 'hand props': things belonging to, or handled by, a character: such as Boromir's horn, Frodo's backpack, Sam's cooking paraphernalia and, of course, the Ring…

These were what Chris calls the 'must-have' props: the ones that *had* to be there. The next priority was for those items required for specific environments such as Weathertop, Saruman's Chamber, the Golden Hall and the Houses of Healing.

Then the calculations began: how many extras were going to be involved in the scene in the bustling market-place outside 'The Green Dragon'? How many of them would require things to sell? How many would need stools to sit on or baskets to carry? Multiply the props by the number of people and draw up another list…

'In the end,' says Chris, 'familiarity with the script was the only answer. Once we'd read the script a couple of hundred times we started to get the hang of it!' She reflects for a moment and then, with an ironic laugh, corrects herself: 'I mean, once we'd read *three scripts* a couple of hundred times!'

In between sketching designs for settings, weapons and monsters, Alan Lee and John Howe turned out hundreds of ideas for Middle-earth artefacts. These sometimes took the form of finished concepts such as a detailed drawing of the serpentine ironwork holding the highly decorated cooking vessels over the fireplace in the Golden Hall; while on other occasions they might be little more than preparatory sketches that would then be developed by Props Designers Gareth Jensen and Adam Ellis.

Since almost all the items were going to be hand-crafted, and often in significant quantities, the Art Department set up in-house workshops, including a glass-blowing studio where, over a period of six months glass-maker Robert Reedy blew delicate, sinuous Elven goblets for Rivendell and assorted jars, bottles and tumblers for the folk of Hobbiton.

There was also a blacksmith's shop ('primitive but functional') which turned out everything from hinges, locks and doorhandles to cutlery for the King's table in Minas Tirith; but *not*, I discover, those enormous pewter tankards that Merry and Pippin drink out of at the Prancing Pony Inn. 'They would have been *far* too expensive to have crafted from metal,' Chris explains, 'so we cheated! We made them as ceramics and then plated them to *look* like pewter.'

The tableware for Bag End was specially produced by the established potter Mirek Smíšek but rather than use his established patterns the production hand-decorated them all with original designs.

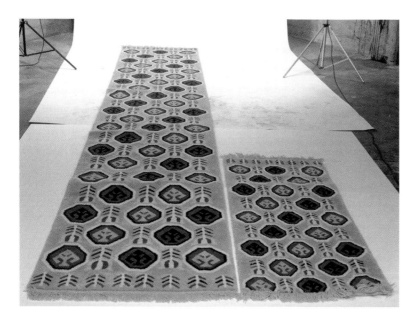

'We even made our own rope,' says Chris, 'and if that sounds like hard work, just remember that we didn't just make rope – we made rope to several different scales!'

As for everyone working on the film, the issue of scale was a continuing ordeal. Supplying props that matched in look, but which were made in different sizes, depending on whether they were to be used by the regular-size actors or by their small- or large-scale doubles was, to say the least, perplexing: 'It took us some time to get our heads around it and even when we'd eventually figured out the logistics of what we'd need – and in which scales – we still had to find people who could actually produce those things!'

Yet find them they did: rug-makers Vita Cochran and Hugh Bannerman who were able to re-create the patterned rugs in Bag End to both large and small scale; a cooper in Christchurch, David P. Bain, who turned out extra-extra-large wine and beer barrels for Bree; and New Zealand's premier silversmith, Jens Hansen, who grappled with the task of producing versions of the One Ring in a surprising variety of sizes.

It was a challenge that was to affect virtually every prop and item of set-dressing from curtain materials (woven in different scale-weaves) to the mugs and plates used in those scenes where Gandalf is sharing a meal with Bilbo or Frodo at Bag End and which involved normal-sized crockery and utensils for the hobbit actors at one end of the table and scaled-down versions for the other end to make Gandalf appear bigger.

Turning a corner in the prop store we come upon an item that perfectly exemplifies the difficulty of dealing with questions of scale. Standing side by side are two of Gandalf's carts: both in all respects identical, except that each looks as if it is being viewed through the opposite end of the same telescope. One is the cart ridden by Ian McKellen alone or in shots in which he appears with Elijah Wood's small-scale double, while the other was used for shots in which Elijah appears alongside Ian's large-scale double. 'Yes,' admits Chris, 'The cart was quite a task: the wickerwork panelling had to be woven using two different thicknesses of willow; the wheelwright had to make two pairs of accurately-scaled, metal-rimmed wheels; and there had to be two sets of all the things stashed in the back of the cart, like Gandalf's battered chest and all those bundles of fireworks.'

Take the challenge of building the Elven boats in which the Fellowship leave Lothlórien: as with all props used in sequences involving the hobbits, Dwarves, Elves and men, these had to be built to both full-and half-scale. We come across the work of Master Boat-builder Wayne Roberts stacked up in the store: silvery-grey, practical yet elegant, with graceful leaf-shaped paddles, the Elven boats come in a variety of scales, each a perfect match in shape and ornamentation. There is also an Elven prow which was specially constructed to fit over the front of the boat carrying the camera crew in order for shots to be filmed of the River Anduin as though from one of the Fellowship vessels.

We've moved on from the carts, when Chris stops, suddenly remembering yet another requirement: 'Oh, yes! How could I have forgotten? Two sizes of cart – *and* two sizes of carthorse!'

I shake my head in astonishment. 'We always followed this one principle,' she adds, 'no matter what we were making we never spared any detail simply because it was difficult.'

Our tour continues. We are now in a curious Tolkienesque furniture-store: a high-backed wooden settle from the hallway in Bag End; large-scale stools and benches from the bar of the Prancing Pony Inn; Elrond's intricately-carved throne; Arwen's day-bed; and assorted cabinets, chandeliers and candlesticks. No two items have been made or decorated in quite the same way: close inspection reveals that the detailing on some

pieces of furniture has been achieved with the use of mouldings, while others – like the chairs for the Council of Elrond in Rivendell – are all hand-carved.

Next we discover a bundle of Gandalf's staffs: I am, by now expecting various sizes (obviously the one which Bilbo takes from the wizard when he first arrives at Bag End is going to be considerably larger than the one Gandalf himself carries), but why are there so many? 'We had eight staffs,' explains Chris, 'because while Ian McKellen was filming scenes in one place, other units filming different scenes, often miles away, might need a staff for a Gandalf stand-in or double.'

Nor was anything particularly special about Gandalf's staff in this respect, since – staggering though it seems – every single unit was provided with a full set of main, or 'hero', props. For Props Master Nick Weir it was a full-time job keeping ahead of the shooting schedule. Eight Gandalf staffs pales into insignificance when you consider, for example, that there were 139 'Fellowship bags' (as carried by the company on their onward travels from Rivendell) all made not only to different scales but also in various conditions, reflecting the wear and tear of the journey. 'We had to anticipate every possibility,' says Chris, 'we could never allow ourselves to be responsible for holding up the shoot – everything had to have been thought of – and ready to hand!'

Chris and I are joined by Dan Hennah (right), who has been overseeing the building of a small part of a set for the doors to the Mines of Moria, needed for a pick-up scene in which Aragorn looks out and sees the Watcher in the Water attacking Frodo.

My attention has, meanwhile, been caught by another pile of boxes: 'Greenery (mainly oak and ivy)'; 'Cherry sprays (mainly blossom)'; 'Pears and apples (red and green)'; 'Peaches, plums and mandarins'. 'Those,' says Chris, observing my interest, 'are just some of the

artificial props; there were plenty of real ones, too, including giant-sized vegetables for the gardens and market-place in Hobbiton and the scene in which Merry and Pippin plunder Farmer Maggot's crops.'

'As for the food,' adds Dan, 'that was most certainly real!' Notably, it seems, the sumptuous spread prepared for Bilbo's eleventy-first birthday party where, in addition to a roast pig on a spit, the tables were seen to be groaning with cakes, pies, scones and muffins, all of which had been hand-made by food technician, Harriet Harcourt.

'We checked out the local bakers' shops,' says Chris, 'and often found interesting-looking loaves, but we really couldn't risk any shots of hobbits scoffing cakes that had obviously been shop-bought!'

With home-baked food on offer, the hobbit extras at the party didn't take much encouragement to tuck in! 'There was a time,' chuckles Dan, 'when you could stop movie-extras from eating the prop food by telling them that it was covered in fly-spray! But actors have wised-up to that one and anyway in this film it was really

important that the food was seen being eaten – *and enjoyed!*'

The one exception was the Elves' *lembas* bread on which Frodo and Sam subsist while journeying into Mordor. *Lembas* was needed with such regularity and frequency that, between producing more appealing food, Harriet Harcourt prepared substantial batches that were frozen for future use. Thin, and somewhat resembling pitta bread, it became for the actors as much a trial to eat as it does for the characters in the book. 'I think it's fair to say,' Chris laughs, 'that by the time we'd finished shooting, Elijah and Sean had pretty well had their fill of *lembas!*'

'Apart from all that food,' remarks Dan, 'there's another category of props that you won't find here in the store – the animals! To help create the illusion that hobbits are small, Head Animal Wrangler Dave Johnson scoured the length and breadth of New Zealand to find outsized cows, sheep, pigs and even chickens.'

Perhaps the most unusual 'living prop' however, was the gum emperor moth which carries the message of

Gandalf's captivity at Orthanc to Gwaihir the Eagle. 'For reasons of animal welfare,' explains Dan, 'the scene had to be shot to coincide with the moth's life-cycle. So we kept the larva in a cupboard with a hot-water tank until it was ready to hatch and, within just a few hours, we had filmed that stunning close-up of the insect in Gandalf's cupped hands and the insect released into the wild.'

The Art Department also had responsibility for the horses used in the filming, both living and dead. A full-time saddler, Tim Abbot, produced seventy elaborately-tooled and decorated saddles for close-up shots as well as 250 background saddles; while a team of farriers were responsible for seeing that the horses were properly shod – on one occasion with rubber horseshoes! Dan explains: 'We had to shoot a sequence in which galloping horses were to be ridden up and down concrete ramps on the Minas Tirith set, so we sent for a supply of rubber horseshoes of the kind used by American mounted police. They duly arrived and on the day of filming the farriers were up at six in the morning in order to have one hundred and fifty horses shoed in time for an eleven o'clock shoot.'

At which point, my thoughts return to those model horses. I look at them again and, even though I know they are fake, they still look remarkably real. Dan and Chris are very proud of their horses, which apparently looked so authentic on one of the battlefield sets that people asked how the creatures had been trained to lie still for so long! 'We took that,' says Chris, 'as a compliment!'

The process began with two full-size sculptures by Head Art Department Sculptor, Brigitte Wuest: one of a horse lying on its left side, the other on its right. Moulds were taken from which forty models were cast, painted with glue and covered in flocking to look like horsehide. The horses were arranged dramatically (their legs could be bent into various positions) and 'dressed' with saddles and bridles and different coloured manes and tails.

'Sadly,' recalls Dan, 'we lost one of the horse models in fairly spectacular style. We were filming the burning of a Rohan village and the building we set on fire burnt rather more dramatically than we had expected, sending out a great tongue of flame that caught one of the fake horses and set it alight! It was a one-off shot, using five cameras to catch the moment, and so, while everyone else was concerned about whether they had got the scene on film, all I could think about was having lost a model horse worth 2000 dollars!'

As he talks, Dan fills a long-stemmed clay pipe of the kind smoked by the hobbits. It is just one more prop which was designed and made by the Art Department.

'Now these,' says Dan as he lights the pipe, 'these are very difficult to find. As a pipe-smoker, I knew that I wanted traditional clay pipes for the hobbits but, apart from a few specialist tobacconists in England, they are difficult to come by. So, I decided that we'd make our own, which was easier said than done, because they are so easily snapped. To begin with, we only had about a ten per cent success rate, but we got better as time went on.

Making a perfect little pipe that could be smoked by an actor on set was one of the many joys of being involved in this film. Every now and again, we just had to stop and allow ourselves to be amazed at all the things – big and small, grand and modest – that we had designed and made, from scratch. It was great!' He contentedly exhales a cloud of fragrant tobacco smoke. 'They do get a little hot,' he adds, 'and you have to be very careful how you knock them out, but they're jolly good smokers…'

'On a Friday evening,' says Chris, 'when we've all finally finished work for the week, Dan often gets out his hobbit pipe and puffs away…'

'The trouble is,' adds Dan, 'they are a bit impractical; unless, of course, like Gandalf, you carry your pipe around in the top of your staff!'

Ring-masters

'The sign over the workshop door in Nelson, New Zealand reads: 'Jens Hansen, Gold & Silversmith'. Jens Høyer Hansen died in 1999, but, like his silver-mark (a shield intersected by an upright and a diagonal cross), his name endures in his reputation as a profound and revolutionary influence on contemporary jewellery in New Zealand.

For more than thirty years, Danish-born Jens Hansen designed and made exquisite silverware: pendants, rings, brooches and bracelets. Whether a tankard or a communion cup, his work was always distinguished by sculptural elegance and purity of line. A note in the workshop window informs fascinated passers-by that Jens Hansen *also* made the One Ring.

It is something of which Jens's son, Thorkild Hansen (above right) – himself a gifted gold and silversmith – is immensely proud: 'My father knew and loved *The Lord of the Rings* and was very excited when he heard that Peter Jackson was going to film it in New Zealand. Then a phone call came asking if he would make the One Ring and he was thrilled and honoured.'

In fact, Jens made *fifteen* rings: prototypes from which the One Ring was eventually selected. Was it difficult, I wondered, working fifteen variations on what is, essentially, a simple gold band? 'Not at all,' says Thorkild, 'after all there are only eight notes in the scale and look at all the music you can compose with them! The variations were not achieved by adding twiddles or frills; every one of the rings had the same simplicity – the variety came from different gauges, weights and finishes.'

One of the curious qualities of the Ring (almost as particular as the invisibility it confers on a wearer) is its ability to change size: it is worn – at various times in its history – by its maker, Sauron the Great, as well as by men and hobbits. As a result, Jens was required to make a number of rings, each scaled for different scenes: whether carried on a fine chain around Frodo's neck or worn over the Dark Lord's iron gauntlet – for which a huge, two-inch diameter version was required.

'It was not always easy,' laughs Thorkild, 'and it took quite some time to get the mathematics right!' Between them, Jens and Thorkild made upwards of thirty special variations of the Ring, many of which were designed to make it appear particularly large and dynamic, as when it acts as a mirror for the various dissenting protagonists around the council table in Rivendell.

'The most difficult ring to produce,' says Thorkild, 'was the one seen in the prologue, spinning and turning through the air. With a diameter of eight inches, it obviously couldn't be made out of solid gold, so we used steel, cutting it on a lathe and then plating it with gold!' Later a scale chain was requested to go with that particular ring for the scene in which Boromir picks it up from where it was dropped on the snowy slopes of Caradhras. 'We also made that from steel,' says Thorkild, adding with a chuckle: 'it was so strong you could probably have used it to tow a car!'

It is, for Thorkild, a sadness that his father didn't live to see the Ring that he made looking so magnificent on screen, but he contents himself with knowing that the very first prototype is safely tucked away in the workshop's safe and that Jens's craftsmanship lives on in *The Lord of the Rings*.

A review of an early exhibition of Jens Hansen's jewellery spoke of the way in which he 'lovingly shaped and polished' his artefacts 'to bring out the very best in the metal so that it glows as if it had a life of its own.' It would be hard to think of a more apposite way to describe the look which Jens later gave to the One Ring.

Penman in Middle-earth

Not only did the bundle of fireworks look *real*, they looked as if they might have been made by a wizard. Still stashed in the back of Gandalf's cart in *The Lord of the Rings* prop-store, the red and yellow paper wrappers were each decorated with an elaborate swirl of Elvish script: 'May the heavens shine with a fire of great brilliance'.

This amazing piece of detailing was, I discovered, the work of calligrapher Daniel Reeve. 'I first read Tolkien's books,' he recalls, 'when I was a teenager and I was immediately engrossed by the various scripts and runes and set about mastering the Tengwar, Tolkien's Elvish script.'

Twenty years later Daniel was working as a computer programmer for a bank when he heard that Peter Jackson was going to be filming *The Lord of the Rings*. Deciding that the film might need the services of a calligrapher who could write in Elvish, Daniel put together some samples of his work and sent them off to Jackson's company, Three Foot Six.

'Almost at once,' says Daniel, 'the phone rang and, within hours, I had driven down the coast to the production offices in Miramar and was on my way back home with my first commission – Elvish labels on Gandalf's fireworks!'

Next came a request to 'write' *The Red Book*, the journal in which Bilbo records his adventures. But what would Bilbo's handwriting have looked like? Daniel prepared sample scripts to be considered by a committee comprising Production Designer Grant Major; Set Decorator Dan Hennah, Props Master Nick Weir, Conceptual Artist Alan Lee, and, of course, Peter Jackson. Everyone eventually agreed on a spidery style, embellished with a variety of characteristic quirks and flourishes. 'It was,' says Daniel, 'at this point that I decided that if the book was to look as if it had been written with a quill, then actually *writing it with a quill* was the only answer.'

After a good deal of experimentation with quill-cutting and ink-holding techniques, Daniel sat down with his copy of *The Hobbit* and began writing out the story in his own words – or, rather, in what he imagined might have been *Bilbo's* words: 'I filled the pages,' he says, 'with maps and illustrations, songs and verses, adding margin annotations and even some crossings-out!'

Drawing on material from Tolkien's books, Daniel created the scrolls which Gandalf pores over in the library at Minas Tirith, penning them in various forms of Elvish and English, including specially devised 'Gondorian' and 'Rohan' lettering styles.

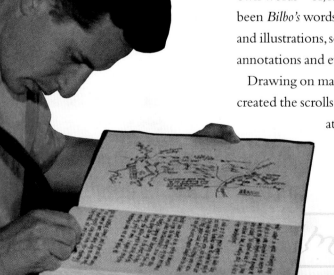

His calligraphy can also be glimpsed on the spines of the volumes on the alcove bookshelves of Rivendell, in a book of Elvish verse for Arwen and in an ancient volume of herb-lore used in the Houses of Healing in Minas Tirith.

For Saruman, the props department created a sinister tome containing a William Blake-like painting of a Balrog by Alan Lee and, from Daniel's pen, pages crowded with 'drawings and diagrams, musings, scribblings, rantings and ravings', written in a harsh-looking Westron-mode Tengwar.

One of the most satisfying props to create was the Book of Mazarbul, the ancient Dwarvish record discovered by Gandalf amongst the debris in the Mines of Moria. Daniel painstakingly created facsimile pages from the book – as if damaged by Orc weapons and charred by fire. 'I emulated Tolkien's style,' recalls Daniel, 'inserting appropriate text where the original is incomplete and, for the filler pages, wrote runes in a variety of hands and styles.'

This document, along with such items as Thorin's Map at Bag End, had to be made to look old and worn. 'My techniques,' confides Daniel, 'involved using lots of watercolour paint, washed, dribbled, run, splattered and thrown. Tools employed included brushes, rags, sponges, tissues, hands and jersey-sleeves!'

For the walls of Moria and Cirith Ungol, Daniel even devised scratchy Orc-graffiti which, as with many details carefully created by the Art Department, will doubtless go unnoticed by most film-goers. 'A huge amount of work,' reflects Daniel philosophically, 'ends up on the cutting-room floor, is on-screen only for fleeting moments in the deep background or is never even shot.'

Desperately trying to hold down his day-job while spending evenings, nights and weekends working at books, scrolls, maps and inscriptions ('At one point I found myself designing an Elven telescope!'), Daniel eventually decided to leave the bank, after fifteen years service, and become a freelance artist.

'I always thought of art,' admits Daniel, 'as just something I could do. I took it for granted and never thought of it as a viable career.' *The Lord of the Rings* has changed all that and he is now kept busy with his pens – creating elaborate lettering for an engraved Elven bowl or simply designing 'Cloakroom' signs for premiere screening parties. 'I'm confident that it will turn out well,' he says. 'And anyway, there's nothing wrong with a bit of uncertainty!'

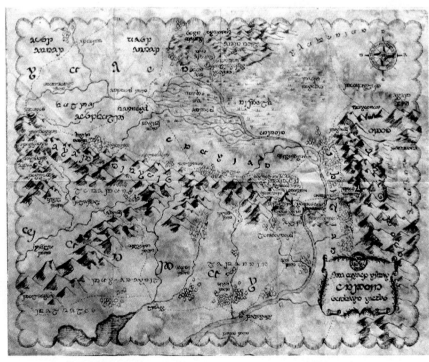

CHAPTER 6

Regal Robes and Big Girls' Frocks

'There's two things that I love: I love fittings; and I love the first time I see the actors on set in their costumes and everything comes together.'

Principal photography is virtually complete and Costume Designer Ngila Dickson (pictured below right) is talking to me in what has become the film's temporary costume store. All I can see, for as *far* as I can see, is rack after rack groaning under the weight of jackets, waistcoats, regal robes and flowing frocks.

This staggering array of costumes – 10,800 pieces for the extras alone – is now sheathed in plastic bags and carefully labelled: 'Théoden (decrepit at Edoras): undershirt with gold-braid trim; velvet overcoat; wool coat with fur collar; fur-fabric foot-wraps; crown and belt.'

Here: a pair of rose-pink, beaded slippers for Arwen; there: a bag of 'goblin knickers' – actually, a designer-brand of briefs with the all-too-familiar logo artfully concealed by a ragged loin-cloth!

Ngila Dickson is elegant and enigmatic; centred, focused and with a smile lurking at the corners of her mouth and at play in her slightly hooded eyes.

'I'll tell you how it starts,' she says, recalling the time before each item in this vast collection had been cut from an idea and stitched into a real garment. 'To begin with there is just a sketch and an idea and a mock-up of the costume, made out of acres of calico, that you've shoved on someone. It looks ghastly and the actor doesn't understand it at all: it hasn't had any embroidery, it's not the right colour – not even in the right fabric! In fact, there's nothing about it that suggests the final costume, but – in that moment – I can tell whether it is going to work or not. I walk into the fitting-room and say (*mentally*, of course) "Oh, my God!" or "Ah-ha!" And from that point on, it's just a big conversation with the actor.'

Exactly how many of those conversations Ngila had with the actors in *The Lord of the Rings* only becomes apparent as you go exploring among the costume-racks laden with ravishing dresses (all drifting clouds of silk and heavy swathes of gem-encrusted velvet); fabulous silvery-grey cloaks for the Elven-army; disgustingly blood-and-sweat-stained leather jerkins for the Uruk-hai.

The detailing – whether exquisite or ugly – is extraordinary: the buttons on Aragorn's tunic embossed with the Tree of Gondor or Saruman's belt braided in white wool, interwoven with gold thread.

We pause by Merry's costume as a captain of Rohan: it is made from a dark, rich green material with deep maroon piping; the belt and collar-edging meticulously embroidered with intricate horse-head motifs. 'I can't make half-arsed outfits,' says Ngila with gutsy directness, 'for me, it has to be what it *would* be. I have to make costumes as real as possible – however small the scene – because a costume is the actor's "pass" to a character. Whether it's royal get-up that's incredibly elaborate and weighty, or some ghastly, scratchy, woollen outfit for the local yokel, the actor wearing it will be in no doubt as to who they are.'

There is also, of course, the director to consider: 'It's vitally important that there is no part of the garment that can't be filmed – particularly where Peter is concerned! You never know what he's going to do: if the script says a scene will be shot "waist and above", you can lay money that Pete will shoot from the front, the back and every which way!'

Making the costumes look 'real' means taking great pains to ensure they don't look *new!* Costumes are clothes and should feel lived-in, worn, grubby, old and battered. A close-up of Bilbo's waistcoat pocket, when he is toying with the Ring, shows – by its slight bagginess – that it has obviously been *used* as a pocket. The secret? Simple: stuff it full of stones and leave it for a while!

Like much of Ngila's art, it all comes down to experience: 'The golden rule in ageing or "distressing" any costume is when you think you've reached the point where it looks right – go one stage further! The *real* trick, however, is not to go *too* far. *That* is the great temptation; and, when you are dealing with 35mm film, your eye is everything: what you see is exactly what you are going to get on screen – *in spades.*'

We are passing the costume bags for 'Gandalf the Grey' comprising, according to the attached list: '1 bag; 1 belt; 1 box with tobacco and scrolls; 1 pair of boots; 1 pair of rain boots; 2 scarves; 1 hat; 1 silk robe and cloak; 2 green robes; 3 undershirts; 3 culottes; 2 oil-skin capes.' Attached to the hanger, I notice, is a small bag of grey darning-wool for running repairs.

'I adore Gandalf the Grey's costume!' says Ngila. 'The material was specially woven for us in Indonesia and, whilst it may look like a lot of old grey raggedy stuff, I can tell you that a huge amount of work went into making it look like that.'

The process began with a good washing: 'Several good washings, actually. Next we over-dyed it until we got to what was the agreed Gandalf costume colour and *then* we washed it again – to dull the colour down. After that, we put it through another dye-bath and washed it *yet again*. Then we *really* got started!'

Sand was used to roughen the surface and oxides were worked into the folds of the cloth to give those variations of colour that only come with fading. The costume was then put on an 'Ian McKellen substitute', so that the natural wear-points could be marked – elbows, knees, hems and down the front, 'where hands and life happen!' – areas which then received *serious* attention: creating stains, making holes, snagging threads.

'When we'd done all *that*,' says Ngila with a smile, 'we stepped back and took a good, long, hard look. Then we very probably stuck it back in the wash and started the whole damn business all over again!'

It took up to three days to create a convincingly 'broken-down' costume and the same laborious process would then have to be applied to however many versions of the costume were required for filming – in the case of Gandalf, some fifteen – all of which had to match as well as show varying stages of wear-and-tear.

Identical sets of the costume were also made for stunt-doubles, riding-doubles and scale-doubles which – in the case of the tall actor standing in for Gandalf when Elijah and the other hobbit-actors need to look small – required a costume in the same fabric but made to a *larger-scale weave!*

The issue of scale caused some of the worst headaches on the project. 'It was,' says Ngila, 'like a puzzle in which, just as you think you've got it worked out, another piece that you've somehow overlooked suddenly pops up!'

This is a view confirmed by Emma Harre, a member of Ngila's team, who happens to be passing with a bag of shoes ('Gondor boots: size 10 and 11'; 'Orc boots size 12 and 13'): 'It near enough killed us!' she laughs. 'We took Polaroids whenever we were on set so that we could keep track of which particular version of a costume the character was wearing at each stage of the journey. Unfortunately, they weren't exactly filming that journey in sequence…'

Working from the scripts, Emma and her colleagues made graphs, charts and maps: 'It was the only way. When Frodo and Sam are in Mordor, for example, their outfits go through twenty-seven different continuity-changes!'

Ngila nods in agreement: 'Honestly, if I had known *then* what I know *now*, I really think I might just have turned down the job, gone home and gone to bed.'

Luckily, she didn't. Ngila accepted the assignment, arriving in Wellington, from her home town of Auckland, in April 1999 – ominously, as she points out, on All Fools' Day!

The perfect choice for the task, Ngila had previously worked with Peter Jackson on *Heavenly Creatures*, and was an old friend of Richard Taylor, having designed costumes alongside Weta's armour and prosthetics on the *Hercules* and *Xena* television series. From the start, Ngila knew that *The Lord of the Rings* was going to be a tough schedule: shooting was just six months away and

it was to be another three months before she would have a team with whom she could start working on what was clearly a hugely ambitious wardrobe.

However, within hours of her arrival, a sobering realization dawned: 'I saw that the look of the film had already been more or less established by Alan Lee and Weta Workshop. So virtually all my own design ideas went straight out of the window! I became incredibly pragmatic, deciding that the best I could hope to be was a facilitator and trust that good-will and naivety would somehow carry me through.'

As it happened, the film went through so many evolutionary stages during shooting that Ngila's personal contribution turned out to be far greater than she originally imagined. Even at the outset there were compensations: since a style for the hobbits had not yet been established, it was a responsibility that fell immediately to Ngila. It was, however, a challenging task with which to begin. The chief difficulty was that of situating the hobbits within a realm comprising a motley collection of cultures and, in consequence, many different styles of costuming. Whilst the reader may not be conscious of the fact, it is almost as if

characters from a novel by Dickens set out on a journey that takes them into a variety of Shakespearean settings. 'The hobbits,' says Ngila, 'walk through time and you really have to believe that they can cross this landscape and meet all these other different people without anyone looking at them and saying: "What a funny outfit you've got on!" I think, in the end, we only get away with it through the sweet poetry of those little guys.'

Working against the clock, Ngila established a hobbit-look: 'I saw them as rustic, unrefined, cheerfully colourful and childlike as they head into a world that grows increasingly blacker and bleaker. So, I decided to dress them in an English style – somewhere in the region of the late seventeenth and early eighteenth centuries – but mucked about with so that it was slightly off-kilter: sleeves and trouser-legs that were short, pockets that were high.'

Here, as with all the costumes, the design process began with the players themselves: 'First, I draw the actors. I need to know them and I need to get a handle on how they're going to portray their characters. Once I have fully understood the physicality of the actor and what that person is going to bring to a role, then I can take full advantage of both.'

As with many other departments, shopping for materials was not easy: 'Distance in New Zealand makes it difficult. We had a blueprint, of course; we knew, for instance, that we wanted silks and silk-velvets for the Elves and high quality wools and true velvets for the people of Edoras but then we looked for as many other interesting fabrics as we could find.'

What is left of those original materials ('Less than 5% of everything we bought!') is now stacked neatly, shelf upon shelf, along one wall. There are silk-crepes; gold polyester-nets; brocades; wools; ginghams for hobbit children; gem-coloured velvets for Bilbo's waistcoats and any number of bales of glittery, shimmery stuff. 'We bought quite a lot of white velvet,' Ngila explains, indicating a particular bolt of cloth. 'That way we could dye it in a whole range of colours. But we also found a *grey* velvet that we could dye to a wonderfully deep midnight-blue. We pretty much dyed everything: stripping out the original colour with repeated washing; pushing in other colours; bleaching-in patterns – essentially taking *new* materials and making them look *antique*.'

Once the initial designs had been agreed, the wardrobe department – which began as a team of eight people, but rapidly grew to fifty – made three variations of each costume for Peter, Fran and Philippa's consideration.

One of Frodo's costumes, for example, might consist of a jacket, waistcoat and trousers made in soft grey

fabrics ('quiet but very rich'), as well as a set in blues and maroons ('fuller and more cheerful') and another in a different choice of fabrics and tonal range that was somewhere between the two. 'The differences,' says Ngila, 'were often quite subtle, but *always* noticeable to Peter. That was the challenge: producing something that matched whatever ideas he had in *his* mind. For my own sanity, I made absolutely sure that all the options were ones that *I* was going to be happy with. Whichever one he went with was, for me, an "A" choice – there were strictly *no* "B" choices allowed! And as for the rejects, they usually ended up (suitably adapted) on one of the extras.'

The demands were high – to start with, more than one hundred hobbit costumes: not just for the principles actors and their various doubles (finding a formula for the scaling-down of hobbit buttons was just one tiny hurdle), but also all the Hobbiton villagers and party-goers.

Time was fast running out. Wardrobe Manager, Janis MacEwan, overhearing our conversation, puts down the box she is carrying (intriguingly labelled 'Galadriel – spare underwear'), and relives the horror: 'The preparation period before the beginning of filming was originally going to be twelve weeks; then it was cut to seven weeks and the race was really on! Fifty people working flat out with no more than two days to get a costume finished and looking right. Everyone feverishly embroidering; quilting and braiding; covering buttons; making eyelets; threading thonging…'

'You know,' says Ngila, 'I can actually feel the hysteria rising as we talk about it!'

Small wonder that whilst Janis, Emma and others started out *and finished* on the project alongside Ngila, there were those who simply couldn't stay the course. Across the most frenzied period of filming, Ngila lost ten to fifteen per cent of her staff: 'It was the men who tended to drop out first. I believe women work much harder than men, they have huge amounts of resource; but it is always a more emotional, highly-charged, atmosphere: there is more laughter, but there are also many more tears!'

There were crazy days – dressing fifteen hundred extras on three different locations in Queenstown – and, perhaps the worst, the thirty-six-hour-long day during which the wardrobe department grappled with designing, making – and *re*making – a costume for Legolas.

'That,' recalls Ngila, 'was heartbreaking for everyone. Shooting was about to start and no one could agree on how Legolas should look. We worked through one night and halfway through the next day; people went home for a few hours' sleep, came back, somehow kept going. It was not a place anyone wanted to be, but

sometimes you just have to walk the plank and try not to think about the sharks that are circling…'

The Elves *were* troublesome: 'They are tall, androgynous, centuries old, yet ageless! How do you convey all that on film? Then, thank God, in waltzed Cate Blanchett followed by Hugo Weaving and, suddenly, we knew that we had found a couple of the perfect Elves. Between the two of them, they defined "Elf" for us at last and we were able to create a design language that was rich and sumptuous and which we knew would work.'

It was a look that also influenced the costume design for Aragorn who, whilst not an Elf, had been raised by Elrond among the Elves of Rivendell.

'In total contrast to Boromir's costume,' observes Ngila, 'which is weighed down with the customs and observances of Gondor, I wanted Aragorn's costume to have something of the "lightness" of the Elves – as though it were a quality which, through long years of living with them, he had taken to himself.'

When Viggo Mortensen – who was thoroughly immersing himself in the character of Aragorn – asked if he might take care of his own costume it came as a something of a surprise to the wardrobe department. 'It was an unusual request,' admits Ngila, 'but it was

important to Viggo and, therefore, important to us. Who knows, perhaps it was because he washed and repaired Aragorn's clothes himself that he so perfectly came to inhabit them – to a point, indeed, where the costume seemed almost blended with his body.' Ngila pauses a moment in thought. 'You know,' she says at last, 'I really do think that particular costume is incredibly beautiful. It seems funny, perhaps, to talk about something that is so worn and broken down, so darned and patched, as being *beautiful* – but to me it is…'

Maybe for a designer, the true essence of beauty lies in texture – it is certainly something that Ngila talks a lot about. 'It's incredible what texture can do,' she says, gathering up an armful of Saruman's white robes, 'look at this: *moiré* silk, woven silk, embroidered silk, texture on texture on texture, until it almost takes on different colours.'

Various techniques and precision skills were employed to create such multi-textured effects: some materials were screen-printed with designs, others were embellished with cornelli, a craft in which patterns are delineated with string and then over-stitched to give the rich look of raised embroidery.

With the introduction of the Rohan civilization in *The Two Towers*, new opportunities were afforded to Ngila and her team, particularly with the character of King Théoden, played by Bernard Hill. A broken monarch, Théoden is held in thrall by the evil Gríma Wormtongue, until he is released and rehabilitated by Gandalf the White.

'When we first meet Théoden,' says Ngila, 'we see him as a crumpled old man, incapable of any kind of decision-making. I wanted him to have the appearance of someone who never got out of his bathrobe! So we made him three layers of gowns, all of which were bled of their colour – so that deep browns became musty and rich golds a sickly-yellow, while the elaborate embroidery was aged down until only the subtlest hint of the original opulence remained. On top of everything we heaped a vast coat with a ratty-looking fur collar.'

The costume department's jeweller, Jasmine Watson, made a beautiful crown which was then ruthlessly stripped of all its patina. 'We only had one crown,' explains Ngila, 'so we had to be very careful that whatever products we used could later be removed and the crown buffed up to its full glory for Théoden's transformation. We actually had a terrible moment on set when the tiny horse emblems on the crown began unexpectedly pinging off!'

Once reclaimed from the spell that has long imprisoned him, the middle-aged Théoden is vigorously reborn and sheds his long, dusty robes in favour of a shorter, more active, style of tunic and cape made in colourful, richly embroidered fabrics fitting for the warrior king he has once more become.

As for the costume designed for Gríma, Théoden's duplicitous counsellor portrayed by Brad Dourif, Ngila relished the task: 'I wanted him to have the look of a hunched, feral creature who was clothed in finery but who never washed. His linen shirt was greasy, dirty and utterly repulsive – I'm happy to say it was a near perfect example of costume breakdown!'

Every aspect of the costume helped convey the

monstrosity of Gríma's character: 'The sleeves of his under-robe came to points on the hands, heightening the sense of evil intent, while the over-robe – black velvet flecked with gold – had a fish-tail extension that dragged along the floor behind him. With the addition of a high, ruched-velvet collar his neck seemed to disappear into his shoulders, creating the illusion of humped-backed deformity.'

For all their textural complexities and subtleties, these costumes are representative of Ngila's determination to resist over-complicated designs: 'I am not,' she says emphatically, 'a designer who wants my work to overwhelm on screen! *Except…*' She stops in mid-sentence and laughs. '*Except*, of course, when it's some girl's *big frock!*'

Whilst Galadriel's gown may have been the solution to the 'Elf problem', creating costumes for Liv Tyler as the Elven princess Arwen – was a continuing quest, driven this way and that by an ever-changing perspective on how the character was going to be represented on film. To begin with, the script had her as a warrior princess in a long, flowing dress: 'It just buried

her,' Ngila remembers. 'Liv was encumbered with all these weapons and every time she turned around she'd be tripped up by a long skirt or whipped in the face by a long sleeve.'

As Arwen's role changed into the one finally seen on screen, the wardrobe department began to achieve what Ngila refers to as a 'whole string of successes'. These resulted from the use of a palette that was less in harmony with the greys, greens and yellows used for the Elves (colours that did not work well on Liv) to full reds and deep blues. 'When she's clothed in those costumes,' says Ngila, 'the effect – with that wonderful face and those luminous eyes – is *amazing*.'

The decision proved pivotal. 'It was fantastic and – at the same time – *terrifying*, because as Peter started to enjoy the direction in which we were going and as he became more confident in these big frocks, he started planning more scenes for Arwen that, in turn, required *more* costumes!'

Similar demands began to be made for Miranda Otto's character, Éowyn, who embodies both the feminine and the heroic. 'Miranda was a dream,' enthuses Ngila. 'She slipped into those frocks and she became the character. I remember watching her put on this huge green velvet number and seeing her sheer excitement at feeling beautiful and feeling herself take on the personality of Éowyn.'

It is an experience with which Ngila is very familiar: 'Actors are often nervous when they first come in: they feel that they're at the very ends of the earth and they don't know me from a bar of soap! But once I get them into costume, I can see the relief beginning to settle on their faces as they realize that they can *work* in these clothes, *be* their character. That's when I get my adrenalin rush!'

Looking back over two years of work on *The Lord of the Rings*, it is not altogether easy to forget those times when tensions ran deep and passions high. There were tedious week-in-week-out challenges such as having a laundry that was a time-consuming trek away from wardrobe, at the opposite end of the studio buildings. There were also those, thankfully rare, moments of out-and-out disaster, such as a telephone call in the middle of the night reporting the fact that the costume tent at the Helm's Deep location had just blown away, scattering Orc gear the length and breadth of the local countryside.

But there are also plenty of good memories: 'Cate, dressed as Galadriel but wearing platform granny-boots (for added height) and stripy socks (for added warmth) goofing around in Lothlórien; Ian McKellen, wrestling with that wretched hat; Elijah in wardrobe at five in the morning, every morning, six days a week; exhausted dyers taking fabrics back to the dye-bath for the umpteenth time… And everyone doing it for Peter! It's extraordinary!'

Ngila gives a low laugh. 'And – *look!* – we survived!'

The Hat in the Bin

'The black dustbin is boldly labelled: 'GANDALF'S HAT. THIS WAY UP!''

'How the hell are you supposed to store a hat like that?' asks Ngila Dickson. 'Eventually we came up with the only answer: in a dustbin, upside-down, stuffed with newspaper! The label is a symptom of an on-going nightmare that one day someone would do what you are *supposed* to do with a dustbin – *empty* it!'

Modelled on the hat worn by Gandalf in illustrations by John Howe, it was a problematic creation: 'Twenty variations before we got it right,' shudders Ngila, 'and a good many "bad hat days" thereafter! How Ian McKellen coped with acting in the thing, I'll never know!'

'I *loved* the hat!' laughs Ian. 'It had to look as though it had been pulled through a hedge backwards – several hedges, in fact – and by the time we were through, that's *exactly* how it looked!'

The hat was remarkably adaptable: 'During Bilbo's party scene, I did some magic using it, rather like a conjuror, in order to produce various things to entertain the hobbit children; whereas, in the snow scenes, it proved a very useful umbrella. In fact, I came up with a number of ideas as to how I might use the hat when I wasn't wearing it – including thinking of it (since it could be a magic hat) as a kind of bottomless knapsack that I might carry over my shoulder and into which I could keep all manner of things – rather like Mary Poppins' carpet-bag.'

I mention that John Howe had observed that Gandalf's hat was the last vestige of the wizard's persona as originally described by Tolkien in *The Hobbit* and that the artist had noted that Ian casts it aside in the Mines of Moria – as if finally casting away the old Gandalf.

'Well,' responds Ian, 'it was obvious that I wasn't going to keep the hat when I was falling in the arms of the Balrog, so there had to be a point at which I discarded it and just before Gandalf is caught up in the heat of battle in the Mines of Moria seemed as good a moment as any.'

Giving an affectionate glance at the dustbin-hat-box, he adds: 'There was, of course, no question of the hat being worn by Gandalf the White, it really wouldn't have gone with the rest of his gear!'

The White Lady of Rohan

'In creating costume designs for Éowyn, shieldmaiden of Rohan, Ngila Dickson turned to Tolkien's initial description of the character – golden haired, robed in white with a silver belt and looking 'fair and cold'. The result: a simple, yet dramatically effective, white gown in which Miranda Otto would make her first screen appearance in *The Two Towers,* photographed in a sweeping shot, from a helicopter circling high above the courtyard of Edoras.

'From there,' says Ngila, 'we took that slightly tomboyish, feisty young thing to the full weight of royalty at the funeral for her cousin, Théodred, clothing her in layer upon layer of rich, regal fabric. Veils, jewellery and a crown completed an ensemble that was redolent with age and ritual.'

For Miranda, these costumes were the beginning of finding and understanding her character: 'I turned up in New Zealand burdened by various personal problems and wondering how on earth I was ever going to become this emotionally complex, fearlessly determined character. Quite simply, Ngila transformed me. She spent a long time perfecting necklines and sleeve lengths, every possible detail, to get it exactly right for me. It was really in the wardrobe and the sword-fighting classes that I began to see, in a very physical sense, who this woman was.'

Actor and designer quickly found themselves simpatico: 'After a fitting,' recalls Miranda, 'I might go away and find myself thinking that we ought, perhaps, to go back to some fabric which we had looked at earlier – only to turn up for my next fitting and find that Ngila had already done exactly that!'

It was in the choice of colours and materials that Éowyn's personality was differentiated from that of Arwen. 'We decided,' says Miranda, 'that since Éowyn was human you needed to feel as if you could reach out and touch her, unlike Arwen and Galadriel who are Elves and, therefore more illusive, more like a trick of the light.'

Ngila's use of natural fabrics (wools, hessians, velvets and brocades) suggested warmth, earthiness and royalty as well as a sense of imprisonment – a woman bound and trapped by duty.

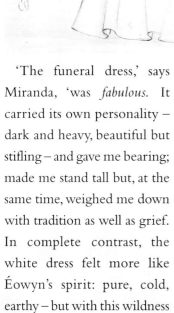

'The funeral dress,' says Miranda, 'was *fabulous*. It carried its own personality – dark and heavy, beautiful but stifling – and gave me bearing; made me stand tall but, at the same time, weighed me down with tradition as well as grief. In complete contrast, the white dress felt more like Éowyn's spirit: pure, cold, earthy – but with this wildness inside.'

'As a child,' Miranda recalls, 'I used to fantasize about being a medieval princess and, what do you know, I got to be one – thanks to Ngila's genius!

Waging the War of the Ring

'This is "the Sword that was Broken",' says Richard Taylor, 'and broken, and broken, and broken – and *broken*!' It seems that Weta Workshop made no fewer than five versions of Narsil, Elendil's sword that was smashed by Sauron and then used by Isildur to cut the One Ring from the Dark Lord's hand. Richard explains: 'We needed to be able to have up to five goes at breaking it without keeping the camera crew waiting.'

We are surrounded by suits of armour and piles of custom-made boxes containing a small part of the arsenal of weapons used in filming *The Lord of the Rings*, all of which are now stashed in one of twenty-eight huge walk-in containers stacked two- or three-deep in the yard at Weta Workshop.

It's a lot of storage space, but then there's an awful lot to store: 'We designed and made 48,000 pieces of armour and had four people working ten hours a day just producing chain-mail. We also produced 2,000 weapons, including swords, spears, pikes and maces, long-bows, cross-bows, daggers, knives and axes.'

As with everything at Weta, the statistics are staggering, the philosophy uncompromising: 'The requirements were unbelievably complex – in terms of the quantities involved and the different scales to which they had to be made, but we were determined that our work would never have the predictable "fantasy" look used in dozens of movies designed by the art departments of Hollywood. This was never going to be a *Conan the Barbarian*-style film: we wanted audiences to feel that when it came to warfare, life in Middle-earth was real and earnest. A sword, first and foremost, is something with which to defend oneself against a foe;

so, regardless of any decoration and embellishment, it had to be totally functional.'

The prospect was a demanding one: 'A tricky balancing-act is how *I'd* describe it,' says Richard, 'attempting to create objects that have a really individual look while, at the same time, mass-producing them, cost-effectively, at an incredible rate. Amazingly, despite churning out items on a daily basis, we somehow managed to create the trappings for a number of very different cultures, all with a ring of authenticity.'

The decision was taken early on to establish a foundry that would employ modern-day power sources to replicate the bellows-driven forge used by medieval swordsmiths and to then look for skilled craftsmen who could work with anvil, hammer and red-hot metal.

It didn't take Richard Taylor long to find Peter Lyon, a swordsmith who forged weapons for historical re-enactment groups and who had only recently started his own workshop a few hundred yards down the road from Weta.

Richard next came across *Heathen Irons*, the catalogue of another New Zealand armourer, Stu Johnson, and invited him to visit Weta. He was a little surprised when Stu and his girlfriend drove up to the gates of the Workshop and got out of their car wearing full plate-armour. 'For the next two hours,' laughs Richard, 'I took them on a tour with them clanking along in their armour until I became seriously worried that they might keel over from exhaustion. But they didn't; and, needless to say, I hired Stu on the spot!'

Peter and Stu – working with Art Director, Kayne Horsham; Head of Armour and Weapons, Gary Mackay; Armoursmith, Warren Green and Leather Craftsman, Mike Grelish – began producing designs and prototypes. At which point, Conceptual Artist John Howe joined the project.

In addition to being steeped in the lore of Middle-earth, John is actively involved with the Companie of Saynt George, a mediaeval re-enactment society in his homeland, Switzerland.

'John's arrival,' recalls Richard, 'was a fundamental, life-changing event for Weta. For those of us who had grown up in New Zealand – a young country with a culture that lacked any of the traditions of European history and literature – we couldn't hope to do more than draw our inspiration from books, museum photographs and the kind of movies made in the past. Then John stepped into our lives – like a living emissary from the Middle Ages!'

'We know nothing about sword-fighting!' observes John Howe in a quiet, but unequivocal, tone. 'We know nothing at all – other than what they do in the movies! Anything historical seems so much less interesting, glamorous and flashy than anything Hollywood. To most film-makers, history is *boring*!' As a result, John believes, we have failed to grasp the realities of medieval warfare: 'Our idea of combat is little more than hitting each other with dull sticks! You cannot, for example, clash two swords together without seriously damaging both; nor will one blade slide down another if it's at any kind of an angle – instead, it will catch, and you'll end up with two jagged notches.' He continues: 'In movies, you see warriors leaping about all the time, turning this way and that! It drives me *nuts*! You would *never* turn around when you are having a fight with someone, simply because, if you did, the other guy would hit you on the back of the head!'

At Weta, John immediately found himself discussing such issues: 'We talked about what made historical things interesting and what made a lot of fantasy –

especially *film* fantasy – so awful! We focused on trying to design weapons with the unambiguous purpose of being used to ram into someone's guts and building armour that is intended to protect your own guts from being rammed into by somebody else!'

For the craftsmen, it was an exhilarating, yet daunting, experience to submit their handicraft to John's uncompromising scrutiny. Any apprehension, however, was unfounded: 'There's one way to see if an armourer is any good,' notes John, 'you ask to see the pieces he's done for the lower leg. It is a difficult, almost *impossible*, thing to understand the shape of the calf, the tibia and the ankle and then create something to fit it – out of metal! If he can do that, then he can probably do anything. Pete Lyon showed me examples of his work and I knew, at once, that he understood.'

The Weta craftsmen warmed to John and welcomed his tutelage: 'We got on well together and they quickly grasped the idea that the *real* use of swords could be equally as exciting as the crazy stuff they do in movies! In fact, they picked it up *so* quickly that they would wander into my room, look at what I was drawing and say: "Are you sure that would work?" or, "That looks a bit *naff*!" That was *really* exciting!

With John Howe providing valuable and challenging inspiration, Weta began crafting an extraordinary range of armour and weaponry: beaten out of steel, much of it was then embellished with intricate designs (as with Éowyn's sword above) or etched with runes and Elvish script.

To create sufficient weapons and armour components for the vast armies featured in the films,

the original, hand-crafted items were then moulded so that they could be mass-produced in polyurethane. Similarly, the key weapons made for the central characters were replicated for use by stunt- and riding-doubles and – for safety reasons and to reduce the weight carried by the actors – in scenes filmed in long-shot. All close-ups, however, featured the original, or 'hero', weapons. The one exception to this rule being Viggo Mortensen, who insisted on carrying Aragorn's hero weapon *at all times* during filming. 'We were very fortunate,' says Richard, 'that Viggo was so dedicated in his portrayal of Aragorn that he treated his sword if his life really depended upon it.'

Richard sets great importance by the relationship between an actor and the weapons he or she is required

to carry. For example, a sword was created for Denethor, Steward of Gondor and father to Boromir and Faramir, even though it would never be drawn on camera. 'Of course,' says Richard, 'we could have simply given Denethor a scabbard with a hilt attached, but you know damn well that the moment the actor grabs the sword-hilt *and it doesn't come out*, he is going to feel like he's only an extra! Because we wanted John Noble, who plays Denethor in *The Return of the King*, to have the authority of his position epitomized by the Steward's sword, we made it for him.'

Richard draws Denethor's sword, swings it so that it catches the light and then returns it to its scabbard. 'Apart from John Noble and the folk at Weta,' he smiles, 'you're probably the only person who will ever see that blade!'

The range of blades created for the films is impressive, from the sword Aragorn carries as a Ranger (which Richard describes as 'A plain, functional design, light enough to be carried over long distances, but very, very powerful'), to the fine Elven-knives which the hobbits are given in Lothlórien. Hung from belts ornamented with a motif of interwoven leaves and buckles like opening flowers, their hafts are made from South African wood with exquisite inlaid decorations in brass which, in the case of Merry and Pippin's knives, survive to be found by Aragorn amongst the ashes of the Rohirrim's bonfire of orc-corpses.

'Our design philosophy for all the weapons,' says Richard, 'was to avoid the fantastical, yet, at the same time to come up with new approaches, such as the daggers we devised for Gríma Wormtongue's henchmen.'

Since weapons are not allowed within King Théoden's Golden Hall at Edoras, these weapons are curved to the shape of the arm and hidden within the sleeves of the henchmen's long, monk-like robes. 'They are like tigers' claws,' says Richard. 'The handle is integral to the blade with a thumb-hole that allows a backwards-cutting motion.' He gives a rather too convincing demonstration. 'Basically, they are designed so you can hook someone from behind and quickly and efficiently slit their throat!'

The potential effectiveness of these unpleasant implements is all too clear. 'Whether crude or beautiful,' remarks Richard, 'a weapon is a work-a-day object that has to undergo almost as many rigours on a movie-set as on a battlefield. Hence the fact that we awaited the arrival of the film's Swordmaster with some trepidation.'

They needn't have worried…

'A job's only as good as the tools that are used, a fight's only as good as the weapons.' Swordmaster Bob Anderson (seen right rehearsing with Sean Bean) is reflecting on his work on *The Lord of the Rings*. 'Fortunately,' he continues, 'Richard Taylor and the guys at Weta are quite simply geniuses! *Absolute geniuses!*'

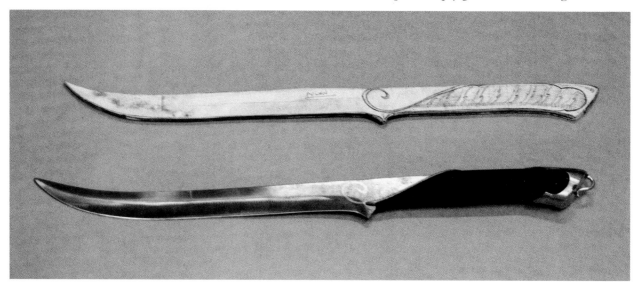

It is the view of an expert: an Olympic fencing-coach, whose fight and stunt work on movies ranges from James Bond's 1963 adventure, *From Russia With Love* to 007's most recent exploits in *Die Another Day*. En route, Bob contributed to such pictures as *Barry Lyndon*, *Highlander*, *First Knight*, *The Mask of Zorro* and the first three *Star Wars* movies.

'Weta made better swords than anybody I've ever worked with,' comments Bob. 'I told them what I wanted and they gave it to me. There were fine fighting swords and rough, hacking implements; there were swords with saw-edges and others with barbed ends – all kinds of unexpected, but imaginatvely useful, weapons!'

Not only was Bob impressed with the type of weaponry, but also with their durability: 'I'm used to fifteen to twenty blades getting broken during a film. On *The Lord of the Rings*, we made *three* films and only broke *one* sword. And that was only because it got so battered and bent that it finally fell apart!'

Nevertheless, regardless of their quality, weapons still need to be wielded by people who look as though they are used to handling them. So, I ask, do the principle cast-members do their own swordwork? 'They do on *my* pictures!' Bob replies emphatically. 'The fact that I only want the best seems to bring out the best in others: Sean Bean worked damn hard on his sword-play and looked good doing it. And why? Because an actor will always have a personal interest in how he looks on film and, since he's already able to act, if you can train him in the swordwork, he'll do it far better than any double ever can!'

Bob is particularly complimentary about Viggo Mortensen: 'He came onto the project late, threw himself into it heart and soul, picked it up in no time and never once stopped rehearsing. His first fight was at Weathertop – which wasn't *too* demanding – but by the time he reached Helm's Deep, boy, was he in trouble!

Surrounded by hordes of Orcs, all clamouring to get at him, Viggo fought and fought like a seasoned trooper!'

There are, however, some occasions when a stunt-double will be required to stand in for an actor: 'Basically, you never take a chance with an actor if it's going to get dangerous. That's when you use stunt guys, whose *job* is taking risks.'

And the essential qualities for a stunt-player? 'The same as for an actor: agility, co-ordination, quick reactions, timing and an ability to remember. Memory is *essential* – not just memorizsing *how* to do it properly, but *what* to do *when*! Despite having little or no experience on film work of this kind, the New Zealand stuntmen worked hard, learned quickly and did a magnificent job!'

Bob Anderson was determined to create a particular 'look' for the fight scenes: 'I have what I can only describe as a sense of drama that won't let me accept mundane, automatic swordplay – it has to look *real* and it has to convince *me*. For *The Lord of the Rings*, I wanted to create a mood that felt medieval: a wild time when fighting was brutal and heavy-handed. So, having spent

a long time training the actors and stuntmen to fence properly, I then told them to let it go and become as bestial as they could!'

It was an instruction that was helped by the fact that the Orcs and Uruk-hai were cushioned by heavy prosthetic make-up: 'Wearing those thick suits and leather armour may have made wielding weapons difficult and tiring, but with so many layers of protection, they could really hit out at one another with very little inhibition! It certainly added to the temper of the film!'

In choreographing a fight-sequence, Bob would plan and video the action using doubles and, where possible, the chosen location. The video would then be discussed with Peter Jackson and, once agreed, the fight would be thoroughly rehearsed with the actors.

'You simply keep doing it and doing it,' explains Bob, 'until every single move becomes a reflex-action. In a fight, things always happen faster than you can think and, anyway, there's no time for thinking or it becomes slow and ponderous. However, once those reflexes have been conditioned, it's too dangerous to make any changes: you can shoot it from different angles but – when you're dealing with swords – what you've rehearsed is what you do! Mind you,' adds Bob, 'Peter always manages to add something: like the arrows in the fight between Boromir and the Uruks at the end of

The Fellowship of the Ring. Those are Jackson embellishments.'

'We made no less than 10,000 arrows,' says Richard Taylor. 'Two thousand for the Rohirrim alone, of which – due to loss and breakages – we've got only 78 left!'

Opening a bag, Richard takes out one of four bows designed for Arwen: 'Bows are incredibly difficult things to make and we pursued many different techniques. To start with, we made them in wood, but that didn't work because a bow is under massive poundage and the actors were often required to "dry-fire" them, so that digital arrows could be added later. If you dry-fire a wooden bow, the energy is absorbed through the wood rather than the arrow, and the timber shatters. For that reason – and because of the elaborate shapes we were designing – we came up with a system of injection-moulding them in rubber.'

Five hundred bows with hand-wound bowstrings were made using this method and, even in rubber, they are a potentially lethal weapon. 'God, yes!' exclaims Richard. 'Not only will they shoot real arrows, if they were properly aimed and fired, then they could kill.'

Apart from the digital arrows there were those 10,000 *real* arrows: some actually fired, others seen in quivers or lodged in enemy bodies. Richard hands me one of Legolas's arrows: it has a wooden shaft, hand-tinted from dark green to light brown, a plastic 'nock' (the groove into which the bowstring fits) wood-textured so as not to *look* plastic; and a tip that has been cast in ship-metal and then plated. Like all the arrows seen in close-up, it has been hand-fletched, using turkey feathers dyed to a greeny-gold colour.

Like the weaponry, the armour made for the films shows the same attention to detail and encompasses a similar range of styles, from the grotesque to the beautiful: ugly armour for Grishnákh the Orc, made from leather decorated with warg-teeth and trimmed with shaggy animal hair disgustingly matted with dried blood; and, in contrast, exquisite 'leaf-mail' armour for the Elven warriors, each leaf of which has been cut from sheets of PVC plastic, individually hand painted and folded in order to create the central vein of the 'leaf'.

'This,' announces Richard triumphantly, 'is my favourite suit of armour!' Made for King Théoden, it is constructed from steel with beaten-copper ornamentation and a chain-mail skirt. 'I love it!' says Richard, pointing out the decorated rivet-covers hiding the modern rivets, 'and Bernard Hill loved it, too! All armour not only has to fit and be comfortable, but it also has to make the actor feel as if he or she were the character who would wear that armour.'

All of which was a challenge, since most of the armour was made long before the actors arrived in New Zealand. 'We would work from the players' measurements, "test-wear" them on similarly-sized Weta technicians and then, when we finally got it onto the actors, often only a few days before shooting, make one or two slight adjustments – or, sometimes, *massive* adjustments!'

Richard produces trophy after trophy as if excavating the treasures of some ancient burial-mound: this is Théoden's shield, etched with interlocking flower-patterns and designs representing the Rohirrim hunting boar; and this is Éomer's helmet with a nose-guard in the shape of a horse's head and a white horse-hair plume behind as if the emblem of the riders of Rohan were offering symbolic protection to the wearer.

'All these images of horses,' notes Richard, 'are a reminder that, in addition to the human cast, *The Lord of the Rings* featured a large number of equine actors.'

'Having horses galloping at full speed down a very steep ramp was certainly interesting!' Mark is remembering a sequence from the Battle of Helm's Deep. 'Whenever you train horses, there's always one who thinks he knows better! On this run, a horse decided to launch himself from the top and landed half-way down with only one more stride before having to make a sharp turn at the bottom. There was next to no margin for error and that horse pushed it to the limit!'

I am meeting with three of the horse team: Mark Kinaston-Smith, Wrangler and Make-up Artist (yes, even horses require make-up!); Stephen Old, Horse Co-ordinator; and Len Baynes, a retired farmer who enlisted as a rider on the film.

When Len wasn't thundering along in a Ringwraith costume (with zero peripheral vision), he was doubling for Bernard Hill and riding King Théoden's horse, Snowmane, played, incidentally, by a horse named – Sno*worries*!

'It was a bit different from my twenty years in farming,' laughs Len, 'riding around in costume and make-up. Fortunately, they seemed to think I was a good enough lookalike, so I grew my own beard (which was a lot easier than having one stuck on) and, whenever riding was involved, there'd be *two* King Théodens on set at the same time. To begin with I did a lot of riding for Bernard, but he would keep training and, as a result, became so damn good that – apart from dangerous stuff – I spent more time sitting around than in the saddle!'

A number of other leading actors, including Orlando Bloom and Karl Urban (below as Éomer), were trained to a level of competence that allowed them to undertake some of their character's riding scenes. Viggo Mortensen, as one would expect, was already a capable rider when he arrived and did virtually all his own riding which provided an irresistible incentive to the younger members of the cast – and one that the specialists somewhat dreaded!

'If a horse is going any faster than a trot,' explains Stephen Old (pictured below right), 'then it can be dangerous. Anything can happen to the best of riders and any fall can result in broken limbs. You can double an actor on a horse, you can't double him in a dramatic close-up if he's in hospital with a broken leg!'

'Frankly,' says Mark, 'it was quite a relief when an actor *didn't* want to ride!'

The horse department was overseen by Head Animal Wrangler Dave Johnson and included trainers, riding-instructors, vets and riders from a diversity of backgrounds including horse-racing, showing and eventing as well as pleasure-riders and people with rodeo skills. Seasoned horsemen and women, they took on some risky assignments. Legolas, for example, is seen riding at a gallop with Gimli seated behind him – a shot which was eventually achieved by having a dummy dwarf attached to both the back of the saddle *and* to the Legolas riding-double!

There was also the problem of Gandalf riding Shadowfax bare-back, at speed, while carrying his staff in one hand. That particular challenge was met by providing the riding-double with a small saddle that could be concealed beneath the wizard's voluminous robes, and by training the white Andalusian steed (and its double, for horses *also* require doubles!) to respond to a low-slung control-wire around its neck.

With no previous film or television production ever requiring as many horses as *The Lord of the Rings*, the team, under the guidance of Horse Trainer Don Reynolds, Technical Advisors John Scott and Lyle Edge and Horse Stunt Co-ordinator Casey O'Neill, specially trained the seventy-six horses who are featured in the film.

Employing similar techniques to those used by mounted police, the horses were trained not to react to sudden and loud noises, flapping flags and banners and the unlikely creatures that might be encountered on a battlefield in Middle-earth.

'It's about repetition,' says Mark Kinaston-Smith, 'some horses will pick it up in a couple of days and

you're confident about putting them on set; others may take two or three weeks and you still can't predict how they'll react when the director shouts: "Action!"'

What proved difficult, as Stephen Old explains, was having horses that were so well-trained that they weren't even remotely bothered by a small thing like an Orc-attack: 'We couldn't have them standing there completely unmoved by the fact that there was a battle raging all about them and yet that was *precisely* what they had been trained to do! So the rider would have to act as if he was trying to control his horse when, in fact, the horse was totally in control! The more takes we did the worse it got: after ten takes, nothing could faze them!'

Finding horses wasn't hard, finding animals that could work well under pressure was a bigger challenge, as – once again – was the difficulty presented by scale. There were, for example, two Bill ponies: a genuine Shetland for scenes with Sam's small scale-double and a small horse for those shots featuring Sean Astin, so that hobbit and pony remained in proportion to one another.

Similarly, Gandalf's cart-horse came in two sizes: a Welsh Mountain pony to pull the regular cart driven by Ian McKellen, and a thoroughbred hack for the bigger cart ridden by Ian's large-scale double, Paul Randall.

'Both cart-horses,' explains Mark, 'had bushy manes, white blazes and two white socks on their hind quarters. As long as they are reasonably well-matched, one horse can usually be dressed to look like another.'

That process, involving Mark's skills as a make-up artist, might include hand-plaiting hair-extensions onto tails and manes, even literally creating a 'horse of a different colour' by the use of special dyes and shampoos normally used for show horses. In the case of the Black Riders' horses, make-up was applied to create the impression that they did not look after their steeds.

'I discovered just how effective our make-up was,' recalls Mark, 'when I was leading the Ringwraiths' horses off the truck at the first location. Our Veterinary Surgeon, Ray Lenaghan, who took the welfare of the horses very seriously, looked at them in horror and, thinking that something had gone wrong, yelled: "What the hell happened?"'

The daily schedule for the wranglers was tough: beginning at three or four o'clock in the morning when they would arrive at the stables, an eighty-acre site an hour north of Wellington. They would then round-up thirty or more horses from their paddocks, put on their make-up, dress them for transportation (fitting the animals with bandages and travelling-boots) and be ready for an 8.00 a.m. drive to the location. At the end of the day, the horse-wranglers were usually the last to get to their beds.

For the Battle of the Pelennor Fields in *The Return of the King*, fifty-four horses had to be transported by lorry and ferry – along with a number of sheep and goats – to the location on the South Island. For the same sequence, seven hundred riders (and their horses) were auditioned

to find the 250 riding-extras needed for the battle scenes: 'That was hard work!' recalls Stephen Old. 'Enjoyable, but exhausting: getting that many people – none of whom had ever worked on a film before – through make-up and costume and trying to keep them quiet and entertained and make sure, when filming was over, that the women riders dressed as men didn't throw away their false beards and moustaches… Exhausting!'

'*This* is something that will never be seen on camera,' says Richard Taylor. 'Engraved on the *inside* of the King Théoden's breast-plate is the horse motif of the House of Rohan. I wanted it to be the last thing that Bernard Hill saw as he put on his armour and took on the persona of the King!'

Richard is in his element opening box after box: 'You know, we had someone practically full-time making boxes like this in which to store and transport all these things…' Things such as Gimli's utility backpack; Sam's frying-pans; and a collection of branding-tools, made for Orc-workers to burn the 'Eye of Sauron' onto leather armour, but, in the event, never used.

'There are all sorts of little treats in here,' says Richard, 'like *this*: a dead Uruk-hai on a stick!' He brandishes the charred remains of a severed head impaled, totem-like, on a Rohan spear. 'And,' opening another box, 'this is the Witch-King's mace, hand-ground from a block of aluminium, it's pretty weighty!' I try lifting it, and it is, indeed, extremely heavy. 'You could get hurt wielding that,' says Richard, as he rummages once more and produces a second, identical-looking mace. 'So we also made this light-weight stunt version –' he gives me a playful bonk on the head, '– in *rubber*!'

Such things were, after all, a necessary consideration on a film that involved so many stunts.

'We did it all! Fights, battle-sequences, wire-work, high-falls and stunts with fire and water. The challenge was not repeating ourselves from film to film.' Stunt Co-ordinator George Marshall Ruge is a veteran of more than sixty motion-pictures from *Zorro, the Gay Blade* in 1981 to *The Mask of Zorro* in 1998 and including *Mars Attacks!, George of the Jungle, Perfect Storm* and *Ocean's Eleven*.

'I didn't want any of my actions ever to be gratuitous,' explains George, 'and I wanted all of it to be layered, like a mosaic. Whenever you are doing a battle, there are a hundred stories within the one story. I developed many such scenarios and believe that if you look at any square inch of frame you'll see this mosaic in place and know that you are witnessing an "in-the-moment experience" with dozens of encounters and clashes and life-and-death struggles being played out simply as a backdrop for the bigger drama of the Ring Quest.'

George's initiation into the project was, to say the least, daunting: 'I arrived in New Zealand without having seen a script or a storyboard and, within two days, began nine weeks of night shoots for the Helm's Deep battle sequence in *The Two Towers*! Before I knew it, I was working twenty-hour days in an effort to bring that action to life as well as planning, choreographing and rehearsing future work. The few hours in which I would "try" to sleep, were invariably passed in a dream-world of Orcs, Elves and Uruk-hai!'

Apart from the challenges of filming three movies simultaneously, there were additional anxieties: 'I began with a team of just twenty stunt performers who had been training for the project but who, with a few exceptions, had little or no film experience. One or two left and others joined, but there was a core team who stayed the course. What they lacked in experience they more than made up for with heart and dedication – special people brought together in extraordinary circumstances.'

Working with Bob Anderson and assisted by Assistant Stunt Co-ordinator Daniel Barringer and Stunt Rigger Paul Shapcott, George contrived sequences that would make the most of the available talent: 'It's not easy, delivering epic imagery with limited resources! We managed to increase the average number on the stunt team to around thirty, but I really needed three hundred! Thirty stunt-performers might be fine for a given sequence, but there were often three or more units *all* asking for thirty people! For one or two major sequences, we reached as many as sixty-five performers and that really *was* luxury! However, by training everyone to multi-task and by making our numbers seem like more, we somehow got by…'

Whatever the difficulties, being involved with *The Lord of the Rings* was, for George Marshall Ruge, an experience not to be missed: 'Whenever the stunt-team showed up on the set, the crew knew we would deliver the goods. A lot of unseen work went on, but my view was that Peter Jackson had invested his life in this project,

There is also an elegant, yet deadly, spear designed for Gil-galad (shown left): made in sprung steel, its head is etched with Elven script and further decorated with hand-brazed filigree vinework in copper. Alongside it, a duplicate spear is covered in blood! 'Once a weapon or armour gets bloodied up,' explains Richard, 'we have to leave it in that condition so as to ensure continuity of blood-stains if, for any reason, the scene has to be re-shot.'

'Blood' is a topic which Richard relishes: 'We had staff whose daily responsibility was taking care of the actors' blood. They all had some "gore requirement" – either subtle or totally over the top – such as old battle-scars that had never been washed off. It was vital that we give the characters the appearance of living in an age when it was virtually impossible to wash either themselves or what they wore. So, the moment we arrived at a location, we'd dig dirt, mix it with food-thickener and wallpaper-paste and daub it onto the costumes and armour.'

There is still much to look at and we're only in the first of twenty-eight containers. 'Exciting, eh?' enthuses Richard. 'You can just imagine what's in the other twenty-seven! More boxes! More cool stuff! There were so many extra bits and pieces that we threw in… For example, we made travelling-bags for every character in which they could carry whatever their particular requirements might be…' he thinks for a moment and then laughs, 'you know, loose change, credit-cards, that sort of thing!'

Picking up one of a number of helmets made for Arwen, but never worn, Richard becomes momentarily thoughtful: 'We did an awful lot of stuff that has never been seen – and never will be… That's always a little bit dispiriting, but there's so much else to take pleasure in: not least the amazing process by which big flat sheets of steel would arrive at the Workshop and, in a matter two or three weeks, have been totally transformed into beautiful suits of armour. Of course, that was only achieved by craftsmanship and bloody hard work, but there's also something more… Something that can only be described as magical… Perhaps, even mystical…'

and I was honoured simply to pick up a spear and carry it as far as I could to help bring his vision to life.'

'Where does the spear come from which Aragorn uses to attack the cave troll in Moria?' asks Richard Taylor, 'and which the troll then uses against Frodo?' Holding up the vicious trident-shaped weapon (available, as might be expected, in large- and small-scale versions), he explains: 'It's an old Dwarven spear left lying around in the debris of Moria, but designed so that when it hits Frodo, everyone assumes it has gone through the hobbit when, in fact, the outer barbs have passed on either side of his body and the shorter, central spike has snagged against his mithril shirt.'

Other spears, stacked in a corner, include the Rohan implement used by Merry and Pippin to cut their bonds when escaping from the Uruk-hai. 'For obvious safety reasons, very few of our weapons were sharp,' reveals Richard, 'but since this one had to be seen cutting through rope, we waited until the day of the shoot and sharpened it on set, the way medieval armourers probably honed blades on the day of battle.'

Extra Special People

'**B**y the end, I was ready to throw my phone in the bin!' Miranda Rivers is reliving some of the stresses of being an Extras Casting Co-ordinator on *The Lord of the Rings*. 'Every extra in New Zealand had my number and felt they had free access to me twenty-four hours a day, seven days a week. I'd wake up to the phone ringing: "Hi, it's Grant here! Can I be an extra on Monday?" And I'd grunt back: "Grant, it's seven o'clock, Sunday morning! GO AWAY!"'

The running-task of casting 20,000 extra roles during the fifteen months of filming was a demanding one: 'We used between three to four thousand people of all ages, from children upwards, and drawn from just about every walk of life you could imagine. We ended up with a wonderful core group of thirty to forty who worked and travelled with us virtually from the beginning to the end.'

Some extras played so many different roles that there were serious concerns about continuity. 'It got to the point,' laughs Miranda, 'when we'd find ourselves trying to avoid casting someone as a Gondorian soldier because, only the week before, he'd played a warrior of Rohan! As a result, we had to disappoint quite a few guys who had ambitions to play someone from each of the races of Middle-earth. "*Please* let me be an Elf!" they'd beg, and I'd

have to say: "Sorry, but Elves are tall and slim! You're too big!" Or, more often, "You're too short!"'

If they were the right build for an Elf, but had brown or black hair, they quickly found themselves undergoing a potentially embarrassing transformation: 'They didn't know what they were in for, being hired as an Elf! After their wig-fitting, we'd give them a facial make-over and they'd often find themselves going back to work with their own dark hair and a stunning pair of eyebrows newly plucked and bleached white!'

Some days, when large crowd scenes were being filmed, the Casting Department needed as many extras as possible and was forced to cast completely against type: 'When we ran out of blond, blue-eyed extras for the men of Rohan, we would have to cast brown-skinned, brown-haired, brown-eyed Maori boys, stick wigs on them and try to hide them away in the background! We nicknamed them "The Bro'han"!'

Of all the peoples in Middle-earth, the easiest to cast proved to be the hobbits. 'We could spot a hobbit straight away,' says Miranda, 'warm, round, bubbly people with cheerful features, large eyes and, if possible, rosy cheeks. You could write a thesis on the various personality-types represented by the characters in the film. The Elves were generally beautiful but rather aloof; the Uruk-hai were big, strong, "no-bullshit" guys and the hobbits were non-stop talkers! Gorgeous people, but such exhausting chatterboxes, that you wanted to scream: "Will you, please – for just five minutes – *shut up*?"!'

There were even what might be described as tribal allegiances: 'There was great pride involved in being men of Rohan or Gondor and the Uruk-hai had a definite, if good-natured, rivalry with the Elves whom they derisively referred to as "Cupcakes"!'

Despite such competitiveness, there was a tremendous over-riding camaraderie: 'They were so committed that they put up with some of the most extreme conditions without complaint. We had every kind of weather

imaginable; there were times when people were passing out from heat-exhaustion and others when they were almost going down with hypothermia!'

There were also the very particular challenges offered by costume and terrain: 'We had extras running up and down seriously uneven hillsides in armour they could scarcely see out of, carrying swords that were so heavy they could hardly hold them, doing their best not to trip over the tree roots! Occasionally an Orc who had spikes on the knee-pieces of his armour would fall over, stab himself into the ground and not be able to get up again. Totally out of Orc-character, you'd hear a pitiful voice call out: "Can somebody help me, please?" And we'd be yelling: "Improvise! Play dead!"'

For Miranda and her colleagues, casting extras became more than a job: 'We were a family: there were births, deaths and marriages, break-ups, break-downs and suicide-attempts; good times and bad, but we got through them together.'

Dealing with so many thousand individuals there were, inevitably, one or two who were difficult to handle. 'We had our own way of dealing with them: we simply coded their application forms, and they were never used again. There were so many fantastic people we didn't need the other sort.'

So, *what* was the code for the trouble-makers?

'We used the letter "T" – "T" for "Tosser"!'

Hobbit Hair and Wizard Whiskers

 'There were two people whose job it was to make mud. We always had a couple of bucket-loads handy.' It's not quite what you expect to be talking about with a make-up artist but when you're filming in Middle-earth mud is one of those things that really has to be thought about.

Peter Owen is talking to me in the studios of Owen, King and Turner, tucked away in a narrow, cobbled mews in Bristol, in the south-west of England. He and his long-time associate Peter King are the men who created the hair and make-up for *The Lord of the Rings*: from Gandalf's beard and Galadriel's golden tresses to all those bucket-loads of mud.

'You use much the same recipe as blood,' explains Peter Owen, 'but whilst nobody expects to use *real* blood in a movie, I did have to explain to some of the people working for us about mud. If they hadn't been on a film before, they'd say: "What do you want to make mud for? Just go and dig some up!" They thought I was loony! But, of course, you can't go rubbing *real* dirt all over actors' faces; it has to be *sterilized dirt* – so you *have* to make it!'

Peter King chips in: 'Of course, you can understand their surprise: after all, most of the time when we were filming on location, ordinary mud was pretty readily available!'

Having two Peters around is potentially confusing, which is why at the studio – and in the conversation which follows – Peter Owen (shown near right) is 'Peter' and Peter King (far right) is 'PK'.

PK continues: 'The weather didn't make anyone's job exactly easy and every now and then there'd be moans and groans. But you have to get people to laugh at the difficulties because it's the only way to keep them all going. I'd say: "Look, you could be on the dole; you could be in a studio working on some really boring car commercial; or, you could be half-way up this mountain being washed away by snow and rain, making *The Lord of the Rings*! Now, what's more fun – *really?*"'

The fun began – though, in truth, it seemed pretty scary at the time – with a telephone call less than two months before the beginning of filming. PK was away, working with Kate Winslet on *Quills*, Peter Owen was, fortuitously, between movies.

'Other jobs were looming on the horizon,' recalls Peter, 'and when they told me the length of the project and when it was starting, quite frankly, I went cold! I took a deep breath and said: "Well, I think I'd better come out to New Zealand – *now!*"'

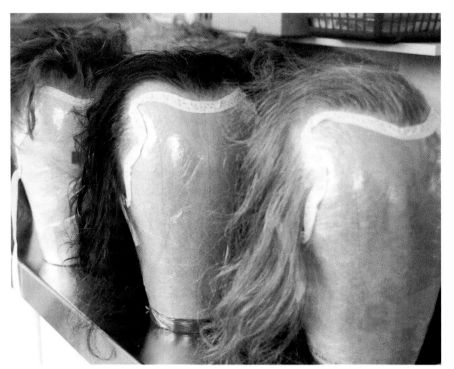

There was no time to get sight of a script, and Peter admits (albeit in hushed tones!) that he had never read the book: 'When I was at university in the late sixties cannabis had arrived and so had Tolkien. Everybody was reading *The Lord of the Rings* – except me!'

Caroline Turner, Peter and PK's partner, dashed out, bought a copy of *The Fellowship the Ring* and a CD-set of the BBC's radio version, starring Ian Holm as Frodo. The following day Peter was on a plane heading for Wellington, passing the twenty-seven-hour flight with a rapid Middle-earth orientation course.

The next few days were a whirlwind: immediately on arrival, Peter was interviewing potential staff, without being entirely sure what he or they were going to be doing. 'I met Peter Jackson,' he remembers, 'and then things started coming together. Tolkien was very specific about looks and so was Peter. My job was less about coming up with ideas than with making the ideas that were in the text work on people's faces.'

There was also the director's specific dictate that this be a film about real people rather than fantasy characters. 'Take Gandalf – he may be a wizard, but since he's also a traveller he needs to look a bit grubby: he's been on that horse and cart for goodness knows how long and he doesn't use hair-gel and hand-cream!'

Next, Peter met 'a lot of hobbits', took head-moulds for wigs and flew back to England wondering whether they could possibly get everything made and ready in time...

On all their film projects – such as *Dangerous Liaisons*, *Portrait of a Lady*, *An Ideal Husband*, *Sleepy Hollow* and *Velvet Goldmine* – Peter and PK only use wigs made on their own premises: 'If anything isn't right,' explains Peter, 'then we've no one to shout at but ourselves!' However, designing and making wigs for such a huge cast production was certainly challenging.

'Although I was confident that our wig-makers would manage to meet our needs,' says Peter, 'precisely what those needs *were* seemed to be changing all the time. Mercifully, we started low-key with the hobbits.'

'Low-key' might actually be something of an understatement since, apart from the central hobbit characters, the staff at Owen, King and Turner also had to make an additional 110 wigs for the hobbit-extras at Bilbo's party.

By the time he was back in Bristol, Peter had worked out what he calls a 'colour language' for the hobbits: 'The best way to describe them is "tweedy"! Given that they are a happy bunch, reasonably well-fed and out-doorsy types (we know that they grow their own fruit and vegetables), I decided they should have fresh complexions, going a bit ruddy, and that their hair colours would be a range of tweedy browns. As for the four young hobbits, Frodo was the darkest, with the others getting gradually lighter, though the difference is slight, almost infinitesimal.' He pauses, then adds: 'Except for Sam, of course. Being a gardener and working out of doors, his hair is rather sun-bleached. In fact, it's a sort of…' he gropes for the right description, 'well, you could say it's a rather funny orange with dark roots!'

Versions of all the hobbit wigs also had to be made for the various stunt- and scale-doubles: 'We always insist on doubles having exactly the same quality wig. Other people use cheaper, acrylic wigs for doubles, but it always shows. They think, because you are only shooting over the shoulder, that it won't – but it *does*! What was exacting was making a scale-double hobbit wig with smaller, tighter curls that were in proportion to the scale of the body. We had to draw up rather a lot of charts…'

Peter brought a number of gifted make-up artists onto the project, including Australian Rick Findlater and, from England, Jeremy Woodhead, who respectively took responsibility for the appearance of wizards Gandalf and Saruman.

Peter then ran a make-up school, in collaboration with the well-known make-up designer Noriko Watanabe Neill that was, in reality, an auditioning centre ('no one got paid but anyone could come') and began assembling a staff for the department. A permanent, core team of eighteen artists was eventually established; although – on big 'extra-days' – their talents had to be augmented by the services of a veritable army of '*make-up extras*'.

'Numbers,' says PK, 'are not a problem. It really doesn't matter whether it's three people, three hundred or three thousand: basically you're doing the same thing – you just have to "scale-up" and get on with it!'

He recalls one of several 'big extra-days' when there were upwards of forty hair and make-up artists working on the set for Aragorn and Arwen's wedding in the third film, *The Return of the King*, while another thirty-five people were working with two other units elsewhere: 'We always found the people and we always found plenty for everyone to do! Of course, you had to move some folk around, so as to make the best use of their talents. If someone said they could do styling, but we then found that they *couldn't*, we'd have them putting-up hair or shoving on wigs. No time for complaining or saying: "We're never going to do it!" Have a laugh, get everything going and keep it moving. "I've got a chair empty!" I'd be yelling at the Assistant Directors, "I can't have a chair empty! I need someone *in* it, *NOW*!"'

It took time to get things organized: installing a boiler so there was always the hot water necessary for dying hair; getting an air-conditioning unit put in so that the staff weren't overcome by chemical fumes from the dyes and changing the abysmal lighting in the make-up room: 'It was pale yellow,' says Peter, 'totally impossible!'

There was also the need for shelves: 'With the exception of one of the hobbit children, played by Peter Jackson's daughter, everybody had a bloody wig on! Well, if you have a couple of hundred wigs on wig-blocks they take up a lot of space, so I kept asking for more shelves. It went on for days. There was a young chippie who was really helpful but he must have got sick of me because all I'd ever say is: "No, I want more than that!" Poor man, he kept coming back and saying: "You want *more* shelves?" And I'd say: "*YES!* More shelves!"

In the end the entire room was lined with shelves and I still didn't have enough!'

The wigs were couriered out from Bristol on a weekly basis, accompanied by cassette recordings of BBC radio programmes (including the long running soap-opera, *The Archers*) as an antidote to home-sickness.

Shooting started in October 1999 and Peter coped alone until the following January, when he was joined by Caroline Turner and PK.

'I'd only recently finished on *Quills*, and had just got married,' PK recalls, 'so I'd hardly had any time to talk with Peter about *The Lord of the Rings*. Until I got there, I had no idea how big the project was – let alone how big it was going to get. Still, it was so yummy being in New Zealand, that I honestly can't say it was difficult!'

Perhaps the biggest problem, as it also proved for others on the project, was deciding how to portray the Elves. 'Both genders had to be over six foot tall,' recalls Peter, 'and had to look ethereal and androgynous – which is not really a great combination…'

'Exactly!' interjects PK, 'Long hair, hardly any facial expressions, floating about a lot, being wise and looking down on everyone else as if they knew everything and nobody else knew anything!'

'Some had long hair of their own that we could dye or bleach,' continues Peter, 'but we had to be terribly careful: too much fussing around with hair-styles, or too much make-up, and you're halfway to drag-queen time!'

'That was the difficulty,' says PK, 'to begin with, they looked as if they had been *made-up to look like Elves*, rather than as if they *were* Elves. We had to find a way of conveying their "otherness", their sense of immortality, and yet, at the same time, make them as real as the Rohirrim or the men of Gondor.'

There were also the limitations imposed by casting – Elves of both genders had to be over six foot tall, although height alone was not enough: 'We had to be brutal,' admits PK, 'If they were too broad or their features were too heavy, it was a case of "He'll be OK as long as he's only in the background… don't like her… can't use him…" Some had long hair of their own that we could dye or bleach, which saved on wigs but, frankly, finding good Elves was not easy!'

With the exception, that is, of Galadriel. 'Cate was perfect,' enthuses PK. 'I can't imagine anyone else in the role: she is so serene and gentle with such a wonderful, forgiving smile. We kept everything on Galadriel very pale: there was almost no colour in her lips or cheeks. I mixed up a special powder to give her the vaguest suggestion of a shimmer – nothing glittery, you understand, that would look ridiculous, unreal.'

It proved somewhat harder to find a look for Galadriel's granddaughter, Arwen. 'To begin with,' remembers Peter, 'she was depicted as a warrior princess – constantly covered in mud and blood – so that determined the look we started with. It didn't really work and by the time she underwent a change in character, I was moving on to other projects and PK was left holding the baby!'

'Liv was very happy with the way in which her character developed,' says PK, 'so it was easy to subtly change how she looked. Essentially, we tamed the make-up down, made her look a lot softer, more beautiful – almost a dark version of Galadriel.'

With so few major female characters in the story it is not surprising, perhaps, that it took time to define their roles and their appearance. As PK explains, the character of Éowyn, played by Miranda Otto, also underwent a significant change: 'When we first shot her at Helm's Deep her hair was a golden red colour, twisted back in a Pre-Raphaelite style to give her a consciously "feminine" look. After we'd shot a few scenes, we changed her look completely: made her blonder (which suited her skin colour better) and let it fly free. Miranda has a fabulous figure so you don't need to make her *look* feminine, she *is* feminine – once we allowed that to come through, it enabled her to enact Éowyn's almost-

masculine strength and heroism; then when she rides out to battle as a warrior it is all the more striking.'

Lest it be thought that only the women were problematical, it should be said that turning Orlando Bloom into Legolas involved a good deal of eyebrow plucking and the shaving back of his hairline. 'Orlando is a mad young thing,' says Peter, 'so he decided to go further and shave off both sides completely! So, what nobody sees is that, underneath that long blond wig, is a lad with a black Mohican haircut!'

Despite the thinning-out of Orlando's eyebrows, they remained curiously dark for so blond a character! Similarly, Christopher Lee, despite being cast as Saruman the White, succeeded in keeping *his* distinctive, pitch-black eyebrows. 'When it came to Saruman,' says Peter, 'I wanted him to look blue-white and icy-cold. But I decided that if I changed those eyebrows, then I'd the lose the face and ruin the look. If there's an essential feature to an actor's face, then you don't mess with it! To make the eyebrows work, however, I left traces of black hair running through the white beard so that it created a triangle on Christopher's face: the dark eyebrows above and the shadow of darkness within the beard below.'

Gandalf's eyebrows, on the other hand, were an altogether different issue. Tolkien describes them, in *The Hobbit*, as sticking out beyond the brim of his hat! 'I'm afraid' says Peter, 'I put my foot down about that! The beard, however, was another story.'

Peter Jackson knew precisely how Gandalf should look and it was exactly as John Howe had painted him. 'So, there we were,' says Peter with a resigned laugh, 'with the famous Gandalf hat and that great long beard.

For *The Two Towers*, Gandalf had to undergo a further transformation. Whereas in *The Fellowship of the Ring* he is Gandalf the Grey ('Not a blue-grey,' says Peter, 'more a sort of filthy-grey'), he becomes, in the second film, Gandalf the White.

'Grey hair,' observes PK, 'drags the face down, whereas pure white hair makes people look fabulous. More than that, we gave his features more colour so that he looked less drawn; instead of the hair being straggly and the beard wispy, suggesting someone approaching the end of his life, it was more luxuriant and closer trimmed, so that he looked rejuvenated. We created for Gandalf the White a feeling of rebirth: he was the same character but renewed and ready to go on again.'

As both PK and Peter are at pains to stress, make-up – like beauty – is only a skin-deep illusion. The success of any character is a combination of the created 'look' and the way in which the actor inhabits that look. 'For Gandalf the White,' notes PK, 'Ian became sprightlier; he lost the hunched and burdened look of Gandalf the Grey, stood up straighter and put his shoulders back.'

The same proved true for the character of Théoden who, when we first encounter him, is a decrepit, feeble-minded king who has lost all his authority through the ensnaring deceits of Saruman's emissary, Gríma Wormtongue, but who is, later, miraculously restored by Gandalf the White.

But my view was that if we gave him a beard that long then that would be all anyone would ever see of him. Instead of Middle-earth, we'd be in Father Christmas-land!'

But the director was loath to relinquish the John Howe look, so Peter Owen agreed to give it to him. 'I understood that he needed to see it for himself, so I said: "All right, I'll show you a really long beard and, I tell you now, you'll *hate* it: it won't work."'

Caroline Turner, who was Wig Technician on the film, sat up all night knotting hair for beard extensions, and Ian McKellen (in an *extremely* long beard) filmed a series of make-up tests. As a result, Peter Jackson agreed to a cut-down version of the wizard's whiskers: 'During the test,' recalls Peter, 'I was cutting it shorter on Ian's face and saying, "Right, let's take off another foot!" Poor Caroline saw all those hours of knotting end up on the floor and it was rather worse than that because it was hours of knotting that we *knew* were going to end up on the floor. But it was worth it because instead of a caricature we had a character.'

'If you've a good actor in a part,' remarks PK, 'you do the make-up and they do the rest. We filmed the two Théodens in quite the wrong order: first, the middle-aged, but brave and vigorous military leader; then his earlier incarnation as the powerless, crumbling monarch. Bernard Hill was quite brilliant: he suddenly became that old person, the stoop, the slight droop on one side of the mouth. Acting is always a much better option than smothering someone's face with prosthetic rubber or gelatine.'

PK digresses for a moment to comment on the prosthetic make-up created by Weta Workshop for the film. 'Weta,' he says. 'did the most amazing stuff! If you look at that wonderful scene between Saruman and the newly-birthed Lurtz, it is completely believable that those two characters exist and are relating to one another. But it works because, like us, Richard Taylor's team had the same aim in mind: whatever you do, you have to be credible; nothing can be so outlandish that it is beyond belief.'

Back to the secret behind Théoden's transformation: filming began with shots of Bernard Hill in full make-up as the aged King of Rohan: wrinkled skin (created using an age-old technique utilizing tissue and glue), a bald wig with thinning hair and hands blemished by painted-on liver-spots. The camera was then 'locked off' and Bernard was given a succession of intermediary

make-ups, for each of which he appeared looking progressively younger and reinvigorated. These images were then 'morphed' into a continuous sequence that shows the king casting off the sickness and frailty of old age.

'When you think about it,' says Peter, 'so much of what we have done on this film has been about transformations. Not just making old Théoden young; or changing Gandalf from Grey to White; but turning sallow-skinned extras into rosy-skinned hobbits and fresh-faced people into porcelain-skinned Elves; making Ian Holm, as Bilbo, look both younger (for the flashback scenes) and then progressively older and older. And, in addition to all that, helping to change Frodo as, step by step on his journey, he too is transformed: by sickness, weariness and grief, as well as the growing weight of maturity.'

'With Frodo,' says Peter, 'we started by working *backwards!* Our first aim was to get Elijah looking as fresh and young as possible: to push that youthful look as far as we could in one direction, so that it gave us the

maximum opportunity to push in the *opposite* direction. The ageing process (it is almost more to do with a loss of innocence) was achieved, very gradually, through shading: making tiny, tiny changes – sinking in that area in front of the ear, so that the cheekbones seemed more prominent and the face began to lose its roundness. Then it was up to Elijah.

Sometimes filming alternated on the same day between scenes featuring the younger-looking Frodo and his more world-weary counterpart. Indeed, there were often occasions when Elijah and the other hobbit-actors had to have their second shave of the day at lunch-time and then be given a different make-up for the afternoon's filming.

'All of which,' says Peter, 'was a continuity nightmare. There were three sets of continuity files: for the key actors, the stunt-doubles and the scale-doubles; and three sets of Polaroid photographs for each and every scene shot. Frequently, different units were filming different scenes (sometimes from the same sequence) on widely separated locations. There was no time, or way, to check one another's scripts for continuity notes, so everything had to be logged: hair wet in this scene, hair blown about in that.'

Charts and graphs were drawn up and meticulously followed: 'We had to determine,' recalls Peter, 'precisely what state everyone was in at any given stage of the journey. Everyone, for example, gets muddy, but you can't just keep piling on more and more grime! So, wherever they stopped, we decided that it was reasonable to assume that they would have had a bit of a wash-and-brush-up. But it all had to be noted down, so

on some scripts you'd find the cryptic instruction: "Cleaner today"!'

Other aspects of the change in the characters' appearance were somewhat harder to quantify, but were, as Peter explains, no less significant: 'There is a tiredness that is symbolic, because it is more than a physical tiredness, it is also a growing-up tiredness. To achieve that, you have to think in terms of a nine-hour film and plot the progression of those changes all the way through; get it wrong, and you'll have used up every look you can create within the first hour and have nothing left for the remaining eight hours!'

Managing continuity was just one of the many demands which Messrs Owen and King had to tackle. How, for example, do you create an army of six hundred Rohan soldiers with long, blond hair when the cost of six hundred wigs is way out of your budget? 'You use weft,' says PK, 'it's blond hair woven onto a string, and we bought a *lot* of it and attached it to the inside of all the helmets. The only thing everyone had to remember was that if anyone lost their helmet, they'd lose their hair as well!'

There were a number of fairly alarming days during the shoot: 'At one point,' remembers PK, 'Peter Jackson had said he wanted fifty Wild Men made up in scraggy-looking hair and beards. Then – *two days before shooting* – he came back to us and said he now needed *two hundred and fifty*! In two days it couldn't be done: we simply couldn't find two hundred extra beards and wigs. So, my solution was to suggest that we placed the fifty best made-up extras closest to camera and fill in the background with other extras whom we'd dress with an approximation to wild-ish hair and use a lot of back-lighting so that they were reduced to little more than silhouettes whilst still giving the illusion of a vast army of people!'

It was something both men have learned in their highly successful careers. 'There isn't a director in the world,' says PK, 'who likes to hear the word "no" and Peter Jackson is no exception. The secret is not to take him a problem, but to give him a solution!'

And to remember that it is fun: 'People worked long days and got very tired, but it *was* fun! Personally, I love those big numbers; I love the challenge of saying: "You've got two-and-a-half hours in which to get three hundred people ready: *GO!*" It's how Peter Owen and I began: doing outrageously adventurous stuff in the theatre and opera – and with no time to do it in. Big extra-days on *The Lord of the Rings* were like going back to that. True, people are throwing problems at you left, right and centre and, of course, you get the occasional feeling of panic, but I absolutely adore it!'

'Of course,' adds Peter, 'you can only do it if you've done the organizational work, figured out the logistics, made absolutely sure that the right Elf ears are in the right place at the right time, and that you've got enough buckets of mud in the fridge for tomorrow!'

So, what exactly *is* the recipe for mud? 'You start,' reveals Peter Owen, 'with corn-syrup, that makes it sticky and stops it drying out; then you add natural earths, such as umber, to give it colour (it's important that your muds match with the earth-colours found at each location); and finish off with plenty of fuller's earth to give it its essential gloopiness. The only problem is that it contains so much sugar that it's a really good bacterial-growth medium. So, we had to store it in the fridge and keep an eye on it – leave it for more than a couple of days and it starts to go off!'

'In fact,' adds Peter King, 'there was a use-by date on every bucket of mud!'

The Grimness of Gríma

'He is creepy and revolting!' Peter King is describing the appearance of the poisonous Gríma Wormtongue who poses as the trusted counsellor of Théoden, King of Rohan, whilst being, in truth, the servant of Saruman. 'We wanted a look that was nocturnal, reptilian; a creature that lives only in the shadows.'

This succulently unpleasant character is given screen-life by Brad Dourif, an actor whose early film portrayals in *One Flew Over the Cuckoo's Nest* and *Wise Blood* earned him a reputation for playing disturbed and obsessive characters: a notoriety since enhanced by a catalogue of oddballs and weirdos in a succession of horror fantasies – including the *Child's Play* series, for which he provided the voice of the demon doll 'Chucky'.

Helping to create Gríma's persona were the combined talents of make-up and hair designers, Peter King – or PK – and Peter Owen…

'Brad arrived on set only a couple of days before filming his scenes,' remembers Peter Owen, 'so we had little time in which to establish Gríma's look. Weta Workshop took a head cast and created a spiky nose for him and we set to work making him as unsettling an individual as possible.'

The process was begun, as Peter explains, by subtly

disrupting the natural balance of Brad's face: 'None of us have perfectly symmetrical features, but people who have noticeably asymmetrical faces tend to make us

particularly uncomfortable.' It is a disquiet which possibly stems from some ancient superstitious belief that such looks denote a 'two-faced' nature – as, indeed, is true of Gríma!

So, Peter began accentuating the natural differences between the left and right sides to Brad Dourif's face, using gelatine to thicken one set of eyelids. It was a look that was then further enhanced by the eyes themselves: 'We were fitting him with a pair of slightly cloudy contact lenses; we had got one lens in and I thought "Oh! That looks nicely strange!" so we left him with just the one and it gave his face a curiously lop-sided appearance.'

'I suggested,' says PK, 'that we give him a skin-complaint – something that would set him apart, make him feel uncomfortable and self-conscious.'

'We had chosen a wig for him: lank, straggly, unkempt hair that we made greasy with hand-cream and then added horrid patches of pink, itchy-looking alopecia.'

Created by make-up artist Jeremy Woodhead, these unpleasant latex embellishments came complete with weeping pustules: 'The moment you saw them,' shudders Peter, 'you wanted to scratch!'

'In addition,' observes PK, 'we felt that Gríma should look as though he seldom saw the light of day: dark circles around the eyes and a pale and pasty look.'

'The skin,' adds Peter, 'needed a waxy translucence with a slight blueish tinge – rather like portraits of Queen Elizabeth I. So, once we'd painted him almost completely white, Gino Acevedo, Weta's brilliant Prosthetic Supervisor, air-brushed veins onto Gríma's face. It looked as though his skin was porcelain-thin when, in fact, he was probably wearing a pound-and-a-half of make up!'

'Then,' interjects PK, 'there were the eyebrows. There are some things that we only question when they're *not there*: so, if you want to make someone look *seriously* weird, just get rid of the eyebrows!'

'Brad was amazing,' says Peter. 'I told him that I really wanted to shave off his eyebrows and he was perfectly relaxed about it. But I was hesitant, only because – well, once they're off, *they're off!* You can't stick them back on again!'

Peter decided to defer the decision until he had seen the actor on camera: 'We are standing on the set and, shortly before they are ready to shoot, Brad looks at me and says:

"Go for it, Peter! Get rid of them!" So, right there and then, I shave off his eyebrows! At first, no one notices: they know there's something very disturbing about Gríma, but they can't quite place what it is.'

'Everyone responds,' laughs PK, 'tells us how weird he looks but, at the same time, are asking what we've done. Then, suddenly, they realize and start yelling: "Oh, my God! His *eyebrows* have gone!"'

There was, Peter recalls, a final unpleasant touch – a snow-fall of artificial dandruff on Gríma's shoulders: 'There was a time when we used soap-flakes for dandruff,' he reveals, 'but they don't seem to stick and they really don't work that well under the lights. So *now*,' he says, pausing to add emphasis to the unlikely revelation that follows, '*now* we use – *instant potato flakes!*'

CHAPTER 9

Making Faces

'Once you're in there,' says Jason Docherty (shown below), 'time stands still.' Weta Workshop's Supervisor is giving a few last-minute hints to stunt-performer, Winham Hammond (nickname 'Moo'), who is about to be subjected to a process known as 'head-casting', from which the Workshop will create a prosthetic make-up to transform Moo into a scary, snarling Uruk-hai.

'You'll still be able to hear,' says Jason, 'but it will sound distant, muffled, drum-like. At that point you'll probably feel a bit closed-in and claustrophobic.'

'No worries,' replies Moo with some difficulty, on account of the fact that he currently has a mouthful of vicious-looking teeth.

'Last week,' Jason tells me, 'we made Moo a set of Uruk-hai fangs and he's wearing them now because, once in, they radically distort the line of the jaw and we need an accurate mould of Moo's face – with his teeth in!'

Moo also has a bald cap. 'We can't mould him,' says Jason, 'without getting rid of his hair. The stuff we use – alginate – *loves* hair, it gets matted into it and pulls it out.' Moo gives a slight wince. Jason continues: 'We can deal with eyebrows, moustaches or even,' casting an expert eye over *my* face, 'a fairly close beard. With stiffer hair we simply massage Vaseline into it so it lies flush to the face.'

Right now, Jason's colleague, Xander Forterie, is smoothing Vaseline over Moo's hair-covered back and shoulders. 'You know, Moo,' jokes Jason, 'you've actually more back there than you've got on top of your head!'

'I'd have shaved if I'd known,' replies Moo through his false fangs; then, as Xander starts giving his equally hairy chest the Vaseline treatment, he adds: 'It's hard work being a man! Just better not show I'm enjoying this!'

The next indignity for Moo is having black bin-liners taped around his body. 'When the alginate first goes on,' Jason explains, 'it is pretty free-flowing, so we need the bin-liners to catch some of the spillage.' Peering down at the band of plastic wrapped tightly around his upper body, Moo laughs and shakes his head: 'Look's like I'm wearing a boob-tube! Good job my mates can't see me now…'

With Moo ready, Xander begins preparing the alginate, using a power-drill fitted with a mixing-tool. The result is a bucketload of thick, blue-grey, slurpy material normally used – in smaller quantities – by dentists to take impressions for dentures.

'You'd better watch out!' warns Xander. 'We're going to be running around with handfuls of this stuff and it tends to fly about. Once it's dry, it comes out of pretty much everything – except clothing…'

Telling Moo to close his eyes, Xander and Jason begin snatching great dollops of alginate and slapping it onto the top of their victim's head, sculpting it across his back,

water and begin winding them around Moo's head, shoulders and upper arms to form a thick casing. Two bandages are wound into ropelike lengths: one placed from shoulder to shoulder, across the top of the head; the other from the nose, again over the head and down the back of the neck. Together they will hold the plaster cast and the alginate mould securely in position.

Working quickly – Jason in front, Xander behind – they continue to swathe Moo in bandages until, with the exception of his nostrils that are still open, he has the look of an Egyptian mummy. Jason is keeping Moo informed: 'As the plaster hardens,' Jason shouts in a cheerful voice, 'it feels a bit like someone's grabbing you round the neck and it gets quite hard to swallow.' As if that wasn't bad enough, he then adds: 'Also, the bandaging under your nose makes the air get warmer, so you might feel as if you're not breathing – but you *are*! OK?'

Now it's all about waiting…

Just when I had supposed that I had discovered all there was to know about Weta, Richard Taylor and Tania Rodger whisk me off to an area of the Workshop which I had not previously explored. We started out in the 'Urethane Moulding Room', where surfaces were

shoulders and chest. Such is the weight of the alginate that it immediately begins sagging and sliding, but it is also rapidly hardening, necessitating speedy work.

Jason is now concentrating on Moo's face – coating the eyes, the ears, the lips – while all the time talking to him, reassuring him. Eventually, only the nose is free and then that, too, is covered and Jason works with a spatula, sculpting into the curl of the nostrils.

His head entirely coated with alginate, Moo resembles some fantasy movie-monster: a creature of clay, subjected to cataclysmic heat.

Before the material completely hardens, patches of brown hessian are put onto the material in order to strengthen the alginate and hold it in place. Next comes the plaster…

Jason and Xander take plaster bandages, wet them in a bucket, squeeze out the excess

littered with pieces of moulds and a motley collection of equipment: much of it clearly pillaged from the kitchen: 'You noticed!' laughs Tania. There is a microwave oven caked in burnt-on urethane and a bread-making machine, the almost-obscured brand name of which looks for a moment like 'Hobbit' but is really *Hobart*… There is a sign on the wall – 'CLEAN UP YOUR MESS' – a pair of rubber gloves and a kitchen-scale. 'All ingredients,' Richard explains, 'have to be incrementally measured.' However, I can't help noticing that the dial on the scale is so gunk-encrusted to be impossible to read.

Next it's on to the 'Foam-Latexing Room'. Is that a food-mixer? 'Certainly,' says Tania, 'perfect for mixing foam-latex.' 'Exactly,' adds Richard, 'not unlike making a Pavlova…'

Passing the ovens ('Home-built in the workshop, they ran twenty-four hours a day for three years!') we reach what, for more than a year, has been the 'Foot Manufacturing Room': 'Yes! We actually had a room "solely" for feet,' puns Richard, 'that's how many we were producing.'

There are still a few in evidence. 'One used pair of Frodo feet!' laughs Richard, handing me the well-worn items. There is a hole in the toe of one of them (rather like a sock that had seen better days); the other has a glued-on patch of hair. 'There were painting patterns to be followed for each of the hobbits in order to ensure continuity. Some of our folk felt as if they'd been painting feet for years!'

Once you've seen your first hobbit in *The Fellowship of the Ring*, you more or less stop noticing their feet, which is how it should be. Nevertheless, as Richard explains, they were a considerable challenge: 'It took us six months to figure out how to make them so that they were pliable and soft as human skin, yet still tough enough for the actors to be able to run about on all kinds of difficult terrains.'

Whilst the feet have a hard, solid rubber sole, the area around the ankle is amazingly thin. 'They need this fine edge,' Tania tells me, 'so that they can be subtly blended onto actors' legs, yet at the same time they had to be made from one type of material – a tricky blend of foam latex – and moulded as a single component, so that we could manufacture them fast enough.'

Why the hurry, you might ask? The problem, it seems, is that you can only get a couple of days' wear – three at most – out of each pair of hobbit feet before they either get damaged or that vulnerable blending-edge starts to break down. The four lead hobbits alone managed to get through 1,600 pairs of feet, to which figure can be added the feet worn by Bilbo, various featured hobbit characters, a number of scale- and stunt-doubles and a great many extras.

And here are all the moulds, one of which for a Frodo-foot to be worn by Elijah Wood's scale-double Kiran Shah – Richard picks up and takes apart. The outer mould, when separated into its two halves, reveals a hobbit-foot-shaped-cavity within. Into this space – and locked in place – goes the 'core', a cast of Kiran's own foot. The gap between the human foot and the hobbit

foot is then injected with silicone, resulting in a sock which, on the outside, will be a perfect Frodo foot but which, on the inside, is a perfect fit for Kiran.

'Weta became the biggest users of silicone in New Zealand,' says Tania. 'We were getting through at least a 44-gallon drum every single day!'

'Every pair of feet,' adds Richard, 'had to be sculpted, moulded, foamed, trimmed, primed, painted, hair-knotted, hair-punched and then – eventually – glued onto someone's *real* feet!'

Not just feet, either. 'There were also the ears!' continues Tania, '1,600 pairs of lead hobbit ears. *And* Elf ears, of course. We had thousands of those! The hobbit ears were moulded in latex, but the Elf ears were made from gelatine. You really ought to meet Norman…'

The sign on the door of Norman Cate's office – otherwise known as the Gelatine Room – is really only a label from a packet of 'Gummi Bears', a popular confectionery item in the form of bear-shaped jellies. The 'B' of 'Bears' has simply been crossed out, so that it now reads: 'Gummi ears'!

'It has been a truly mind-numbing experience,' laughs Norman. Blond, bespectacled, with a fresh-scrubbed, schoolboy complexion, Norman is the chemist who concocted the mix of sorbitol, gelatine and other materials that went into making all those thousands of ears as well as quite a few noses: 'There was a lot of research to begin with to find a recipe that would give flexibility. Get it right and it would have the same "memory" that enables human skin to stretch and then go back to how it was before. After we got that right, it was largely about trying to find ways to stop it from melting off people's faces!'

Noses particularly have a habit of getting a bit runny. 'After about fourteen hours,' Norman tells me, 'the nose goes. As the body gets hot – and under studio lights, it can get *incredibly* hot – sweat leaches under the edge of the appliance and the nose starts deteriorating from beneath. You have to try to keep the actor cool – hand-held blowers are really useful – and just hope the director will shoot the close-ups in the morning.'

Weta's mascot, Gemma the dog (shown below, guarding the Helm's Deep miniature set), pads in to join us. 'Norman,' says Tania, 'became Gemma's very best friend! As soon as she smelled Norman cooking up his gelatine, she'd be down here like a shot. We'd find her, in the corner, chewing Elf-ears!'

'She was certainly partial to those,' grins Norman. 'Personally, I'd say they were the toughest of the lot – especially Legolas's ears: we went through six different sculpts before we got *those* right. For some reason it was always the left ear that gave us problems.' 'Well,' quips Richard, 'maybe it was the side he slept on!'

Laughing, Norman, continues: 'There was always a lot of pressure to get things right but then, we could afford to spend half an hour being frustrated over Legolas's ears; the make-up artists were the ones in the firing-line: they *couldn't* afford that time – if an ear needed to fit, it had to fit!' He looks around him and shakes his head. 'This room! The days, weeks and months that I sat here screaming: *"Please! Not ANOTHER PAIR OF EARS!"'*

'Which explains,' jokes Richard as we move on, 'why we had Norman's room *soundproofed!'*

The conversation turns back to noses. Tania: 'No one got around to telling Ian McKellen that Gandalf was going to have a false nose. The first he heard of it was during one of his frequent visits to the Workshop.

He was wandering around, chatting to the sculptors, when one of them, Mike Asquith, happened to mention that he was currently working on Ian's nose!'

'He wasn't exactly amused,' adds Richard, 'and who can blame him? Ian had lived through the daily frustration of having a false nose applied when he made *Richard III*, and he didn't relish the prospect of spending at least another hour in the make-up chair each morning – especially since he was already going to be starting at a pretty ungodly hour. However, he was a real gentleman about it and, five noses later – they were either too short, pointy, hooked or bulbous – we found the perfect fit.'

So, what was wrong with Ian's *own* nose?

'Nothing,' laughs Richard, 'but when you put someone in a huge beard and a moustache that protrudes heavily off the upper lip, the nose gets diminished in relation to the facial plane; by bringing the nose out by as little as six millimetres ensured that it wasn't lost in a mass of hair.'

Peter Jackson wanted 'the strong-nosed' Gandalf depicted in John Howe's paintings, which is what he eventually got from Mike Asquith, a sculptor with a talent for recreating the detail of human skin-pores. 'When I applied Mike's final nose,' says Richard, 'it floated onto Ian's own nose, matched his skin-colour perfectly and was imperceptible.'

Tania takes Gemma back to the office while Richard tells me about the *other* wizard's nose: 'Although Christopher Lee has played a great many evil characters, he has an open, warm face; so we decided to create a bump on his own incredibly distinctive nose and to draw down the tip so as to create a slight hook which made his face look a little more bitter and pinched.'

Giving an actor a prosthetic nose is, it seems, a tricky

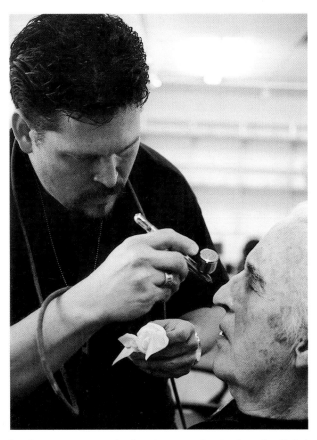

air-brushing kit for his fourteenth birthday: 'I used to marvel at the way in which the air-brush artists used to paint T-shirt designs at my local shopping mall in Phoenix, Arizona. That was when I knew I had to have one!'

From modest beginnings – designing and air-brush painting Hallowe'en masks – Gino graduated to Hollywood where his first job was helping to apply the grotesque features of Freddy Krueger in *Nightmare on Elm Street, 5.*

It was for his exceptional air-brushing skills that Gino was brought onto *The Lord of the Rings*, adding colouration and detail to the character make-ups once they were applied. Air-brushing, which is now used not just in the field of special make-up effects but also by beauticians, offers a far smoother method of application than can be achieved with the conventional use of brush or make-up sponge.

The elderly King Théoden was given age-spots and veins (the addition of the latter being an effect almost unachievable without the aid of the air-brush) while various refinements were made to the noses created for Gríma Wormtongue, Gandalf the Grey and – as Gino proudly related – Saruman the White: 'My air-brush, which is Japanese, has a special feature which allows me to "speckle" on the colour, a technique that is perfect for duplicating freckles and skin textures.

Christopher Lee was fascinated with my chrome-plated gizmo and told me that throughout his entire

business: once attached, using prosthesis glue, the 'join' has to be 'blended' onto the actor's face by subtly melting – or 'burning down' – the edge of the gelatine appliance. Since water tends to eat away at the gelatine too quickly, the prosthetic make-up artists use warm witch-hazel to melt the gelatine gently onto the surrounding skin.

'If it's a good blend,' says Richard, 'you don't use make-up on the edge, because it will only highlight the surface difference between the skin and the appliance. With gelatine, the best way to work it is with an airbrush.'

Which brings us to the office of Gino Acevedo – a genial, American giant with a trim beard and deep, chuckly laugh – whose film work has included make-up and paint effects on *Alien 3*, *Death Becomes Her*, *Demolition Man*, *Wolf*, *Independence Day*, *Godzilla*, *The Nutty Professor* and *Men in Black*.

Gino (pictured above, detailing Saruman's nose) is a master with the air-brush, a medium he's been experimenting with since he got his first

career of being made up, he had never been "spray-painted" before!'

Not that 'spray-painting' is a term Gino would use: 'Whilst a lot of people are now using the air-brush for make-up effects, there are only a handful who really know how to do it without its having that "too soft" appearance, as if it had been done with a spray-can! The hardest thing is to make it look like it *wasn't* done with an air-brush.'

This particular project provided Gino Acevedo with a rare opportunity to share in a sensation experienced by the actors whose make-up he applied. Donning full prosthetics, Gino portrayed one of the seven Dwarf Lords (pictured left, as the right-hand of three Dwarves with Richard Taylor) seen in the prologue to *The Fellowship of the Ring*: 'What was amazing – magical, really – was sitting in front of the mirror, looking at myself and not seeing *myself*, but another person looking back at me – with my eyes!'

Richard and I continue with our tour. 'Thanks to Gino's very particular skills,' he comments, 'and those of the other Prosthetic Supervisors, Marjory Hamlin, Kym Sainsbury and Dominie Till, we managed to keep on top of the most impossible schedules. There were boxes and boxes going out of here every day full of feet, ears

and noses – along with quite a few other body-parts as well…'

Richard generously offers me the opportunity to hold Lurtz's tongue and then proudly displays a set of ugly Orc-teeth that, despite being jagged, yellowed fangs are, in fact, custom-moulded to fit the mouth of Orc-actor, Lee Hartley, as snugly as any set of conventional dentures. 'Give any actor rotten teeth and you'll put them back in time five hundred years. Good teeth are a feature of twentieth century life, so we were always striving to create a convincing level of tooth-decay!'

Having taken head-casts of all the actors – leads and doubles – a set was produced to serve a similar purpose to a wig-block. Lying down, as if in sleep, the heads provide a personalized resting-place for the prosthetic moulds of the various facial features – noses, chins, cheeks, brows and eyelids – of each character, thereby preventing them from getting pulled out of shape. 'This, by the way,' Richard tells me, 'is the chin of Clint Ulyatt, our Hero Orc 2.' And Clint's chin is just one of a staggering 10,000 individual foam-latex appliances that were produced for the three films.

In addition to some ten 'hero Orcs' who might be seen in close-up shots on any one day, there was also a requirement for as many as fifty mid-ground Orcs wearing foam-latex, pull-on masks. Richard hands me one to examine and I immediately notice that, even though it may never be spotted on screen, it has been sculpted with an exceptional degree of detailing including, in the case of this ugly character, serious acne scars.

But there's more to an Orc army than a lot of gruesome faces – there are also a lot of gruesome *bodies*! And here they are: rack after rack, hanging up like rows of outsize wet-suits in a rather unappealing colour that might politely be described as 'earthy-brown' – or just 'mud'. These are Uruk-hai: barrel-chested torsos; dangling pairs of bulging, muscular arms linked by a lycra bikini-top that keeps them together and, when worn, closely-fitted to the actor's own body.

A demonstration follows: 'First the arms… Then the body…' Richard now has monstrous weight-lifter muscles. Curiously, there were also straps with clips hanging, suspender-like, from the trunk. 'These,' he explains, 'clamp the outer body and legs together without wrinkling…'

Richard grabs a pair of legs – great, sinewy thighs – but limits himself to a verbal explanation: 'Basically, you put one leg in, then the other and after that…' putting one arm between his legs, 'you reach round and grab a zipper

the various film units, creating realistic effects from sword cuts to lopped-off limbs. 'We did some cool stuff!' enthuses Richard, 'making and applying hundreds of prosthetic wounds. We were limited as to what we could show because of the film's classification – that's why Orc blood is so dark, so that it doesn't look like human blood – but whenever we could get away with a gore-effect, we had a bloody good chop at it!'

With a sudden start, I catch sight of the Ring-crazed Bilbo from that 'jump moment' at Rivendell when the old hobbit makes a grab for his former possession. Picking up the puppet-head, Richard explains: 'We took lots of photographs of Ian Holm in scary mode, and then sculptor Jamie Beswarick created this spooky caricature with which we replaced Ian's face for a couple of frames.'

Next to Bilbo – and twice as terrifying – is the prosthetic mask of the Witch King, the spectral leader of the Ringwraiths. Standing on a wig-block, it might have been the head of some long-decapitated monarch. 'We worked hard to get a look that was wraith-like,' says Richard, 'and yet was *not* the standard movie-zombie. Perhaps the best way of describing his final appearance is that he looks as if he's been sucking lemons for a thousand years!'

that's at the top of your bum and you zip it right around under the crotch! They're incredibly hot as you might imagine.'

I *can*! And, unless you are a serious fetishist, fairly uncomfortable. 'Getting people into these things,' admits Richard, 'did involve the use of quite a lot of talcum-powder…'

Even when an Orc has been strapped and zipped into all these components, there are still hands and the head-mask to be put on, not to mention armour and whatever shreds of raggedy costuming go with his rank in Saruman's army. 'It's like the "before" and "after" illustrations in one of those old body-building adverts,' laughs Richard, 'your average, weedy guy really *can* become a huge menacing Uruk-hai!'

Weta were also responsible for all the 'wounds' sustained by characters in the film: from that inflicted on Frodo at Weathertop through to full decapitations. 'I love it!' chuckles Richard. 'Don't forget we worked on the ultimate training-ground – *Braindead*!'

Equipped with their own truck, the Gore and Injury Rig Department, headed by Dominic Taylor, followed

The most complex masks are those worn by the hobbit-doubles: on the exterior, scale-likenesses of Elijah Wood and the other lead hobbit actors, inside a face-fit of Kiran Shah and the other doubles and, between the two surfaces, a thin air cavity carrying a network of wires operating a series of mechanized facial movements for the brow, eyes, eyelids, cheeks and mouth, worked from a power-pack under the actor's wig-line.

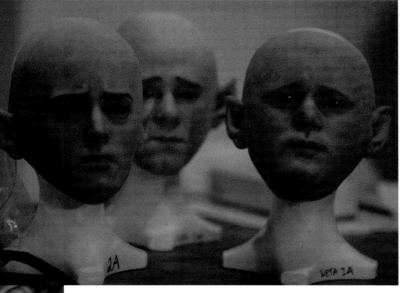

Hanging up along one wall are swags of lank, grey hair which are being prepared for the prosthetic make-ups that will be worn by the Army of the Dead in *The Return of the King*. 'Talking of armies,' says Richard, 'we had a tiny army – nine women and one man – who knotted all the hair for the goblins and the Uruk-hai as well as hundreds of Gimli wigs and beards, and vast quantities of hobbit foot-hair!

Called 'ventilating', it's an intensely focused job: the 'hair-knotter' takes a single strand of hair that's been chewed on – in order to soften it – threads it through the eye of a hook that's about the size of a small needle and sews it into a sheet of fine mesh, ensuring that every strand falls in the same direction. Though skilled workers are able to knot hair with exceptional speed and efficiency, it takes at least eight or nine days' intensive work in order to produce one Dwarf-beard.

'And, where do you suppose the hair comes from?'

Richard asks me, though I know better than to guess. '*Yak!*' he grins. 'Commercially grown yak belly-hair! Which, in case you wondered, just happens to have the springy nature of human facial hair. It's fascinating what you discover on this job…'

John Rhys-Davies as Gimli had to endure daily marathon make-up sessions. 'If we had simply presented Gimli as a man in a wig and a beard,' says Richard, 'it would not have been true to Tolkien's creation. We needed to play around with John's physical shape in order to create a Dwarvish look. Through the design of his armour and the use of make-up we created the illusion that his arms and legs were considerably shorter and that his head was a good deal larger.'

It proved a testing experience for the actor, who was spending six hours in the make-up chair beginning at 4.00 a.m. each day. 'We went for full head and facial silicone appliances,' Richard explains, 'including eyelids so that the only bits of John which are visible are his eyes and the inside of his mouth. I believe he only put up with all this, because he realized that, together, we were creating a totally convincing character.' Richard laughs. 'John was really amiable. Mind you, he'd quite often remark: "If I ever take another job involving prosthetics, you have my permission to shoot me!"'

The single most complex prosthetic make-up, however, was created for the sequence showing the 'birthing' of the Uruk-hai in the pits beneath Orthanc.

'How does Saruman breed his army?' asks Richard. 'Tolkien doesn't tell us, so our concept was that these creatures – incapable of thinking as individuals, but only as a group; perfect to Saruman's eyes, but apt to age and deteriorate – were, in fact, born of the earth. They develop within an embryonic sac filled with mud and slime and they are dug up by the Orcs – rather like living potatoes!'

Special birthing-tools were designed for the Orcs, resembling the implements used by Japanese fisherman to cut the blubber from whales: 'Because there are so many Uruk-hai, the Orcs don't care if any are maimed or killed as they are ripped out of the ground!'

A hugely elaborate sequence was eventually focused on the birthing of a particularly monstrous Uruk-hai, whom the film-makers would come to refer to as Lurtz. It was a truly bizarre scene, set in a nightmarish environment. For the stunt-performer involved, it was a gruelling test of endurance: a nine-and-a-half-hour make-up session, followed by a fourteen-hour shoot and, at the end of the day, another two hours of make-up removal.

'We started at midnight,' recalls Richard, 'every single millimetre of his skin – with the exception of his tongue – had to be covered in prosthetic appliances: a full chest, crotch-piece, thighs, hands and feet – even the inside of his ears. Finally, we applied a blind face-piece with closed and swollen eyes. His mouth was forced open in a scream by a set of dentures, so that he could only breath through the back of his throat.'

In addition to being unable to see, the prosthetics robbed the actor of all sense of touch: 'For several hours,' says Richard, 'he was completely encased in an embryonic sac of liquid – simulating the birthing matter – and buried beneath a pile of dirt. After every take, we'd get him out of his sac, lead him blindly to the showers, wash him off, re-do the make-up, lead him back, return him to the sac, fill it up with goo and ooze, and start again. Months of preparation and over twenty-four hours of hell for just one sequence that would eventually be cut from the film to help with the running time... Still, that's the stuff we do!'

It is time to liberate Moo…

Xander has marked a line on the plaster across the shoulders and head. Using a round-ended spatula he now cuts through and – with a lot of pushing and pulling – he and Jason prise off the plaster.

Finally, the back half is wrenched off and Jason starts cutting through the alginate beneath, sliding his hand under the rubberized material to ensure that the blade doesn't come in contact with Moo's back.

Once cut to the crown of the head, they begin to ease it off, Moo leaning forward and supporting the heavy face-part with his hands. 'OK, Moo,' calls Jason, 'squidge your face up!'

Moo duly starts pulling faces which helps release the mask. Suddenly he's free! He looks around blinking, spits out his false teeth and accepts a welcome drink from Xander, while Jason immediately puts material into the nostrils of the mask in order to complete the detailing of the mould.

Everyone relaxes. The Weta technicians can now begin the creation of the prosthetic appliances which Moo will wear when the time comes for him to join the Uruk-hai and go rampaging through Middle-earth.

The Body on the Floor

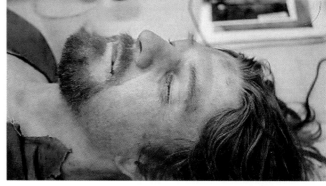

'There are Orc skulls on the shelf beside Gino's desk *and* a decapitated Uruk-hai head. But they're nothing compared with the shock-factor of noticing that there's a dead body lying in a corner of the room. And it's not just *anybody's* body… it's *Boromir's* body!

'We get strange requests here at Weta,' says Prosthetics Supervisor Gino Acevedo, 'including five days to produce a "lifelike dead Boromir"!'

The body was required for the scene in which the fallen warrior is laid in an Elven boat by his companions, prior to being sent on his final journey over the Falls of Rauros.

It is unnervingly authentic, but how was it done? Gino explains: 'We already had a head cast of Sean Bean from which our Workshop Supervisor, Jason Docherty, made a silicone mould. By pouring melted plasticine clay into the mould he got a perfect copy of Sean's face which was passed to one of our top sculptors, Ben Hawker, who worked on the features in order to make them a little more gaunt.

'From this amended sculpture, Jason made another mould of the whole head, and I mixed up a pale silicone that we use for replicating skin and poured that into the mould which was left to "cure" overnight. The next day, Jason demoulded the head and I painted it in very pale dead skin-tones.

'Once it had been painted, Boromir's head then went to Gavin

Skudder, one of our hair technicians, who meticulously punched in the hair, beard and moustache, a strand at a time. This painstaking work is done using a sewing needle that has the "eye" cut at an angle so that it forms a "u" shape. A single hair is placed in the middle of this "u" which is pushed into the silicone. When the needle is removed, the hair remains inside, giving the appearance that it is growing out of the skin.'

So authentic was the result, that when the body had been lying around on set for an hour or two, an unsuspecting technician thoughtfully enquired whether Sean oughtn't to be offered something to drink!

Talking to Treebeard

'So, tell me: how exactly does a tree talk?' John Rhys-Davies asks the question which has been plaguing him ever since he was asked to record the voice of Treebeard the Ent.

'What is essentially difficult about Treebeard is – well, how can I put it? He is a walking, talking tree! And that is what we have to create – without its being utterly risible.'

The on-screen manifestation of Treebeard is achieved through the combined use of a towering animatronic-figure created by Weta Workshop (big enough for Merry and Pippin to sit in its branches) and computer-generated imagery.

'That's one good thing,' says John, giving a boom-blast of a laugh, 'at least I don't have to physically play the role! That would have been too much! First of all smothering my face in make-up to play Gimli and then covering me in bark for Treebeard!'

There is, however, still the challenge of creating the Ent's vocal personality: 'Tolkien describes Treebeard as one of the oldest living beings on Middle-earth and, as such, he takes his time to think and speak – he has a great many memories but a methodical, unhurried central nervous-processor with which to access them. Then there's his voice, which Tolkien describes as sounding like a deep wood-wind instrument. Now, when you think of "old" and "deep", you think of "slow", but we're working with film and the one thing we really can't afford to be is ponderous. Yes, I can see fifty ways of making it work filmically, but making it work so as to be true to the book is a nightmare of difficulty!'

In truth, John is relishing the task: 'Actually, I'm in that position I like most with a part: I've thought a lot about it and played around a bit with it and am dead scared because I haven't made the final choice! Which, from my experience, is always the right pre-creative state in which to make the jump. I love that moment of taking a deep breath and committing!'

So, how does a tree talk? 'Well,' chuckles John, 'by the time people are reading this, they'll know, won't they? These are a few of the thoughts I've had, so far: there are sounds: the rustle of leaves, bark rubbing against bark, a noise that suggests the movement of roots coming out of and delving down into the earth. As for the voice: this tree – this Ent – can talk; he has travelled all over Middle-earth, so his language might well have picked up different regional colouring – a touch of accent here, a trace of dialect there. One game-plan might be to see if we can layer the sounds and the voice so that some lines are deep and rooted and some are soft and breathy, like wind in the high leaves…'

John breaks off, looks at me with deadly seriousness and bursts into a peel of laughter. 'And, when we've listened to all that and found that it's nonsense, then – then we go to plan "B".' He pauses for a moment. 'The trouble is, I don't know what plan "B" is yet!'

I offer a suggestion: might there be some link between Treebeard and the Green Man, the ancient mystic image found across countless centuries, amongst many different cultures. A human face, benign or mischievous, made out of leaves or peering from a pattern of foliage, the Green Man is, after all, a symbol of the eternal life-death-and-rebirth cycle of the natural world.

'Hmmm,' says John with an Ent-like slowness. 'Hmmm. You may just have given me the germ of an idea… A seedling of a thought… Yes… I need to think…' There's a twinkle in his eyes: 'You see, I'm already turning into Treebeard!'

CHAPTER 10

Filming
a Masterpiece

'"A masterpiece!" That's what I told them: "We are making a masterpiece!"' 'John Rhys-Davies gives a big, beaming smile. 'After a couple of days of filming, I am proud to say, I was the first person to be saying: "Gentlemen, we are making a film that will be bigger than *Star Wars*, a film that, in twenty years' time, people are going to list in their Top Ten movies!" I've seen nothing since to shake me from that belief…'

Christopher Lee agrees: 'This project is phenomenal. There has never been anything like it. Never, ever – *ever*! It will create new audiences for the cinema and it will make an impact on the history of motion-pictures that will be titanic and enduring.'

For many, the potential classic status of *The Lord of the Rings* is due to the vision, inspiration and dedication of one man: 'I spent my first few days in New Zealand,' recalls John Rhys-Davies, 'watching Peter Jackson direct. I saw how he handled actors, how the crew responded to him, how he solved problems. And I *liked* what I saw: his attitude, his low-key evenness, his focus. He is *magnificent*!'

Ian McKellen reflects: 'Peter's talents and gifts were there, fully-formed, right from the beginning. Constantly good-natured and welcoming, he was always expecting to enjoy the day ahead. As a result, we shared that expectation…'

It would be a simple task to produce several dozen other equally glowing testimonials. So, what is the 'Jackson Recipe for Success'?

'I am a general,' says Peter, 'in charge of a huge army. I try to be a *good* general because a bad general will never get the best out of people. My strategy? Try to make sure there's not too much tension around and that if people

screw-up they don't get told off, because mistakes are always going to be made on something this big. Get to know those who are working with you, treat them as individuals with different egos and different temperaments and create a stable environment in which everyone can work together in a friendly, civilized way.'

Peter thinks for a moment and continues: 'If I don't do those things then I'm failing in my job, because everyone on this team must always feel inspired to give of their very best.' He breaks off and laughs: 'I don't want them to be doing the finest work of their career on their *next* film. I want them to be doing it here and now – on *this* film!'

Long before that team was assembled, the film was shaping in Peter's mind: 'It may sound mysterious, but from the day we started working on the script, I could see the entire movie in my mind: the setting, the lighting, the angles, shots: what would be a close-up, where I'd use a wide shot – and ways in which those

or exciting than I *ever* imagined!" So, then I would start slotting *those* images into the picture and, suddenly, my little "mental-movie" begins changing shape.'

It is a process, as Peter explains, that continues with the casting: 'I visualize the characters, but never a particular actor – I'm never envisaging Sean Connery as Gandalf or Anthony Hopkins as Bilbo – I just see the characters in the same way that anyone does when reading the book; then, finally, the actors come on board, take on those characters and define them. What the actors do is, once again, always better than anything you'd imagined!'

In taking on – or 'owning' – their characters, the actors initiate a further stage in the film's evolution. 'You may have had an idea in mind that when Gandalf is talking to Frodo about this or that, you'd cut to a wide two-shot; but, the moment you film a close up of Ian McKellen doing it, you don't want to cut to a wide-shot any more, because Ian is so compelling; and, when you cut to Elijah, his eyes are conveying so much information and emotion that you *now* want to film the scene as two close-ups and, though it was a nice idea at the time, the wide-shot doesn't matter any more.'

shots might eventually be cut together. Of course, how a scene ends up in the movie is probably nothing like it was when I saw it for the first time on the page, because it will have *evolved*.' He gives an example: 'I imagine a scene and how I'm going to shoot it and then Alan Lee or John Howe come along with their sketches and it's totally different from how I'd seen it in my mind's eye – but *better*! I had all these mental images that I'd lived with for years – the Council Chamber at Rivendell, the Mines of Moria, Helm's Deep – and then I'd look at a drawing by Alan or John and think: "God! That's fantastic! That's so much more beautiful, dramatic

For Peter, the actors' arrival also signals a release: 'You have been through all the stress and turmoil of the pre-production period when you've had to shoulder the responsibility for every single character in the film and answer a thousand questions on their behalf: "How would Frodo react in this scene?"; "What shape is Gandalf's staff?"; "Is this the right sword for Aragorn?"; "Which of these waistcoats would be best for Bilbo?" Then, all of a sudden, the actors are there and starting to "own" their characters, and if somebody wants to know whether Gandalf would do this or that – they can now go to Ian McKellen and ask *him*!'

The casting, from Elijah Wood as Frodo (eighteen years old when filming began) through to septuagenarian Christopher Lee as Saruman, was inspired. Elijah remembers: 'When I first heard that Peter was going to make *The Lord of the Rings*, I thought: "How perfect!" I was so excited by the idea of playing Frodo, partly because there was nothing *ordinary* about role or the story and because it was going to be filmed over such a long period of time that it would almost be like setting out on as long and exacting a journey as that taken by the characters in the book.'

'When I first read *The Lord of the Rings*,' recalls Christopher Lee, 'I remember thinking: "Wouldn't it be wonderful if this story could be made into a film?" But I dismissed the idea as impossible! When, years and years later, Peter said that he wanted me for Saruman, I thought it was a dream come true – in two senses: firstly because they were going to make a film of this book which I love; and, secondly, because I was going to be in it!'

'We went for the most appropriate actors to play the roles,' says Producer Barrie Osborne (right). 'We weren't under any pressure to cast "star names" simply in order to open the movie because, after all, we had a novel with a hundred million readers that would open the movie! So we just went for the best…'

Drawing on actors from England, America, Australia and New Zealand, Peter assembled his cast. John Rhys-Davies recalls: 'I went into a reading, and there were quite a few of the actors whom I didn't know. But straight away, just from their looks, I guessed who everybody was: "I bet he's Frodo…" I thought to myself; "And *that* will be Merry… And he *must* be Sam…" That tells you something about the casting; and, if a director casts right, then he's already done eighty per cent of his work.'

There was, however, still that other twenty per cent that would demand Peter's attention virtually around the clock, seven days a week for the next year and a half – *and* beyond!

'I don't think we ever doubted we could do it.' Supervising Editor, Jamie Selkirk is looking back to the days before filming began, 'we knew we had the people-skills and the environment in which to do it, but – with the exception of Peter and Richard Taylor – I really don't think any of us realized the true scale of what we were taking on until we were actually doing it. And, even when we finally comprehended the scale, that scale just went on getting bigger and bigger!'

So it did. To begin with, Jamie's department was handling between 5,000 to 10,000 feet of exposed film a day, a figure that rapidly accelerated to 30,000 to 40,000 feet. Most films employ

two units: the first, working with the director, shoot scenes featuring the lead cast; the second devoting its efforts to shots of extras, stunts and such things as the sun setting behind the mountain or an inn-sign swinging in the rain… Filming *The Lord of the Rings* frequently required five and – once or twice – as many as *seven* units, under Second Unit Directors John Mahaffie and Geoff Murphy, *Additional* Second Unit Directors Ian Mune and Guy Norris, and just about anyone else who happened to be available at the time – including producers and screenwriters!

For First Assistant Director Carolynne ('Caro') Cunningham (shown right, directing her troops at Osgiliath), organizing a workable schedule for such a complex project – and then ensuring that everyone stayed on course – ought to have been a logistic *nightmare.* 'I admit it wasn't like anything else I've ever worked on,' laughs Caro, 'but the only *real* difference was that it was *bigger* – so you just had to roll your sleeves up and get stuck in. With three large-cast films being shot concurrently on multiple sets and widely separated locations, there was plenty to get your brain around, but once you'd cracked that, it simply became something you knew and got on with. It really wasn't any great feat – it just required a normal modicum, of common-sense – *times ten!*'

That said, it was, Caro admits, exhausting: 'A normal feature film shoot would take anything from eight to fifteen weeks – not *fifteen months*! There was too much

to do and no time to stop. So, it was up each day at 5.00 a.m., an eleven-hour shooting day, back home to prepare for the next day and bed. There were times when you were so tired, you weren't sure if you could get up and *do* another day. Everything else in life went on hold.'

It doesn't sound much fun: 'I had a *ball*!' laughs Caro. 'It was a *lot* of fun. But it was also damned hard work and, by the end, we were pretty much like the Walking Dead.'

Rick Porras, Co-producer (and sometimes Fifth, Sixth or Seventh-Unit Director!), reflects on the achievement: 'It's amazing that Caro could plan and plot this great chess-game of a schedule and weave us all though it; it's amazing that we were able to assemble all those crews and keep the work going across so many units; but what's *most* amazing is that Peter was able to keep all that information about all those units in his head at any one time.'

So rapidly expanding and accelerating a project placed high demands on Peter and the film crew and resulted in one of two additions to the creative personnel. The production reins were taken up by Barrie M. Osborne, whose previous credits included *Face/Off*, *Child's Play* and *Dick Tracy* and who joined the project after producing the international blockbuster, *The Matrix*.

There was to be another significant addition, this time in the cast. Shortly after the commencement of filming it was decided that actor Stuart Townsend had been mis-cast in the role of Aragorn. Whilst mutually agreed, the timing of the decision to re-cast could scarcely have been worse: Stuart had been preparing alongside the rest of the Fellowship actors and filming was due to begin on the scenes in which the hobbits first encounter Aragorn (as Strider) at the Prancing Pony in Bree.

Executive Producer Mark Ordesky (pictured below) takes up the story: 'I was in London when I got the phone call from Peter. I immediately rang Los Angeles to find out what the knock-on effects would be if the recasting of Aragorn were to cause any delay to the schedule. The answer was a really frightening number of dollars a week. I hung up the phone, feeling about as alone as I have ever felt in this business. We had five days in which to find and cast the right person, make the deal and get him on a plane for New Zealand – for fifteen months! That is an inherently dramatic situation.'

For Mark, there was only one contender for the role of Aragorn – Viggo Mortensen: 'My wife had seen Viggo in *Crimson Tide* and pushed me and harangued me to track him down and meet with him. Viggo doesn't "do lunch" with Hollywood "suits", but eventually I got to meet with him and afterwards told Peter that I was passionate about finding an opportunity to work with Viggo.'

A year later that opportunity arose, but it took

brinkmanship to win the day: 'We got a script to Viggo and his first reaction was to say "No"! It took three more days to convince him. At the eleventh hour, Viggo Mortensen arrived in Wellington, joined the already-bonded cast and stepped into filming almost as unexpectedly as his character, the mysterious, unknown Strider, appears in the story. Peter likes to say that "fate intervened", but he doesn't realize that fate was given a helping hand a year before, when Viggo reluctantly "did lunch" with an unknown "suit"!'

Co-scriptwriter Philippa Boyens reflects on the casting of Viggo: 'We knew that we were blessed in having Viggo – who is of part-Danish descent – step into the role of Aragorn when he arrived carrying a copy of the *Volsunga Saga*, that he had taken from his bookshelf! Viggo not only has a great actor's sense of bringing his character to life, but also an innate understanding of "the warrior code" and Tolkien's philosophy of heroism.'

Back at New Line, Mark Ordesky tidied up the pieces: 'When it was over, I called Bob Shaye and said something had happened – a change had been made – we'd re-cast Aragorn with Viggo. All Bob asked was: "What did you *spend*?" So, I told him; and, without a trace of anger or even annoyance, Bob classically replied: "Well, I guess you've done it then…"'

With filming begun, the cast found themselves in an interesting situation, rarely experienced in film-making. 'Most actors count on having the script in advance so that they can prepare,' notes Sean Astin, 'but much of the time on *The Lord of the Rings* we had no such luxury, simply because Peter, Fran and Philippa were engaged in the awesome task of assimilating the

literature of Middle-earth and building these three movies. The script went through many revisions and changes as we filmed, but rather than view that as a bad thing, we saw it as an opportunity...They counted on us to know the people we were playing and empowered us to be advocates of our characters during what was to be a tumultuous shoot.'

Some roles went through major transitions as filming progressed forcing the players to reassess their characters and their relationships and interactions with others. For example, Liv Tyler's initial portrayal of Arwen as a warrior-princess eventually softened into the more emotional, muse-like role that she now fulfils: a transformation that, in turn, impacted on the evolution

of Miranda Otto's portrayal of Éowyn. It was an exciting, but sometimes confusing and frustrating, process.

Virtually every character-portrayal would pass through a refining process to which the actor would invariably make a significant contribution. For Orlando Bloom it was the challenge of understanding the nature being an Elf: 'Legolas is 2,931 years old; ageless and immortal. He's seen the world, yet you never really know what he is thinking. He's distant, aloof; stands apart from life. The eyes and ears of the Fellowship, he is objective, dispassionate yet incredibly focused and can fire a bow with the deadly accuracy of an assassin! That is a complex range of characteristics to portray.'

In contrast, John Rhys-Davies had to come to grips with playing Gimli: 'If I was to use "actor talk" (which I love), I'd say: "Well you see, I had to find the *Dwarf* in me!"' John gives a great, fruity laugh. 'And, actually, I didn't really have to delve that deep! Dwarves take themselves terribly seriously, they are desperately politically-incorrect and quite forthright in saying whatever's on their mind whether they should or not.' Another bellow of laugh. 'And I happily confess that I had no difficulty whatsoever in finding any of those traits within myself!' Suddenly serious, John adds: 'Of course, Gimli is a *wonderful* character! Suspicious, paranoid, quick to quarrel; yet he shows unquestioned loyalty to Aragorn, and his protectiveness towards the little hobbits is endearing. Above all, there is his fearlessness in the face of overwhelming odds, so that even when confronted with certain death, he will always turn and fight!'

John's portrayal of Gimli was eventually shaped in response to the other members of the Fellowship: 'The disparity in sizes between these characters could so easily be risible, but here was Gimli: halfway between the taller men and Elves and the shorter hobbits. So it struck me that Gimli – a character whose own sense of self-importance is coupled with an absolute incomprehension of the fact that he is *small* – might possibly provide a lightning rod of humour that would

In *The Two Towers*, however, Ian also had to play Gandalf the Grey's *super*human transition into Gandalf the White: 'Despite the fact that, for most of the story, Gandalf is not Grey but White, it is as Gandalf the Grey that you immediately think of him when reading the book – even after his transformation. I had the good fortune to begin by playing the Grey version (in his very first appearance in the story, arriving at Bag End), so it was natural to have a sentimental attachment to him. Gandalf the White was harder to play: sent back to complete a task, he is more grim, more driven. Of course, he *is* more stylish, with a much better dress-sense, sporting an outfit that has something of a Samurai-warrior look to it as opposed to the grey tent which he wears at the beginning!'

On the subject of playing Gandalf, I mention that Fran and Philippa had joked about dreading those occasions on which they would see an approaching wizard with a copy of Tolkien's book open in his hand!

Ian chuckles. 'I don't believe they *really* dreaded it! But it must have been very hard for them, after years of poring over the book and deciding what should and shouldn't be there, to have this bright-spark actor, who'd only just read the relevant chapter in detail, saying: "Look here, you've got it wrong!" And, of course, they *hadn't* got it wrong, they'd made a considered decision to change, amend or ignore Tolkien's text. And they were always happy to discuss the point and, very often, words or phrases were slipped back in. For writers and actors, it was wonderful that there was a "bible" that could be appealed to.'

It's an analogy also used by Sean Astin: 'I treated the books as the Bible for the character and I used the screenplay as the map to understand the direction in which Peter, Fran and Philippa were taking us.' There were, however, many, sometimes passionate discussions about the role of Sam: 'Peter didn't want him to be a Hollywood character, he wanted him to be real; I wanted to focus on Sam's heroic and ennobling qualities. Peter liked the element of comic-relief offered by the hobbits, but I was conscious of not wanting to go

help make the transition between the two group-sizes work.'

In achieving the role there were many discomforts to be endured: 'I lived in prosthetic make-up, which was hell, and spent a lot of time wondering why I'd worked all my life to establish a recognizable face – only to then cover it up in layers of latex! Apart from which I acted so many scenes looking up at Legolas, Gandalf or Aragorn that I had a constant crick in the neck and spent an awful a lot of time down on my knees – and that was *after* getting the job!'

The challenge for Ian McKellen was in confronting the portrayal of a character with iconic status: 'You simply can't act that! You can't think about Gandalf being 7,000 years old because that's beyond anyone's experience: you have to play a man – an old man admittedly – who's got arthritis, who's cold, wet and tired; a man who has a daunting a job to do, who enjoys a drink and a smoke. In short: someone human, human, *human*…'

too far in that direction and so reduce the credibility of the heroism which they display at various times throughout the story.'

There were, as a result, occasional divergences of opinion: 'Now and again,' says Sean, 'I breached protocol and asserted my own views – well, let's face it, I'm a know-it-all-megalomaniac-freak of an actor-filmmaker and there were times when I simply couldn't help myself! But Peter was always patient with me, occasionally took my suggestions and, between us, in the end, I think we achieved a pretty good balance for the character.'

The patience and willingness to discuss character which Sean describes, was a quality which many of the actors were aware of and appreciated. 'He was always reassuring,' notes Ian McKellen, 'there was never a sense that time was running out or that he had to be mindful of a schedule or financial constraints that might restrict the number of times he could shoot a

scene; it was always: "We'll get it right and not move on till we have…"'

Ian Holm agrees: 'With Peter, the word you waited to hear was "Excellent". You knew that "Good" simply wasn't *good enough*. There'd be take after take after take and it would be: "Good…" "Good…" "Good… Let's go again! *Action!* Yep… Good…" And so on until, eventually: "*Action!* Yep… *Excellent!*" *Then* you knew that you'd got there!'

Of all the practicalities involved in the production, 'getting there' – anywhere (let alone *back*) – was often fraught with problems. 'We were here one day,' says Barrie Osborne, 'and somewhere else the next: Wellington, Queenstown, Christchurch, Nelson… North Island, South Island; back up North again… Trucks, vans, ferries, aeroplanes and helicopters.'

For those in the Locations Department there was the added trauma of running on a different time-circuit to the rest of the team. Supervising Unit Locations Manager Richard Sharkey remembers: 'There were occasions when I'd be working all day on the North Island, setting up perhaps ten other locations that the crew would be going to during the next few weeks; then, in the evening, I'd fly down to the South Island to view the day's "rushes" (maybe for no more than an hour),

only to then turn round and fly back to the North Island. There was a standing joke that I collected more air-miles than anyone else on the crew!'

Richard's most unforgettable journey occurred at the end of the first day's filming on the Edoras set on the South Island: 'I had planned to make the three-and-a-half-hour drive from Mount Potts Station to Christchurch in order to catch the last plane to Wellington. Inevitably, as on any first day, there was one problem after another and I was left hanging around, waiting, waiting… In the end, there was no way that I was going to make the flight using my car, so I thumbed a lift with a light-aircraft that was taking the day's film-footage to Christchurch airport and on, via Wellington, to the laboratory. We were running late and fighting head winds and it began to look as if we would miss the connection. But the pilot, who was well-known locally, contacted Air Traffic Control at Christchurch and got them to hold the flight for Wellington and to give permission for him to land not, as usual, on a grass strip *near* the airport, but on the *main runway!*'

Things suddenly got a bit scary: 'There we were in this tiny aircraft that felt as if it was held together with a couple of rubber-bands – if we were lucky! We slotted in behind a 737 and in front of a 747 that was obviously travelling at something like 400 miles an hour (compared with our *fifty* miles an hour!) and which was getting closer and closer, until it looked as if it was about to swallow us up in mid-air. Somehow we landed on the runway and were just about clear before the 747 roared in; then we taxied up to my plane and I leapt out, clutching the rushes, ran across the tarmac, dashed up the steps and into the cabin where I was greeted by a thunderous round of applause from the waiting passengers! For a fleeting moment I felt like James Bond!'

The difficulties of managing transportation were inevitably exacerbated by schedule changes. 'It wasn't that it was changing every week,' observes Richard Taylor, 'or even every day – sometimes it was changing every hour!'

So complex was the jigsaw puzzle of people and places that, as Richard explains, it didn't take much to muddle-up the pieces: 'The merest change would send a ripple-effect throughout the entire system. We might have eight or more containers ready and packed to be shipped off to the locations with as many as one hundred Uruk-hai prosthetic-suits, armour and weapons, and outfits for two hundred and fifty Rohirrim and one hundred Elves, only for there to be an alteration to the schedule and all those containers would have to be unpacked and repacked with different gear before the lorries arrived to collect them.'

The factor most likely to disrupt the logistical equation was the weather. On the first day's shooting in the woods on Mount Victoria above Wellington, conditions were perfect: sunny and calm. On day two, it was cloudy and blowing a gale! It was symptomatic of the changeable weather that was to be encountered over the next year and a half.

'Here we are on the first anniversary of the beginning of filming.' It was October 2000 and Peter Jackson was talking into camera, snow swirling about him and settling on his anorak hood and spectacles. 'That was one year ago today, in the heat of Mount Victoria and here we are at Deer Park Heights, Queenstown, and as a special treat for the crew who have been so wonderful for this first year, we've bought a new snow-machine.

We're just testing it at the moment... It's quite amazing, it can actually cover several miles! Just one little machine blasting this snow out. It's so effective! Anyway, we'll turn it off and get back to shooting!' He turns away and shouts to the crew 'Turn that snow machine off now, please! Come on! Back to work!'

But the snow didn't stop; in fact, it got heavier: 'It looks like we've got a problem with the snow-machine. The button's jammed and we can't turn it off! It's snowing all over Queenstown! I think the police are going to come and tell us off. We've got to try and get this machine to shut down!'

And while the First Unit were coping with snow, the Second Unit were filming at another location outside Queenstown when the South Island experienced some of the worst storms and floods for a hundred years.

Rick immediately ordered an evacuation and, abandoning some of their trucks, the crew loaded up as much equipment as they could and headed out of the area as quickly as possible. At the nearest town, beside a lake, the crew set to helping the local people to sand-bag the houses against the rising flood-water, while Rick was checking out the 'wet-weather cover' – one of the interior venues (often a church hall or farmer's barn) that are always arranged near any location where weather might prevent shooting. The plan was to use the time while waiting for the weather to improve in filming Frodo's scale double, Kiran Shah, for a scene in which the wounded hobbit first sees Arwen arrive in a dazzling blaze of light. It was late in the day when they discovered that Kiran's 'Frodo wig' was in one of the trucks that had been abandoned on location. Rick and a make-up artist jumped in a four-wheel drive vehicle and set out through the rain and flood waters.

'The entire area was now in a state of emergency!' says Rick. 'At the bridge, which was now almost under water, we had to convince an army patrol to let us cross. We reached the make-up truck, grabbed the wig, raced back and were just about the last car out of the place!'

Listening to this experience, I am reminded of Peter Jackson's description of his job as being a 'general' and the military metaphor is one that is shared by others on the production. 'We were a small army,' says Richard Sharkey, 'and quite a lot of the time we were at war with the elements. And, like any war you have to accept that there are going to be some casualties...'

It is dramatic language, but born of bitter experience: 'We worked eight days on Mount Ruapehu, filming the scenes on Emyn Muil of Frodo and Sam coming down into Mordor. The weather was miserable: rain, fog and,

eventually, snow. It was 1.00 a.m. when I received the phone call from a security guard on duty in the marquee we'd set up to serve as our unit base: "Richard, it's been snowing…" Heavily, as it happens: snow on snow, piling up. Apparently, the security guy, who came from Auckland, had never

seen snow before. As a result, he didn't think to knock it off the roof or turn on the heaters. "Richard," he said, "we have a problem…" And, in the background, I heard a groaning of buckling aluminium and an almighty crash as my massive marquee collapsed under the sheer weight of snow. It was probably my scariest moment going up there and looking at a pile of twisted metal and ripped PVC and realizing that I didn't have a unit base and that the full crew were arriving in thirty-six hours' time!'

With the help of the marquee-suppliers Richard managed to salvage the situation but, as he observes: 'Sometimes nature just gets the better of you…'

And sometimes, as Ian McKellen discovered, weather could be equally unpredictable on set! 'Probably the most unpleasant scene to film was the one in which the Fellowship is caught in the avalanche on Caradhras. We were stuck in the studio for days subjected to an artificial snow storm - created with a rice-based product, mixed with eight tons of *genuine* snow - permanently whipped to a frenzy by giant fans and, every now and again, unceremoniously dumped on us from a great height! Now, if you're filming on the top of a real mountain with a camera on a helicopter circling above you, the excitement is such that two or three hours go by pretty quickly, but if you're trapped tantalisingly close to the creature-comforts of your caravan and the lunch period with false snow whirling around you then, believe me, you're counting the minutes for it to be over!'

In contrast, the set for Saruman's chamber in Orthanc proved to be a veritable sauna. 'It was a tough set,' says Rick Porras who directed part of the duel between Gandalf and Saruman. 'It was enclosed and claustrophobic; there were machines pumping out smoke to create the atmosphere and we had to shut off the air-conditioning – to avoid smoke getting sucked out – which made it stiflingly hot even before we lit the burning braziers. Both wizards were dressed in long, heavy robes, beards, wig and prosthetic noses. It was not exactly the easiest shooting situation.'

Christopher Lee sums up the experience rather more succinctly: 'It was,' he says, 'murder. *Murder!*'

Of all the sets and locations, the worst-case scenario was, without doubt, that experienced during the nine weeks of night-shooting for the Battle of Helm's Deep. 'Night-shoot?' says Stunt Co-ordinator George Marshall Ruge. 'The *correct* word is *nightmare!* Over fifty nights in the most arduous conditions: it was a brutal, surreal experience, exhausting to the point of hysteria.'

It is a view confirmed by Extras Casting Co-ordinator Miranda Rivers: 'There were hundreds of Elf and Uruk-hai extras who had been up for fourteen hours and more, standing under rain-towers, being constantly dowsed with water. Everyone was absolutely saturated. It was far worse for the Uruk-hai, because they were wearing heavy prosthetics that trapped in the water and kept them cold. Amazingly, these guys had the most wonderful sense of humour and when they began getting tired and fed-up, you'd hear someone rapping a sword on a shield "Tap-ta-tapta-ta-tap…" Within minutes you'd have a hundred Uruk-hai doing full percussion on their armour to keep up their spirits and keep themselves going. After a while, the crew got the message! Those wet Uruk-hai would start chanting: "Turn off the rain-tower! Turn off the rain-tower!" – until someone would eventually yell out: "All right! *All right!* We'll give you a break!"'

As George Marshall Ruge expresses it: 'The Battle of Helm's Deep was a testament to human will, and to our collective loyalty to Peter Jackson. The survivors of that experience – and you had to be good to survive! – will be forever bonded in heart, soul and friendship.' No wonder those involved were proud to sport crew T-shirts emblazoned with the slogan: 'I survived Helm's Deep!' (with the 'm' crossed through to suggest the word 'hell'). In such a demanding and potentially perilous shoot, there were surprisingly few accidents. Viggo Mortensen chipped a piece off one of his teeth during a fight and famously suggested – to avoid the delay of getting to a dentist – that they stick the tooth back together with super-glue! Sean Astin had more than his fair share of mishaps: a wooden loom fell on him on the Rivendell set and knocked him unconscious and, later, when filming the closing scenes on *The Fellowship of the Ring*, rushed into the river to wade after Frodo's retreating boat, only to impale his foot on a piece of wood sticking up out the river bed. Piercing both the rubber hobbit foot and Sean's *own* foot, the actor had to be air-lifted to hospital. Sean's profuse apologies to Peter Jackson for delaying the shoot were greeted with the response that it wasn't a problem, that the schedule would be changed and that the next day they would move on to filming Frodo and Sam's arrival at the Black Gate of the Morannon – a scene that would only require the actors to crawl!

The most unexpected accident was that sustained by Conceptual Artist Alan Lee (shown below), who was discussing the building of one of the sets for Lothlórien and stepped back onto a part of the base that had not yet been reinforced. Though only a few feet off the ground, he took a hefty fall and broke his arm. Such was everyone's concern that the first question asked was invariably: 'Is it his drawing arm?' It wasn't, and whilst Alan had to spend the next six weeks in plaster, he was back at the drawing-board within a couple of days.

Rather more predictably, perhaps, were the riding incidents. Horse Co-ordinator, Steve Old, recalls the scariest: 'There were two hundred and fifty horses and riders, lined up twenty wide by ten deep for a battle charge. Just as the cameras turn over, something is obviously going wrong for the second rider in on the front row. His saddle begins to slip, and he starts rolling over to one side; he grabs the guy next to him and pushes himself up but by now they're moving and it's too late! He drops his spear, falls to the ground and instinctively curls into the foetal position. The horses are now going at a flat gallop, somehow swerving past or jumping over him. At the end, miraculously unscathed, he stands up and everyone applauds. Not only had he done something no stunt rider would ever have agreed to do, but he had the presence of mind to quip: "If only I'd had a camera while I was down there – there were some great shots of hooves…"!'

A particularly daunting scene, as horse-wrangler Mark Kinaston-Smith notes, was that in which the Ringwraiths are seen galloping in pursuit of Arwen as she flees to the Ford of Bruinen with the injured Frodo: 'Each of the Black Riders was wearing a heavy costume comprising nine layers of raw silk with a cowl which covered the head and which stuck out three inches in front of the face. Under their hoods they wore a gauze mask which allowed little more that peripheral vision.

There were, in fact, times when the horses knew where they were going and what they were doing better than most of the riders!'

Arwen's riding double, Jane Abbot, also had to cope with difficulties: 'Jane had a dummy of Frodo wired to the front of the saddle,' explains Mark, 'and was riding a boundy sort of horse whose first instinct was: "I'm not letting those black horses catch me!" In fact, he had so much speed that there was no way they were going to!'

Len Baynes, one of the Black Riders, agrees: 'We couldn't get near enough and we were going flat-out! Which is how –' Len begins to laugh '– on the first day of shooting, I fell off! We were racing at full-speed amongst trees. Scarcely able to see what was going on, I was weaving in and out. My horse wanted to follow the other horses, I didn't want him to, but the horse won out: we parted company, him going one way and me going the other! I landed on the ground with the costume over my head and found myself, in pitch blackness, trying to fight my way free from all those swathes of material!' After a moment's reflection, he adds: 'But, despite the odd spill, working on that scene was so exciting. There was an incredible adrenalin rush. One minute, you're sitting on your horse, waiting to go, then – "Action!" – and suddenly – *rooooooosh*! *Amazing*!'

Which is how it was for most people working on the film. That sense of thrill and excitement sprang in no small measure from Peter Jackson's own dedication: 'He has an incredible eye,' says Caro Cunningham, 'he understands people, he knows his equipment, he has a clear vision for what he needs to do and how to get it.'

It's a view shared by Director of Photography, Andrew Lesnie: '*The Lord of the Rings* contains just about every trick of the trade. When people ask me whether I mind if people work out how we did things, my answer is that I hope they won't *want to*! If they don't, then that's down to Peter. All the greatest films have been about *script* and *performance*. Peter knows that directing is not

about moving cameras around for the sake of it, or because it might look cool. He's a director who wants to tell a story well and get good performances. And he does both brilliantly!'

To tell this story required, Ian McKellen believes, a particular approach to the original material: 'With any film, you sometimes find yourself asking: "Who *is* this camera? How did it get there to see these events?" Tolkien's imagination was such that he writes, at times, as if he were describing what he himself has seen which is why Peter decided that the camera would live the journey – almost like a tenth member of the Fellowship seeing everything: sometimes focusing on the detail, sometimes with an eye to the grand sweep of things. I can't help feeling that it is an approach in keeping with Tolkien, who is a masterly painter-in-words of landscape – one of the very best – but is also intrigued by detail, the movement of a leaf, the twinkle in the eye…'

And Peter's view? 'It was tiring, physically and mentally, but never dull. Three movies, one big story and so much variety: one day shooting scenes of intimate, heart-wrenching drama; the next, vast battle scenes involving hundreds of extras. Every day bought an opportunity to create something new on this enormous canvas that is *The Lord of the Rings*.'

Hobbit Talk

A conversation with Dominic Monaghan and Billy Boyd

Q: How do Merry and Pippin develop as the story unfolds?

Dominic: Basically they are forced to grow up – grow *older* – a lot quicker than, as hobbits, they normally would… And, in doing so, they learn to embrace what's happening to them… Merry becomes a lot more serious and thoughtful and, later, although he becomes incredibly damaged, psychologically, by the war, he finds a courage that surprises even him…

Bill: Even though Pippin also matures, he still finds a time and a place for humour. The difference is that whereas in the first movie he's a source of unconscious comedy, it's something he grows to understands; to begin with, he doesn't know that the things he's doing are funny, later he says things to intentionally lighten the mood…

Dom: Actually, it was a bit of a 'group-project', getting Merry and Pippin to grow up! Make-up and costume helped a lot – especially wearing armour: the moment you put on gauntlets, strap on a breastplate and start carrying a sword, you not only stand and walk differently, you *feel* different…

Bill: And the armour worn by the men (and hobbit) of Gondor was fantastic!

Dom: But not as good as that of Rohan!

Bill: You say that, Dom, but I did notice the girls on set looking at me quite differently when I had my Gondorian uniform on…

Dom: Hmmm…

Q: What about Dominic and Billy? Did you feel that *you* changed or developed?

Billy: *Everyone* changed! And, because we were so close, everyone *borrowed* from each other – took on some of those qualities that we respected and admired in other people…

Dom: I'm sure that in casting us all they must have asked themselves: 'Can these people survive this ordeal? Do they have the strength of character to get through a year and a half together?' But we did! Elijah was inspiring because he was so incredibly resilient and hard-working; Ian McKellen was like a father figure to whom you'd turn for advice; Viggo was such a strong, powerful character who was always there for people; Bill always made people feel good by making them laugh, and—

Bill: And Dom always made the girls feel good in a special way! No idea how he did it!

Dom: Peter was a good judge of character: sensing that this group could work together and complement one another – not for four or five weeks but, by the time we're finally done, four or five *years*…

Q: If it hadn't worked you could have ripped yourselves apart…

Dom: There'd be times when someone would get tired and lose their temper, but we became such good friends that we got to know when someone was at breaking-point and whether they needed a night out or just a good night's sleep, whether they needed to be left alone or given a hug –

Bill: *I* need a hug!

Dom: Not *now*!

Bill: The great thing was: if there was any danger of losing it, you really only had to remind yourself that you were making *The Lord of the Rings* and that was enough to make you focus: knowing that you are making this movie and that's going to be seen by generations…

Q: Which could be enough to terrify you out of your wits!

Bill: That's true! In fact, for the first three months, I couldn't think about it, every time I did I'd just pass out!

Dom: Fall down, flat on his face, he would!

Bill: One time, in a cactus!

Dom: It was like an 'Itchy & Scratchy' cartoon on *The Simpsons!* Personally, I think it's too dangerous to keep thinking about the future. I'm all about living for the moment and being in the now… If you plan too much, it's boring simply because you know what's coming up next. I always want to be interested in what's happening; I want things to surprise me.

Bill: I think if you're lucky enough to have a choice in life then you have to choose what you feel, in your guts, is right for you at the time… This film, this experience, was right for me – for *us!* There's one day that sticks in my mind: we were on Mount Cook – this incredibly beautiful place where, because of environmental rules, people normally aren't allowed… There was just the Fellowship and a very small crew and I remember sitting, eating lunch and looking over and seeing Aragorn, Frodo, Sam, Merry and these other characters that I'd read about in a book and there they all were – and I was one of them…

Dom: I'm the same as Bill –

Bill: Are you, *really*? Well, I'm tired and I could do with a bath… I *stink!*

Dom: That's true! You do! You stink of elderberries and wizards!

Facets of Frodo

Ian McKellen:

'In creating Frodo, Tolkien may well have been thinking back to the First World War and the lads who went on a terrible journey from which many never returned. Elijah reminds me of those statues of idealized young men on war-memorials throughout the world: more sublime than human and with a complexion of molten marble. He is simply terrific…'

Christopher Lee:

'Elijah Wood will never grow old! With that almost Elfin face, he *was* Frodo. In his gentleness and sincerity – and in his enormous enthusiasm as an actor – he was simply perfect for the part.'

Sean Astin:

'We lived and worked so closely together that he became more like a brother than a fellow actor. I came to feel as protective of Elijah as Sam does of Frodo… In turn, Elijah helped me discover a lot about myself and, I literally might not have survived the journey had this young prince of an actor not taken me under his wing!'

Ian Holm:

'Those remarkable, God-given, eyes! That glorious, good-natured personality! Elijah's Frodo is a dazzling light in the doom and gloom of war and despair…'

Miranda Otto:

'Elijah has the innocence of a child, the wisdom of a ninety-year old man, and the grace of an angel…'

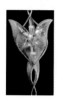

Aspects of Aragorn

'I was afraid!' Viggo Mortensen is discussing the challenge of portraying Aragorn. 'As an actor, you try to find some connection to the story that you are helping to tell, to find what you have within you for the job at hand – often, as was the case in this film, with virtually no time to prepare.

'Practically speaking, within days of joining this project, I was still furiously reading the book and starting to recognize things that I knew and felt were true to my own situation. As I read, I saw that, brave as Aragorn seems to be, he is much conflicted and dealing with a lot of self-doubt… That was a point of contact with the character: here I was, thrown into a situation where I didn't yet know the story; didn't know the country I was going to be working in or any of the other people on the project. Like Aragorn, I realized that I faced a long and uncertain journey.'

As Viggo began studying Tolkien's writings about Middle-earth, his discernment of Aragorn's character deepened: 'I see Aragorn as a bridge between the past and the present. Having travelled extensively in Middle-earth, he's familiar with the landscape, with its sounds and smells; he knows its people and speaks their languages. That understanding, combined with Aragorn's knowledge of how weak even the strongest of his forefathers were – how even the bravest and most honourable

among them were unable to master their potential for greed – makes Aragorn a link, between what's good and what's scary about the past, and what is good and potentially scary about the present, and the future.

'Whereas Frodo, for example, is in a continual process of learning about the world, Aragorn knows it well; whereas Frodo is coming to terms with what he is learning, Aragorn is coming to terms with what his learning dictates that he must do.'

Being half-Danish, Viggo had an awareness of much of Tolkien's source material – the great medieval Nordic sagas – which enhanced his appreciation of Tolkien's mythology: 'On one level, Aragorn is the heroic archetype that you find in the sagas, but with the striking difference that he is a man who seems almost to have lost his tongue! In the sagas, the hero will brag about what he's going to do, do it and then brag about what he's done. Aragorn, in contrast, is a modern character with qualities more like those of the Samurai hero who must often learn difficult lessons and endure much hardship on his journey, and whose eventual triumph is usually as much in the service of society as it is for himself.'

In seeking to comprehend Aragorn's character, Viggo draws parallels with many literary and filmic resonances: 'I recognize something of the roles played by Toshiro Mifune in Kurosawa's pictures, among others, as well as something of those taciturn characters played by Clint Eastwood, or Gary Cooper's sheriff in *High Noon*. Although the tone of *The Lord of the Rings* strongly identifies with Northern Europe, its author certainly tapped into the rich literary legacy that connected the Near and Far East with Europe in the early medieval period. The elements of heroism and romantic love in stories as disparate as, say, *The Thousand and One Nights* and the Arthurian legends are obvious in Tolkien's work. There are certain qualities – such as Aragorn's healing powers – which are usually associated with the image of the Christ-like king and with other leader-characters whose true nature is "hidden": from the individuals themselves and, for a while, from the world at large. These characters, such as Moses and King Arthur, are raised by people to whom they are not related (possibly, as with Aragorn, who was raised by the Elves in Rivendell, by people of another race) and have to fulfil a destiny that requires them to understand the things of the past and commit to the future.

'Myth – just like religion – is dead unless you keep reinvigorating it, reapplying it. I think that what Tolkien did with some of the elements from the sagas and Celtic legends which I know and love was to forge something new, reinvent a lot of these archetypal stories and characters for his generation. Now Peter Jackson is doing that for ours.

'Seeing a film is not something to be looked down on in comparison with reading a book. There can be millions of identical copies of any book, and yet the copy you hold and read is your personal doorway. It is the same when you go to the movie-theatre: you and the movie have a secret. It might even be a god-awful movie and you could still walk out with this little secret – or a big secret – inside you: a discovery that might stay with you for a day, for a month or two, even years. In those secrets we touch myth and confront universal issues, perhaps even draw new strength for our own lives.'

Just such a secret may be found towards the end of *The Fellowship of the Ring* when, following the death of Boromir, Aragorn takes the dead man's vambraces and straps them to his own forearms. It is a gesture Viggo contributed to the scene: 'They serve both as a reminder to Aragorn that he has made a pledge to Boromir and as a way of carrying Boromir's spirit with him as the remnant of the Fellowship continues its journey. In a movie, you can use such symbolism without comment: whether people consciously notice such a detail at the time or not is irrelevant. It still *means* something. And to the actor, it can be a powerful talisman…'

Adding the Magic

'Peter is always taking chances. In fact, he's beyond taking chances. He never stops delving into things that other directors wouldn't want to know about.' With a career which includes work on such films as *102 Dalmatians*, *Star Trek: Insurrection*, *Air Force One*, *Starship Troopers*, *Batman Returns* and *Ghost*, Weta Digital's Visual Effects Supervisor, Jim Rygiel (pictured below), knows of what he speaks. 'When you're doing work like this on a film, you are always "post-production". What's interesting and really great is that, as far as Peter is concerned, this is production. He says that every day through his ceaseless involvement in every single aspect of the making of these films.'

The film footage may be in the can; the wrap-party with all its laughter and tears and parting hugs has been and gone, but for everyone involved in post-production, the work goes on and Peter is in the thick of it.

I'm in a back room of the large, rambling house that is the office of Peter's production company, Wingnut Films. Several hundred yards of shelving is stacked with what look like brown cardboard pizza boxes.

'They are pizza boxes!' laughs Assistant Editor Heather Small. 'Three thousand, eight hundred of them!'

'What you see here,' says Supervising Editor Jamie Selkirk (right), 'is every roll of film that was printed; all the shots that Peter may want to use — which is only about 70% of everything that was actually shot and which, in terms of footage, is about 3.5 million feet of film. Now, that is a lot of picture!'

The 'dailies' arrive from the laboratory as their name suggests on a daily basis and First Assistant Editor Peter Skarratt and his team synchronize the film with its corresponding sound-track and arrange for what are known as the 'rushes' to be screened for the unit directors, editors and anyone else who needs to know what is going on.

When Peter Jackson and others were shooting on location in the South Island, this involved the added complication of having the 'rushes' ready by late morning in order for them to be couriered to the airport for the mid-day flight to Christchurch so that the director could view them at four o'clock in the afternoon. On one bonanza day, the film lab processed 43,000 feet of film, the rushes for which — if anybody had had the time to view them at a sitting — would have taken ten hours!

While Heather logs and codes the rolls of film and files them away in their pizza boxes, a 'telecined' version on digital tape is loaded into the computer hard-drives of the six editing machines which — with their combined disc storage of 2000 gigabytes — are being used to edit the three films.

In one room, Peter is closeted with Film Editor John Gilbert, cutting *The Fellowship of the Ring*; on the other side of the corridor, Editor Mike Horton is in the early stages of putting together *The Two Towers*, while, nearby, Assembly Editor Annie Collins, is already lining up material for *The Return of the King* which Jamie Selkirk will be editing: 'It's an interesting process. To begin with you just have to plonk stuff together, then Jamie comes in and we get to work. I fight my way through all the technical stuff involved with editing on computer while Jamie talks story. Everything we do from then on is about making the film better and better.'

Nevertheless, as Jamie admits, there is a lot of material: 'Peter covers every shot with two cameras: one static, one tracking; one tight, one wide; one from this angle, one from that. There's always plenty of choice!'

As Annie is discovering in assembling a scene in which King Théoden rides out onto a battlefield to address his troops: 'I started out with over two and a half hours of different takes for this scene which I whittled away at until I got it down to twenty-nine minutes. I kept discarding and discarding (sometimes going back to look at earlier choices and reassessing) until I had a core of material which was made up of the best shots, the best angles. I'm now down to twelve minutes and going to have to start chipping and chiselling again until I get it to the length it has to be on screen – which is ninety seconds!'

And what happens when Peter eventually gets to see it? 'Oh, he'll probably say, "That's nothing like what I wanted!"' jokes Jamie. 'Seriously, he could say that we've gone in completely the wrong direction – which is easy to do with all the footage we've got and the number of effects we're trying to figure out – but we've got a reasonably good idea of what he's looking for so, hopefully, we won't be far off-course. You could put four editors in this room with all this footage and they'd all come up with a different way of cutting it, but the essence of the scene would always be there.'

Unlike some directors, who never enter the editing room, Peter loves the process. 'He never tires of noodling away at footage,' says Jamie. 'He might ask to check out one or two other performances, or perhaps change a wide shot for a close-up. But that's because the finished film is already playing in his head.'

As the editing process advances, Heather Small (pictured above left) keeps track of all three films with a master cut of each, put together from the thousands of rolls of film in all those pizza boxes. Using the code numbers which are recorded both on film and in the editing computers, Heather cuts and splices together a working-print that can be screened in the theatre. It's a constantly shifting puzzle. 'If the edit changes, I may

have to find the new shots and cut them in. On the other hand, I may have to take shots out, in which case, I have to find the original rolls of film they came from and put those shots back in the precisely the right place – even if it's only a single frame!' Heather averages between one hundred and one hundred and twenty shots a day.

Meanwhile, the sound for the movie is being created with as much painstaking care and sheer inventiveness as has gone into every other aspect of making *The Lord of the Rings*.

'Frankly, it sounded like a flying saucer coming into land in a 1950s sci-fi picture!' Ethan Van der Ryn (shown below), Supervising Sound Editor and Co-Designer, is talking about early attempts at devising a sound for the One Ring: 'It was just cliché – all high and wavery! The challenge is to come up with something that "says" what it's meant to be, but which you haven't quite heard before.'

Ethan came to the project after thirteen years with George Lucas' Skywalker Sound, working on *Pearl Harbor, X-Men, Saving Private Ryan, Jumanji* and *Terminator 2: Judgement Day*.

The thrill and the danger of what he is doing comes from the fact that most of the sound recorded during the shoot is not really usable, due to various extraneous sounds such as wind-machines (on set) and real wind

(on location) as well as, just about anywhere in the vicinity of Wellington, the drone of incoming and outgoing aircraft.

'We start,' says Ethan, 'with pretty much a blank sheet. We collect sounds, put together a library of effects (some borrowed, most newly-recorded) and then we build, layer upon layer, starting with the basic ambience – the tone and atmosphere – for a scene.'

Sitting at his editing desk where the sounds are mixed, Ethan calls up a scene as an example: the events in Balin's Tomb from the Mines of Moria sequence. The footage plays on a TV monitor, but the focus is on the sound, which is a mix of various winds: a distant low rumble, deep roars, sharp gusts, high whistlings and the chink of chains stirred by a passing breeze.

'Peter talked about wanting "the sound of silence",' Ethan recalls, 'the feeling of a vast tomb filled with dead air. So we went to some old military tunnels on Wrights Hill, just outside Wellington, that dated back to World War Two and we played our wind-sounds through speakers and recorded the results. What we got was a sense of place that could never be so powerfully created by using an electronic reverberation in a studio.'

The sequence runs on to the coming of the goblins. I'm seeing, but mainly, I'm hearing: sword-hits, clanks

Howzat!

Just how do you set about recording several thousand Uruk-hai chanting Black Speech as they march in Helm's Deep in *The Two Towers*? Answer: Go to a New Zealand versus England cricket match!

Post-Production Supervisor Rose Dority tells the story: 'At one of our sound meetings early in 2002 we were discussing the fact that *The Two Towers* featured a lot of crowd scenes with thousands of troops which would require a great many voices. Since our recording stage won't hold thousands I suggested that we might look at recording the cheers at a sporting venue.

'One thing led to another and sound assistant Peter Mills set about getting approval to utilize Westpac Stadium at an upcoming event, which just happened to be a one-day cricket match between New Zealand and England – and which, I might add, New Zealand won convincingly!

'The next question was who would direct the recording? Followed immediately by the thought: "Wouldn't it be fantastic if PJ did it?" Fortunately, the cricket management, the Westpac Stadium Trust and PJ all thought it a great idea.

'Due to international television rights, we had to record in a twenty-minute window during the tea break. We had eight of our sound team with microphones at various locations on and around the field – including the roof. The announcer played *The Fellowship of the Ring* trailer on the field replay-screen and then introduced PJ to the crowd. Well, it was a standing ovation and cheers as he walked on to the field. Very exciting!

'PJ was great directing the crowd with stomping, chest-beating, cheering, hissing, whispering and chanting in Black Speech – with the replay-screen serving as an auto-cue for the words!'

and clunks; a heavy door grating closed, then the splintering of wood as the enemy smashes through; blades being drawn from sheaths (with added metallic 'zings'); sword swishes and the dull thud of falling bodies.

Then the arrival of the cave troll, whose vocal performance was created by Ethan's Co-Sound Designer, David Farmer. 'Dave made the cave troll mostly out of walrus!' Ethan informs me, unfazed by the surrealism of the statement. 'Obviously, you can't show a walrus a picture of a troll and say "OK, now, just pretend you're this guy!" So he recorded a walrus and selected particular sounds that seemed to convey emotion – anger, confusion, surprise or hurt – which could then be used to suggest characterization. Then he started shaping those sounds to the pictures – adding in a few extra

things such as the snorts and grunts of a horse on heat!'

Some of the best sounds, it seems, are found by accident, often while recording for something quite different: 'That's the real fun: trying something completely unlikely and finding that it works. A part of being a sound editor is about playing. It's helpful not to have too many preconceived ideas, but to keep an open mind to serendipity: some of the most alive sounds come from the strangest of sources!'

Ethan plays the scene of the Ringwraiths' attack at Weathertop. 'We wanted the wraiths to have dry, brittle, icy voices and we drew on all kinds of elements to create them.'

Listening, I try to disentangle the sounds. Are those lions? 'Oh, yes!' says Ethan quoting a lyric from *The*

Wizard of Oz: "'Lions, and tigers and bears! Oh, my!'" Well, maybe not tigers and bears, but certainly lions, owl-hoots, possum-squeals, camel-grunts – pitched rather higher than normal – and the sound of a plastic cup being scraped over concrete!'

I can see what he means about playing...

We take a tour of the department and meet Sound Effects Editor Tim Nielsen (also from Skywalker Sound), currently creating an ambience for the top of Orthanc: 'I brought some rain with me from the States, but most of the wind was recorded on a hill-top near Wellington. What makes this job interesting is that you obviously can't go to Orthanc or to Rivendell or Lothlórien and record what it sounds like there, so you get to make it all up, decide what those places would sound like.'

But, with nothing to go on, how do they know if they're getting it 'right'? Ethan's verdict: 'Trust your gut feelings. If it works for you, it should work for everyone else.'

'Essentially,' adds Tim, 'you know it's right when Peter says: "I like that!"'

Tim established the department's database for the sounds which, by spring 2001, were already totalling 11,163 effects but which, by the time the films are finished, could number as many as 50,000! Sounds can be searched for by category ('horses' hooves') or by a keyword which might be very specific ('cold' or 'wet'), suggestive of a mood ('danger', 'fear'), or an abstract notion such as 'sharp' or 'puffy'.

With a few taps on the keyboard, Tim summons up 'single bat-wing flaps', 'deep ethereal hits', 'small twittering clicks' and a 'gooey flesh effect'. Typing in the word 'bys' he plays me a series of sounds made by various things – arrows, spears, rocks – going by!

Vital though sound may be, there is, as Ethan points out, another consideration: 'You need to look for places to put in not sound, but beats of silence. Without them you lose the dynamic range and start to lose the drama. You can create the storm, but before it must come the lull!'

On next to Dialogue Editor Jason Canovas who is 'spotting for ADR'. Sometimes known as 'looping', ADR stands for Automated Dialogue Replacement which will be used in place of up to 90% of dialogue recorded during the shoot. Jason watches the film and transcribes, line by line, the dialogue that will need to be re-recorded.

Later, in a studio – possibly in London or Los Angeles – the original actors will watch film, listen on headphones to the lines as originally delivered and recreate them for the microphone. It can take anything from four to twenty attempts to achieve 'lip-sync' which is when the words are in synchronization with the lip-movements seen on film. 'Even then it won't be absolutely perfect,' explains Jason, 'finally, we can pull it all together: editing or stretching, until it fits down to the very last breath.'

In a nearby office I meet Assistant Sound Editors Chris Ward and Kathy Wood. Chris has been recording

the sounds of costumes: Boromir's leather tunic, Bilbo's mithril vest or a Ringwraith's robes: 'You can get a very particular sound from the flapping of all that ragged cloth!'

The sound department will also use the skills of what are called 'foley artists' to create the physical sounds needed for the various characters. Foley artists Phil Heywood and Simon Hewitt will watch footage and provide such sounds as footsteps, gown-rustles and the clattering of pots and pans on Sam's knapsack. Phil (shown below) spent several hours scrabbling around on gravel to simulate the sounds of Gandalf losing his grip on the edge of Khazad-dûm.

Kathy, meanwhile, has been recording sounds for the scenes with the Fellowship in the Elven boats on the River Anduin: 'We got pretty grubby, cold and wet – jumping into boats and jumping into the water as well as recording the sound of paddles sluicing through the water.'

Next door, Sound FX Editor Craig Tomlinson is working with those sounds: 'Timing is crucial. On film, each stroke of the paddle takes five seconds, so when

they were recording, they timed their paddle-strokes to fit. What I'll do is tweak the sounds here and there to give them a smooth, silky quality and add a sound that suggests the gliding of the boat through the water.'

Our next stop is John McKay, through whose closed door comes the terrifying sound of stampeding horses. John is working on the scene in which the Ringwraiths are pursuing Arwen. So, what, I want to know, does a Ringwraith sound like? 'If you ask Peter Jackson,' says John, 'he'll tell you it should sound as if it's "gargling blood"! At the moment, it's sounding something like this –'

John clicks his mouse and there's a thundering of hooves, a sound of laboured breathing and the jangling of a bridle, with, somewhere in the mix, a high-pitched shriek like a rabbit in a trap and, perhaps, just a hint of blood-gargling!

'There's one or two non-animal elements in there!' John shouts over the sounds. 'There's a wind whipping the branches of a tree and the "whooshing" sound of a firebrand being swung around to enhance the heavy breathing.' Then, to Ethan: 'I just added in a few leather-creaks, could you hear them?'

As we leave John to his horses, Ethan observes: 'You know, in this job you can't have a big ego. If we get it right, people will hear those horses and simply think that those were the sounds the animals made when they were being filmed!'

The same is true of many contributions to this film, including the work of Peter Doyle of The Posthouse, who is responsible for the films' revolutionary Digital Colour Grading: 'Peter Jackson wanted *The Lord of the Rings* to have "a painterly look" that stayed close to the conceptual art for the film. So, what we're doing – and it's the start of a new trend – is extending the art design by digitally manipulating the imagery: we can alter the contrast and change the brightness, pull out certain hues and twist specific colours.'

For the scenes in Hobbiton, Peter Doyle has transformed the stark Southern Hemisphere light of the location into a softer, European look with plenty of strong, clean colours. In contrast, for the scenes shot on the Moria cemetery set he has reduced the reds and pushed the blues, to convey the coldness of the mood.

Peter is currently tinkering with the light cast by

Gandalf's staff and helping to illuminate the wizard's face which was seriously overshadowed by that broad-brimmed hat. He is also planning effects for the rest of the film: 'The predominant colours in Bree will be dirty golden yellows, edging towards green; Lothlórien will be blue, swinging into pastel shades of lavender; while Rivendell will have a crisp, clear Alpine light. "Painterly", yes; but not a painting: that's the secret.'

Next door to The Posthouse is 'the optical motion capture stage', a vast, echoey barn of a warehouse, starkly furnished with an array of black-painted ramps, steps and ladders, all of which are used to simulate specific environments by the Mocap unit.

Motion capture is the technique of recording human action and applying it to animation. Around the walls are twenty-six cameras that are used, in various configurations, to film a variety of performers including stunt-players, dancers, mime artists, people skilled in martial arts and, for *The Lord of the Rings*, the actors playing the nine members of the Fellowship.

To be motion captured, it is necessary to wear a skin-tight black Lycra jumpsuit with small yellow balls spotted onto all the joints to act as reflective markers. In order for the cameras to register the markers clearly, the action must always begin with the performer adopting the 'da Vinci' pose, inspired by Leonardo da Vinci's famous drawing of a man – legs apart, arms at right angles to the body, created to represent the ideal proportions for a human being. The performer then acts out the desired movements for the cameras which translate the images into data that effectively manipulates a 'digital puppet' on screen in replication of the human performer.

I meet Weta Digital's Chief Technical Officer, Jon Labrie, who explains some of the uses for 'digital doubles': 'They might stand in for the actors in a variety of scenes, such as those involving dangerous stuntwork or where they are required to interact with creatures – for example, Legolas riding the cave troll like a bucking bronco – or when the environment is so vast, such as the great Dwarrowdelf chamber in Moria, that it would be impossible to film the actors from sufficient distance to show them in scale with their surroundings.'

Creating digital doubles for the Fellowship actors required them to act out some fifty different motions including a selection of walks, runs, turns and jumps. As Jon notes: 'Replicating human figures – and identifiable actors in particular – is quite a challenge. Creatures are easy in comparison: who knows how a cave troll moves? However, some of our results are terrifyingly good. Even at an inch high, it is possible to distinguish Sean Bean's walk from that of Viggo Mortensen, Dominic Monaghan's from Billy Boyd's.'

It's a complex process that goes beyond capturing the actors' moves into replicating their facial looks, hair and clothes. 'We take head scans when they're wearing their wigs and make-up and use programmes that add shade and textures, but it's time-consuming: we'd no sooner think we were done with a character then we'd find they'd have another prop or a different costume that would have to be dealt with. Gimli is the worst because he wears so many layers of clothing and Sam's almost as bad, because he's carrying so much paraphernalia around!'

Jon runs a sequence on a monitor of the 'Digital Fellowship' running through the great chamber of Dwarrowdelf. 'The more we can do, the more we can get away with,'

he says. 'Sometimes I think Peter has more faith in us that we have in ourselves; certainly he's pushed us farther than we thought we could go – and got the camera in a good deal closer than we ever expected!'

So, with digital doubling, who needs actors? 'There's no need for actors to worry yet,' smiles Jon, 'not until we can do close-ups!'

After one or two anxious exchanges, the stars of *The Lord of the Rings* threw themselves into creating the motion-capture footage for their digital doubles, as Mocap Supervisor Greg Allen remembers: 'They were fun times, but very demanding on the actors because they had to imagine the appropriate environment and the costume they would be wearing: we gave John Rhys-Davies ankle-weights to help simulate his heavy boots and Ian McKellen would mime gathering up his robes as he ran! In addition to all of which, they'd be expected to act out their characters' physical responses to a scene: running through this empty space – nothing but black floor and a few lights – with us shouting: "Look round! There's a Balrog!"'

The actors did have the benefit of props, made by Mocap Prop Designer Frank Cowlrick, who proudly shows me a series of replica weapons smothered in black paint and yards of black sticky tape and dotted with yellow markers.

Stacked on racks like curious items of lost property are Gimli's axe, the cave troll's mace and a telescopic hobbit sword, the length of which can be adjusted depending on which of the four hobbits is carrying it. Some of the swords were simulated with lengths of aluminium piping strengthened with wooden doweling, but Viggo, who had become used to the weight and balance of Aragorn's sword, insisted on carrying a blacked-out version of the real weapon.

Shields and helmets presented a particular challenge: whilst they needed to be represented it was essential that anything carried or worn didn't obscure the markers on the actors' suits. 'You have to think in skeletal terms,' explains Frank, 'what we call "space-frame construction".' So, in this department, a round shield tends to ends up looking more like a bicycle wheel!'

For Ian McKellen, who was already coping with carrying a staff and a sword, Frank made a special 'skeleton-Gandalf-hat' which somewhat resembled the wire frame of a lampshade!

Motion capture was also used to help choreograph the cave troll sequence, as Animation Designer Randall ('Randy') Cook explains when he comes to collect me for a tour of Weta Digital. 'Peter wanted the troll to have a feeling of a mad rhino: so we tried to find a way of taking the attributes of a rhinoceros and translating them – one frame at a time – into humanoid form. Although he doesn't speak, we devised an inner dialogue-track consisting of his thoughts that would be expressed through facial and body movements. His emotions are pretty limited, of course: after all he's only got a walnut-sized brain and about a twelve-word vocabulary of thoughts!'

For Randy, animation – like acting – is a performing art. A veteran of such films as *The Thing*, *Q: The Winged Serpent* and *Armageddon*, Randy took on the task of acting-out the cave troll's movements. A 3-D virtual set was constructed and, wearing goggles which enabled him to 'see' inside the simulated interior of Balin's Tomb, Randy rampaged about for the motion capture cameras. Then Peter Jackson donned the goggles and

used a 'virtual camera' to plot all the moves that would be used in filming the live-action footage featuring the Fellowship.

'The sequence was filmed using a hand-held camera,' says Randy, 'so it's like you're in the middle of a newsreel film about a troll that's going nuts! The cameraman is running around, dodging about and leaping out of the way while this crazy creature is running amok!'

Most spectacularly, motion capture is being used to create the basis for the animation of Gollum, a character which will combine the creative work of artists, model-makers and animators with the essence of an actor's performance. For Greg Allen and Mocap Technician James van der Ryden, working with the voice talent of the creature – Andy Serkis – was a thrilling experience.

They recall Andy's first test-footage for Gollum: 'It was amazing!' says Greg, 'He was down on the floor on all fours, crouching, crawling around, jumping about: one minute vicious and dangerous, the next cringing and pathetic!'

'There were so many contrasts,' adds James, 'he'd be apelike, then froglike; angry, then tearful; and always hissing and sniffing! The dynamic was fantastic!'

'All the time,' says Greg, 'we were thinking: "Oh, my God, we don't want to say *Cut*." We just wanted to go on watching him bring this character so completely to life!"

Andy Serkis's performance is essentially that of a puppeteer: the creature reacts to the motions of the actor and a software programme compensates for the differences in their physical build by imposing Gollum's proportions onto the capture of Andy's body movements. So, if Andy's arms are shorter than Gollum's or his thighs larger, then the computer will process those differences and read and interpret the actor's moves in terms of Gollum's physique. Once 'captured' the Gollum image is then open for modification by the animators.

'The process of creating the essence of Gollum,' notes Randy Cook, 'is finding those points of intersection between the character and the actor – either literally or spiritually. Somewhere they will meet. Where? We don't know yet – but stay tuned!'

We set off to walk the few hundred yards up the road to Weta Digital. 'Basically,' says Randy, 'all you're going to see is a few hundred people sitting in front of computer monitors doing cool things.'

And 'cool' is the word, as I discover when Visual Effects Art Director Christian Rivers (pictured above) reveals some of the trilogy's 1,500 visual effects shots: the digital magic that has such a vital – yet often unobtrusive – part to play in creating Middle-earth on film.

There are, for example, the creatures: not just Gollum and the cave troll, but the Balrog, the Watcher in the Water, Treebeard and the Nazgûl fell-beasts that become the flying steeds of the Ringwraiths. 'A lot of digital creatures,' says Christian, 'are nothing more than skin and bone which is why they tend to look fake and plastic. There's more to our creatures than meets the eye!'

The process begins with conceptual designs and the sculpting, at Weta Workshop, of a detailed three-dimensional model known as a maquette. Scanners are then used to record the surface of the maquette and convert its bulk and texture into computer data which will enable three-dimensional animation of the figure in all its sculptural detailing: folds, wrinkles, veins, warts and all.

'Every creature needs a skeleton in order for the animators to be able to articulate it, but, equally important is the building of a muscle-system working beneath the skin to give the creature the dynamics of movement and weight.'

Weta Digital is also responsible for the scale-trickery involved in bringing Gandalf and Bilbo together in Bag End, ranging from simple false-perspective set-ups to the complex use of 'composites' that combines footage from different sources into one shot.

The latter technique is also being used to assist in the creation of the various environments: action filmed on a set, such as Frodo standing on a balcony looking out across Rivendell, will be composited with shots of a miniature model of Elrond's House, still photographs by Craig Potton, and background paintings by Visual Effects Art Director, Paul Lasaine, into which will be incorporated moving footage of waterfalls.

Next, Christian throws in what he modestly describes as 'a few little doozies' by which he means such effects as the reflection of the Ring inscription on Frodo's face; the fiery cat's-eye of Sauron; the vision of Wraithworld in which reality becomes a swirling mass of shroud-tatters; the firing of a digital Legolas arrow and (less likely to be spotted) the throwing of a digital Boromir knife.

I marvel at Gandalf's fireworks: dancing butterflies, a torrent of spears and a dive-bombing dragon – the biggest challenge, apparently, being to stop the effects artists from trying to make the firework-dragon look too convincingly like a real dragon! 'To make any effect work,' remarks Christian, 'you can't have it draw attention to itself. If you're not aware of it there's nothing to stop you believing in it.'

This has been possible because of the many

technological breakthroughs in the creation of the special effects for *The Lord of the Rings* – such as development of the software programme called 'Massive' which has enabled the creation of vast fighting armies of Elves, men and Orcs.

'We've used every trick in the book,' says Christian, 'and quite a few more that people don't even know are *in* the book! If you want to see just how complex this film can be, look at the flight down the collapsing staircase in the Mines of Moria. In that one sequence there are miniature models, effects of fire, smoke and falling masonry; actors, stunt-doubles, scale-doubles and digital doubles. So many tricks and devices that the viewer can no longer be sure what we're getting up to. They'll never pin it all down – or, if they do, they're going to have a very, very long list!'

It's tempting to think that therein lies the magic; but it doesn't, as I discover in following Peter Jackson on his daily tour of Weta Digital. Awaiting Peter's arrival, Visual Effects Supervisor Jim Rygiel observes: 'Quite often in a facility like this one would try to keep the director out of the way. It would be a case of: "No, don't let him come in yet – not till we've got it right!" But you couldn't keep Peter out – nor would you want to. It might seem like the film's finished and the director's job's done, but Peter's in here, down in the trenches with all these people – and still directing!'

Peter pounds barefoot up and down stairs, moving from one unit to the next, talking with each animator in turn about whatever shot he or she is working on. His absorption in the story and characters is absolute, the precision of his direction is unwavering, his ability to communicate his ideas with perfect comic timing is refreshing…

'What we've got to remember is that the troll is a kid who's gone berserk… And he's *tired*! He's an incredible out-of-condition cave troll…!' 'He's looking down at Legolas as he advances and he's panting…' *(Peter pants breathlessly)* 'He's exhausted! He can't believe what's happening… It's like: "I'm trying to kill these guys, I've just had my guts slit open and *now* what…?" Can you put in a breath there…?'

'You've put in a little bob of the head there - after Legolas fires the arrow… It's like he's thinking: "Why have I got a headache? Why is it getting dark?" If you're going to do that, then try getting in close, so we see him wince… He could give a squeal – but with his mouth shut, lips tight…' *(Peter demonstrates with a pathetic whimper)* '…Let us see that look of pain… Then you can go from pain to anger… He's like a child: he's sore and he's going to take it out on someone… It's good… It's cool… It's all coming together nicely…'

As the suggestions flow, I realize that *this* is where the magic happens: not with the tricks themselves but with the conjuror…

Massive Achievement

'It can take a month to build a brain!' It may sound like a line from a Boris Karloff movie, but the speaker is Stephen Regelous, who is responsible for developing and supervising the crowd software used by Weta Digital on *The Lord of the Rings*. And once Stephen's team have built that brain there is no limit to what it can be programmed to do.

It all began several years ago when Peter Jackson asked Stephen to put together a computerized crowd system for use in what was then going to be *The Hobbit*. The working title for the software programme was 'Plod' (the aim being to allow an animated character to walk), but it soon outgrew that pedestrian title to be re-named 'Massive'. Simply put (and the mathematics and technology are anything but simple) Stephen and his colleagues are creating nothing short of artificial intelligence. 'Massive' enables characters – or 'agents' – to react to their situation and environment through sound and vision, using a 'brain' to access and use, in real time, upwards of 250 body moves.

Stephen explains: 'Every little snippet of motion joins up with another so that there is a logic to what they can and can't do at any one time. The agents make their decisions in "real time" and the "thinking" process can undergo a change every twenty-fourth of a second!'

Certain conditioning influences apply – much as they would in any organized group in the real world – so agents follow a 'spec' (specification) which establishes what they are required to do (firing arrows, wielding swords, throwing spears) and what is in character for them – if they are Elves, to fight Orcs; or, if they're Orcs, to kill Elves! 'Within those general constraints,' admits Stephen, with a somewhat scary calm, 'we never really know how they're going to react!'

This is demonstrated, on screen, by a single Orc swordsman. He moves: left foot forward, sword outstretched; a second later he might encounter an Elf-warrior who reacts to the sword-thrust and responds with his own weapon. At that point, the Orc might block the blow with his sword, punch with his shield, go to 'wind-up' (getting ready for another strike), step forward with the right foot, retreat a pace, turn and run away or 'go to death'.

All agents are well prepared to meet their end by the application of a 'rigid body dynamics simulation' by which they fall and react in relation to the terrain on which they are fighting, whether rocky plain, steep hillside or cliff-edge.

'We've a lot of variations in our deaths,' says Stephen, obligingly bringing up on screen a series of Orcs falling to Elf-arrows. One keels over backwards, another goes down on one knee, while a third does an extravagant back-flip. 'I have to say,' laughs Stephen, 'his reaction is a bit over the top!'

The godlike creation process taking place at Weta Digital is two-fold: they build a body and they build a brain. All the bodies are constructed with a programme called 'Orc-Builder' (shock revelation: even Elves are created this way!), and share a common skeleton, depending on their race or species, but with variations of height, build, stance and stride-length. The brains are developed on what is called a 'motion tree', which comprises a grid of moves and actions interconnected by nodes which feed a central vortex.

The models for the movements are created with the aid of motion-capture and the skeletons are then fleshed over and supplied with 'secondary dynamics' which simulate the movement of clothes and hair in relation to how the figure moves.

Using the Massive programme these AI armies are then ready to march into battle. 'You hit the "go" button,' says Stephen, 'and the programme writes the animation data for every single agent in each and every frame of film.'

How many agents are there? '100,000 if you want them! That's what's so wonderful: you couldn't possibly get 100,000 people in order to film a scene, but you can have 100,000 of these guys! In fact, you couldn't even animate 100,000 characters, but what we're doing is letting them animate themselves!'

Capturing Gollum

'I played Gollum as an addict!' Andy Serkis is talking about his approach to playing one of JRR Tolkien's most memorable characters. 'The thing to remember about Gollum is that he hates the Ring and he loves the Ring – just as he hates and loves himself. He's an addict in need of a fix, and that fix is the Ring.'

Andy originally auditioned to provide the voice-over for the computer-generated Gollum, but the actor whose film work includes *Career Girls, Mojo, Among Giants, Topsy-Turvy, Shiner* and *24 Hour Party People* gave such a physical reading of the part that Peter Jackson videoed the performance 'every which way' and decided that Andy should act out Gollum's scenes with Frodo and Sam, both to integrate his performance with those of his fellow players and as to inspire the artists in the animation department who would be subsequently replacing him with a digital Gollum. The animated Gollum began with a maquette (right) which was scanned into the animator's computer. It was at the point at which this digital creation was brought to life that Andy's involvement began.

Every scene was shot three times: once, on set or location, with Andy acting alongside Elijah Wood and Sean Astin as Frodo and Sam; then without Andy in frame, in order to provide the shots into which the digital Gollum would be placed; and, finally, with Andy working alone at the motion-capture (Mocap) unit – wearing goggles in which he could watch the other actors in the scene – in order to provide footage that could be digitally translated into computer data for the CGI animators.

'The challenge,' says Andy, 'is to come up with a fully-integrated character on screen.

Even though Gollum will be created by technology, Peter was determined that the part would be actor-led; something which is symptomatic of a production in which effects never take precedence over story, character or performance.'

Despite considerable experience within the disciplines of physical theatre, Andy found the process of embodying

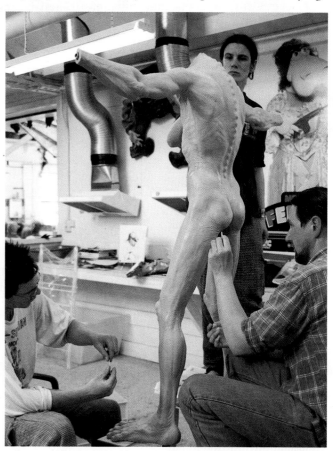

an absentee character somewhat scary: 'The others would be acting in a conventional way, in full costume and make-up and there's me as this weird creature, crawling around on the floor in a skin-tight lycra suit with padded knees and shoulders – it was quite exposing stuff!'

Nevertheless, the sense of vulnerability which was induced aided Andy's portrayal: 'Being hunched over, almost on the ground, certainly affected how my voice came out. Tolkien tells us that, long ago, Gollum had been

a hobbit-like creature named Sméagol and that he acquired his new name because of the unpleasant swallowing sound that he made. I figured that a lot of Gollum's pain was in his throat: everything that has happened to him – murdering his friend, Déagol, in order to get the Ring and then becoming addicted to it – was trapped right there in his craw. The physicality and the voice were one.'

Both voices. For there are times when the character becomes an arena for two warring personalities: the pre-Ring Sméagol and the corrupted, distorted Gollum. 'Sméagol is higher and more nasal,' explains Andy, 'Gollum is lower, throaty, more guttural. Physically, Sméagol is gentler, less domineering; Gollum is tortured by his craving for the Ring and his anger at having lost it. His body-shape doesn't change, only how he holds himself. You see the tussle going on inside him: wanting to be loved, wanting to serve the Ring-bearer; yet, at the same time, giving way to his own self-seeking motives and schizophrenia.'

When Andy was additionally cast in the role of Sméagol, he had the opportunity to act out the character's transformation into Gollum as he retreats deeper into dark ways beneath the Misty Mountains. The sequence –

seen, in flashback, in *The Two Towers* – involved extensive use of prosthetic make-up, but it helped lock the actor into his role.

Andy drew much of his inspiration from the book: 'I got an image of Gollum always looking down rather than up, digging, burrowing, hiding… Tolkien suggests that he was something of a kleptomaniac: finding and hoarding things – fish bones and trinkets – stuffing them away in his "pocketses". There are also a number of references to Gollum's animal qualities and picking up on one of these – that he could be cat-like – gave me the idea that, when Gollum speaks, his body would have those convulsive movements a cat uses when it is trying to regurgitate a fur-ball.'

Ultimately, however, Andy Serkis's Gollum is an addict, a Ring-junkie, who is perceived with great compassion by the actor who portrays him: 'Gollum is the dark side of humanity, but I tried to look at him in a non-judgmental way – not as a snivelling, evil wretch but from the point of view of "There but for the grace of God, go I". My view is simply this: we can choose to demonize anyone with uncontrollable obsessions, but if we don't seek to understand them, then we can never hope to grow as human beings.'

Knowing the Score

'Opera. That's how I'm thinking of it: as if I were composing an opera.' Howard Shore is talking to me during a break in one of the music recording sessions for *The Fellowship of the Ring.* 'The book was written as a single story that was later divided into three volumes. The film tells a single story, though it will also be released in three parts. So I'm approaching the music as if it were a three-act opera.'

The musicians are finishing off their teas and coffees and making their way into the studio. Howard Shore turns to go; then, looking back with a wry smile, adds: 'And *this* is just the first act! A *two-and-a-half-hour* first act!'

Air Lyndhurst in North London is an unusual place. If you didn't know that these were the studios where they recorded the film scores for *Gladiator, The English Patient* and various James Bond pictures, you might easily take it for a church. Which is exactly what it once was.

Built in 1884, Lyndhurst Hall was designed by Alfred Waterhouse, the eminent Victorian architect, whose Gothic-styled buildings include London's Natural History Museum with its fantastical façade encrusted with birds, beasts and prehistoric creatures. Lyndhurst Hall's striking Romanesque exterior remains unchanged, but inside is a state-of-the-art recording studio, created by the legendary producer of the Beatles, Sir George Martin.

Here, along with four other studios (one in Wellington, three in London) is where the score for the movie has been recorded. In the control room there is an intense atmosphere of busyness and concentration. Sound-engineers and dubbing-mixers sit at consoles which bristle with knobs and switches: seventy-two channels, with flying fader automation, film matrix and recall. Producers and editors pore over stacks of music manuscript, checking the scoring and logging the various takes. And, at a table directly in the centre of the stereo spectrum, is Peter Jackson.

Despite the cold, wet weather of a London autumn, Peter is dressed in shorts and T-shirt and is, as usual, bare-footed. He looks remarkably relaxed for a man at the mercy of a punishing schedule.

'I find this relaxing,' he confides, 'Howard's got the hard job... Normally, when I'm on set, I'd be having to do something similar to what he's doing now: you film a shot and have to decide whether it works or it doesn't; whether you want to do it again, and, if so, whether you should do it differently: maybe change this...? Possibly try that...? It's nice to be able to sit back and enjoy the music without having to carry the responsibility of recording it!'

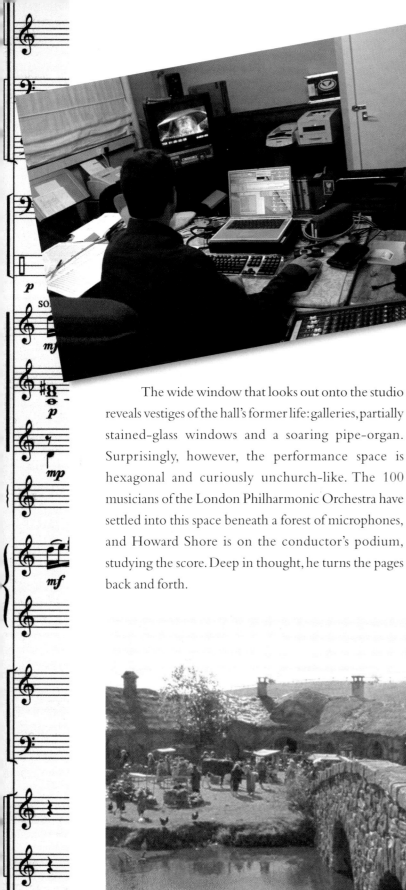

'Howard has hand-crafted the entire score,' says Peter, 'and the result is very exciting. It has one consistent musical voice; yet, at the same time, it reflects all the different cultures in Middle-earth. It's a big undertaking.'

'OK, ladies and gentlemen...' Howard's voice fills the control room via a huge bank of speakers above our heads. 'Let's try another take of 1G, shall we?'

Four grey-faced television monitors come suddenly alive, as does the one on the conductor's music stand. A freeze-frame close-up of Gandalf: the beard, the twinkling eyes beneath the beetling brows, and everyone is ready to begin again – after, that is, a word or two of advice: 'The musette might be just a little *too* loud –' The musette is a French accordion. 'It seemed to be hanging out a bit too much... And Rachel, have you adjusted the tightness of the drum?'

She has. The take-number is recorded by the control room for identification purposes: 'Take 961 of 1G-43...' Howard raises his baton: 'Here we go...'

He hesitates. 'A strong bar 3 would be great...'

The wide window that looks out onto the studio reveals vestiges of the hall's former life: galleries, partially stained-glass windows and a soaring pipe-organ. Surprisingly, however, the performance space is hexagonal and curiously unchurch-like. The 100 musicians of the London Philharmonic Orchestra have settled into this space beneath a forest of microphones, and Howard Shore is on the conductor's podium, studying the score. Deep in thought, he turns the pages back and forth.

There's another pause. 'And a really nice attack on the flute as well...' The orchestra are poised to begin, but the composer still has one or two last-minute suggestions: 'And strings, you could accent the downbeat of that bar a little bit... A *little* accent... Not much... Just so that it feels like we've arrived together...'

A voice in the control room murmurs onto tape: 'This is still Take 961 of 1G-43...'

Then: 'Hang on a minute, I've just remembered one thing. Cellos, there's a part where it went up an octave, don't play that: don't play bar 35... Oh, and French horns, don't play 36 and 37, OK? All right, let's try that...'

On the monitors, Gandalf begins speaking, although no dialogue is heard. For this screening only, we are watching a silent-movie version of *The Lord of the Rings*; the pictures and the music. No one will ever see the film like this in the cinema – shorn of its words and sound-effects – but it is essential for everyone needing to concentrate on what is being recorded musically. But it is also the best possible way in which to appreciate Howard Shore's remarkable creative achievement.

Again and again, over the next few hours, a comment which Howard made to me months ago runs through my head: 'I want the score to have a feeling of antiquity, to sound old – as if it had been discovered somewhere, in a vault.'

A yellow line, followed by a green line, wipe the screen; a dot appears in the centre of the image; the baton descends and the music begins.

As requested, the orchestra give it plenty of 'attack'. Gandalf is driving his cart along a narrow country lane, Frodo sitting beside him. The music is full of lyrical sweep: a flute theme trips gaily across the strings' melody like a breeze rippling through the grass. The music has an English pastoral sound that nods courteously to Elgar and Vaughn Williams with a hint of the Celtic that securely locates us in an older, gentler, quieter age.

The cart passes through the sunlit fields of the Shire on the way to Hobbiton. The hillsides are dotted with little round doors, smoke rises from chimneys, lines of washing dance in small, neat country gardens. There is

an easy, rustic feel to the music now with an insistent fiddle tune chirping away and demanding to be taken notice of – rather like hobbits themselves!

Gandalf crosses the bridge by the mill and makes his way up the meandering track. A group of hobbit children run excitedly behind the cart – after all, this is Gandalf, the maker of legendary fireworks! An elderly hobbit watches the youngsters with a wistful look as if remembering his own childhood. But the cart passes on and the children gaze after it in disappointment. The music seems to have reached a full stop. Then, suddenly, it erupts again, as fireworks whiz into the air, exploding in a shower of sparks! The children laugh and clap with glee, the strings subtly underscoring Gandalf's mischievous chuckle.

Next stop: Bag End, for the reunion between Gandalf and Bilbo. As the two old friends contemplate one another for a moment and then affectionately embrace, the hobbit-theme reappears now a little slower and, perhaps, just a little sadder.

Inside Bag End, the music speaks of comfort, warmth and a reassuring cosiness; but as Bilbo potters off to fetch tea, Gandalf wanders into the study and finds, amongst a pile of books and paper, an ancient map depicting a mountain and a fire-breathing dragon. A note of unease,

played on the high strings, edges into the music. Gandalf's brow furrows in thought, for the journey represented by the map was the one on which Bilbo had come into possession of a certain *ring…*

The music reaches a climax and that is the end of the take. The orchestra relax: one or two chat quietly, another picks up the newspaper and scrutinises the crossword, one of the violinists is reading *Harry Potter and the Goblet of Fire.*

Howard considers. 'We need more volume from the whistle – it's really not loud enough at bar 49: make this *mezzo forte…* And the same with the piccolo and the clarinet – and you can even go to *forte* on the last half of 50…' He hums it.

They do another take. 'Let's not use the accordion on the wagon going over the bridge…' And another. 'I'm wondering whether the harp and guitar at 52 should continue the arpeggio. Try that, because the motion seems to stop there…' And yet another…

Coming into the control room, Howard joins Peter in listening back to the sequence against pictures and sound, seeing how the recording works alongside the dialogue and effects.

Peter is happy: 'That was sounding good.' Howard is taciturn: 'It's getting there…'

'I really don't have any director-type notes,' Peter tells Howard. 'It's up to you to wrestle with the performance of it…' Then, glancing in my direction, he adds: 'I'm tone-deaf and really don't know a thing about the creation of music. So I limit my input to saying things like: "Could that be a little bit quieter?" or, "Maybe that can be a bit more exciting," and, amazingly, Howard always seems to find a way to make it happen…'

Howard smiles. 'I'll spend maybe another half-hour, on this section – once I've sorted out the dynamics of the thing. We must keep the emotion in there...'

I remember an earlier conversation with Howard, six months ago in Wellington, New Zealand. It was a warm, late summer morning and we were talking in his apartment on Marine Parade looking out over Worser Bay.

'This is going to be a very emotional score,' he told me. 'Of course, there'll be passion, and mystery, and action, and intrigue; but, essentially, it has this emotional heart to it...'

At that time he had just begun composing, although he had been thinking about the music since he joined the project in the summer of 2000. 'Hiring a composer,' observed Howard, 'is rather like casting an actor: a lot of research is done in order to find someone with the right sensibility to work with the director of a project.'

Fran Walsh had been listening to a lot of film music and kept coming across scores by Howard Shore that not only fired her imagination but which were, in a number of instances, from literary adaptations such as Shakespeare's *Richard III,* William Burroughs's *Naked Lunch,* Thomas Harris's *The Silence of the Lambs* and J. G. Ballard's *Crash*.

Eventually, Fran and Peter telephoned the composer: 'We talked at length,' Howard recalled, 'about music and film-making in general, and finally they asked if I was interested – and, of course, I was!'

A trip to New Zealand confirmed that view: 'I came down and visited Edoras, Rivendell and Lothlórien, saw some digital animation being done and lunched with the hobbits! It was obviously going to be a challenging project but for me it was irresistible: I could see that Middle-earth would be a wonderful world in which to work.'

That work had begun in the dark, labyrinthine passageways of the Mines of Moria, creating the music for a sequence of the film which was scheduled for screening at the 2001 Cannes Film Festival.

'When you are working with something literary, you have a responsibility to do it right: you are taking the

words from the page and translating them into a musical score. Even more so with this particular book. It doesn't feel as if we are trying to do a "version" of the book, so much as to "create" it on film. The music is a part of that – to create the world in a realistic way, so that the audience feels that they are "in" Hobbiton or Rivendell or Moria.'

The desk was scattered with sheets of manuscript paper (Howard is not only writing but also orchestrating all the various instrumentations in the score) and a well-thumbed copy of The Lord of the Rings.

'The book is always close by when I'm working and I am constantly referencing Tolkien's text looking for musical elements in it and trying to convey them in my music.'

Howard found plenty in the book to inspire his music for the ancient mine-workings of Dwarrowdelf: 'Moria has a very specific sound to it: Tolkien talks about "drums, drums in the deep," and, later, describes the "doom, doom of drum-beats" that shake the very walls. So the music will have drums and voices: a male choir of

Maoris and Samoans singing a low, Dwarvish chant with a guttural – almost Tibetan-monk – sound to it.'

Six months after that music was written and recorded by the New Zealand Symphony Orchestra, three months after the Mines of Moria sequence thrilled audiences in Cannes, Howard Shore is in London to complete the recording of the score for The Fellowship of the Ring.

It is lunch-break at Air Lyndhurst (which takes place roughly around dinner time!) and Howard is democratically standing in line, waiting to be served while most of the orchestra are already seated on old pews, tucking into heaped helpings of toad-in-the hole and apple crumble.

I remind Howard of our earlier conversation about Moria. 'It was,' he says, 'the perfect beginning. I spent a long, long time in Moria and by researching and putting all that together really cracked it open for the rest of the score. It was fortuitous to have begun in Moria because the events there are pivotal. There is much leading up to the Fellowship's journey through the mines and everything that happens afterwards is shaped by what happens to them there. I couldn't have chosen a better route to approach the score: once I'd created that world, I was able to write my way both to it and out of it!'

The journeys to and from Moria involved creating a number of other musical 'worlds': 'They are all,' he explains, 'thematically different: Moria has a drum-driven sound, while Rivendell is brighter and Lothlórien more mysterious; I think of Rivendell as a symphonic suite, whereas in Lothlórien I use more exotic instruments such as Indian bowed-lutes and North African flutes.'

Themes for the Last Homely House and the Golden Wood involve the use of choral music. 'The book,' Howard reminds me, 'is full of music and song, but – simply in terms of time – there wasn't a way to do that in the film. However, I wanted to find a way to put back that missing element with choirs and choruses, using the human voice as another, integral part of the orchestra of sounds.'

The creation of such a complex score has resulted in a tiring schedule: 'It's a long-distance race! I try to pace myself like an athlete. And now we're on the last lap – well, for *this* film, anyway.' This 'last lap' averages sixteen hours a day: 'I spend every morning composing the music for the film's Prologue. It's tricky because it's very detailed and I'm dealing with images and a voice-over, but it's coming along pretty good.' He pauses and, raising his eyebrows, adds, 'it needs to be: we have to record it in a few days!' The rest of his time is given over to working with the musicians. 'When you are finishing a very long work like this you can't imagine doing anything else because you've invested so much time and energy in it. The only thing I do away from all this is maybe go for a walk to clear my brain – but even then I'm still thinking about it.'

There's a lot to think about: '*The Fellowship of the Ring* will contain about as much music as two normal films: partly because of the sheer length of the movie, plus the fact that we have fewer quiet patches than most films!'

So, I ask, how many cues are there in the film? '*Cues?*' he echoes with a hollow laugh, 'Oh, it's gone *way* beyond cues! It's written in suites and, all told, we're talking about more than two-and-a-half hours of music!'

Back in the control room, Howard Shore gets into deep discussion over the talk-back with Associate Music producer, Michael Tremante, and Music Editor, Suzana Perič, who also serves as a liaison with Peter Jackson and colleagues. Together they are an invaluable second and third pair of ears, following the score, note for note, as it is recorded.

Michael tells Howard that the last take of bar 28 was 'very good' and Suzana adds that bars 1 to 12 were also fine. Howard decides to do a pick-up from bar 11. But there's a problem. Dermot, the fiddle-player, has gone walkabout with a couple of other musicians. While one of the cellists runs off to fetch them, a clarinettist hands round a packet of chocolate biscuits and the violinist reads another page of Harry Potter.

During this hiatus, I ask Suzana how usual it is for today's film composers to do all the orchestrations as Howard has done: 'It's almost a forgotten art,' she replies. 'In America, especially, movies are being done so quickly and schedules are so short, that it's often a necessity to have someone else arrange your music. But there are still some composers – like Howard – who insist on doing their own orchestrations, because *that* is where the personal voice comes through the most. We all pick up on a melody when we hear it, but the way in which the harmonies work is what really allows the composer to make an imprint.'

Dermot and friends come scurrying back into the studio. Howard is remarkably calm: 'If you need a break, then take it during a piece in which you don't play, but not, please, in the middle of this one...'

There are profuse apologies from Dermot. 'Yep,' says Howard, 'do you want tuning?' He does and, when everyone is ready for another take, Howard offers a final suggestion to the penitent fiddle-player: 'You could grace-note the A on the sixth beat of 16... Is that all right?' He hums it and the fiddler plays it. 'Exactly so...'

The film runs on the monitors once more and the orchestra plays. At the end of what is generally agreed to have been a good take, there's a conciliatory compliment for Dermot: 'The grace-note was fine and that little turn on bar 18 was very good and really helps. Thank you.' All is forgiven.

On goes the painstaking quest for perfection. It is night outside and the stained-glass windows have become panels of darkness. It is 9.00 p.m. and the orchestra are dismissed for this session in order to make way for the sixty-strong voices of the London Voices and their choirmaster, Terry Edwards.

Howard Shore shows no sign of flagging: there is a new group of musicians to be directed towards giving the best possible sound to enhance this complex score. On the monitors: a still incomplete computer-generated image of a moth flies up from the Orc-pits beneath Isengard to the top of Orthanc.

'This is just the ladies,' explains Howard, 'and it's very brief, just five bars...' The music is played for the choir. 'Hear those high strings? You're singing an octave lower than that.'

The next scene is of the Fellowship setting out by boat from Lothlórien. The choir rehearses, but something is wrong. There are some syllables missing. Howard is mystified:

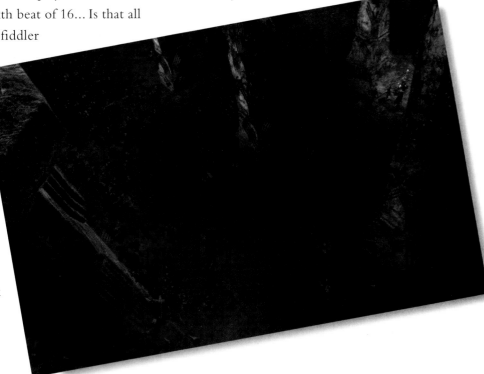

'I don't remember leaving them out. Could you check on my sketch?' he asks Michael. 'Maybe they just got left out of the score...'

Michael says he'll check but it will take a few minutes. 'Ohhhh,' sighs Howard, 'Then we'd better go on to something else.' They turn, instead, to a sequence involving the Orcs slaving away in the fiery pits beneath Orthanc. The music for this scene only features the men and the first take sounds good. But Terry Edwards isn't happy: 'I can hear some of you breathing on the fifth beat.' 'Breathing?' quips Howard, 'I'm not sure we can allow that!'

Terry has the answer: 'Just breathe earlier,' then an even better solution: 'Look, I'll do the breathing for you!' Everyone laughs and tries again. That's good,' says

the composer, glancing at his watch, 'but it's five after eleven. On we go...'

So, on they go. There is still much to be done, but some of us have to go in search of last trains and Peter Jackson is off into the wilds of Hertfordshire to view special-effects footage that's been flown over from New Zealand.

As we creep out of the studio, the choir is tackling another scene. Just outside the door is the recording machine where the master tapes are turning, laying down another element for the final soundtrack of *The Fellowship of the Ring*. Realizing that, right here, is the results of hours and hours of work in the studio, we pause and look at one another.

'Whatever you do,' says Peter, 'for pity's sake don't press the erase button!'

On the Theme of Fellowship

If they have a choice, most film composers would prefer to work with one or two clearly defined central characters for whom they can create strong musical themes. In approaching the task of writing music for *The Fellowship of the Ring*, Howard Shore faced the daunting prospect of composing the score for a film which features – in the Fellowship alone – no less than nine central characters.

'I decided,' says Howard, 'to compose a theme that would run through the film and represent that Fellowship in its varying stages of strength and weakness.

'The theme is heard first, in fragmented form, when Frodo and Sam are setting out from Hobbiton for Bree: this is the first time they have left the Shire and they are afraid, so it is only a tentative reading. Then they meet up with Merry and Pippin and, since there are now four of them, the theme becomes more upbeat, more frolicking. On arriving in Bree, the hobbits are scared and intimidated but once they have encountered Strider, the Fellowship becomes five and the theme becomes a little more formed – although it also reflects their weariness, the arduousness of the way ahead and the danger of their situation. Finally reaching Rivendell, they think

they have completed their journey only to discover that it is just beginning. Now, however, they have help – Gandalf, Boromir, Legolas and Gimli – and as the nine set forth on their mission, we hear a heroic, joyous rendition of the theme.

'As the Fellowship passes through Moria, there are several different readings: after defeating the Cave Troll, there's a victorious version, but then – when Gandalf dies and Boromir is increasingly tempted by the Ring – the Fellowship begins to break apart and, so too, does the theme.

'At Boromir's death, we hear it in a solemn, processional version and as Frodo and Sam go on alone into Mordor, the theme turns to the more fragmentary form in which it began: a fellowship of two, heading into the unknown…'

Epilogue
An End and a Beginning

Judgement Day dawned...

The world premiere party for *The Fellowship of the Ring* had begun late on the night of Monday, December 10th 2001, and had gone on until the early hours. By the time the last guests were leaving Tobacco Dock in the East End of London, the first editions of that morning's papers were being delivered to the news-stands. What would the press make of the film?

There was no need to have worried. In a rave review, the *Daily Mail* described the movie as having 'a mythic grandeur and a profound understanding of human corruptibility that makes the *Star Wars* movies look like kid's stuff', while the *Daily Telegraph*, in an article headlined 'If you don't like this, you don't like the movies', declared: '[*The Lord of the Rings*] brings a panoply of quest narratives up to the very minute; it enjoins them to landscapes of unbelievable density and richness, pastoral idylls to snowy tundra; it choreographs a variety of beings and gives them enduring character – and it does all this with an unprecedented technical verve.'

Several critics compared Peter Jackson with legendary directors from Fritz Lang via John Ford to David Lean, while others looked to the world of art for parallel visions: some seeing the inspiration of John Constable's picturesque landscapes, others detecting shades of Gustav Doré, Hieronymus Bosch or John Martin; while, for the *Financial Times*, Elijah Wood's Frodo had 'the features of a William Blake angel'.

In America, the first wave of critical acclaim rolled in onto the front page of the entertainment weekly, *Variety*: 'Evocatively delineating the many aspects of Middle-earth, Jackson keeps a firm hand on the work's central themes of good vs evil, rising to the occasion and group loyalty in the face of adversity, and always keeps things moving without getting bogged down in frills or effects for effects' sake.'

Screen International described the film as 'visually striking, thematically grave and morally weighty' and declared that it 'not only faithfully captures the spirit of its source material ... but also stands tall on its own merits as one of the most ambitious features to come out of Hollywood in a long time'.

A snippet from a glowing review in the *Los Angeles Times* is typical of the movie's critical reception: 'Made with intelligence, imagination, passion and skill, propulsively paced and shot through with an aged-in-oak sense of wonder, the trilogy's first film so thrillingly catches us up in its sweeping story that nothing matters but the vivid and compelling events unfolding on the screen.'

As the worldwide media response stacked up, so too did that of Tolkien fans who, despite predictable cavils relating to those parts of the film which departed from the letter of the original, were generally approving of the results and websites were soon full of postings from devotees who were heading back to the cinema for second, third or fourth viewings.

But no group of people awaited the coming of *The Fellowship of the Ring* more eagerly than the people of New Zealand and, in particular, the residents of Wellington. That poster of the New Zealand customs desks was reworked with signs that indicated queues for 'Orcs', 'Trolls', 'Hobbits' – and 'Journalists'! 'We placed the posters all through the airport,' recalls Elliott Kirton, who managed the campaign, 'even behind the Customs Desks, themselves! Originally, we had hoped to change the signs over the customs desks for real, but, as you can imagine, that didn't prove so easy! However, during the week of the premiere, we did get away with placing various packaged items on the baggage-carousels with labels that included "Gandalf's Staff", "Bilbo's Ring" and, in the case of a bundle of hay, "Bill the Pony"!'

New Zealand Post marked the release of the film with a set of six stamps, (from 40 cents to $2.00) designed by Sacha Lees of Weta Workshop. Featuring Gandalf and Saruman, Frodo and Sam, Strider, Boromir, Galadriel and the Guardian of Rivendell, the set was also issued as a special first-day-cover, decorated with a Black Rider and franked with an 'Eye of Sauron' mark.

Then came the premiere. 'A Middle earth-quake struck Wellington last night' declared the *New Zealand Herald*. Giving the movie five stars, the review continued: 'If your optic nerves are getting a delightful battering, even better perhaps is the film's capacity to make your heart leap as high as your imagination... A few weeks ago Jackson said he was looking forward to the day when the hype would give way to the notion that after all, it's just a movie. Fat chance. *The Fellowship of the Ring* is incredible. Bring on the next two.'

It was December 19th, the day on which the film went on release across the world. With understandable pride,

In fact, *The Fellowship of the Ring* provided a generous Christmas present to everyone involved in its making and distribution. New Line Cinema reported that the film played in 3,359 theatres across America and had taken an estimated opening-day gross of $18.2 million. On the opening weekend, a few days later, American box-office receipts totalled $66 million with an additional hefty taking of £11 million earned from screenings in 470 cinemas in the UK. Within a month of opening, the film had grossed, in the US alone, $228 million and $850 million worldwide.

the *Evening Post* told its readers: 'Forget London, New York and Los Angeles: the real premiere of *The Lord of the Rings* was in Wellington last night.' Despite overcast skies and icy winds, fifteen thousand people lined the streets to the Embassy theatre – which had undergone a multi-million-dollar refurbishment, and was graced by a huge Weta Workshop replica of the Moria cave troll, towering, Kong-like, above the marquee – to greet the stars of the film and their director on the last leg of their premiere tour. 'It's great,' said Peter Jackson, 'to see the old home town turn out like this!'

Helen Clark, the country's Prime Minister, declared in her speech: 'It's amazing what this movie has done for New Zealand. A lot of movies you see, you wouldn't have a clue where they're made... Everyone knows this is made in New Zealand.' Reading that speech, I recall John Rhys-Davies' observation that 'Peter Jackson is going to do more for the New Zealand tourist industry than any man since Captain Cook!'

Following the premiere, the Embassy instantly became the cinema in which to see the film and soon takings at the 800-seat theatre were estimated to be in the region of $30,000 (NZ) per day; prompting the Embassy's operator to remark: 'All my Christmases have come at once!'

The first indication of glittering prizes to come was the announcement of the American Film Institute Awards which named *The Fellowship of the Ring* Movie of the Year and Jim Rygiel as Digital Effects Artist of the Year. The film also picked up the Best Production Design/Art Direction award from the National Board of Review, which named Cate Blanchett Best Supporting Actress (for *Rings* together with *The Shipping News* and *The Man Who Cried*) and gave a Special Achievement award to Peter Jackson.

Howard Shore won the Los Angeles Film Critics Association award for 'Best Music Score', while Ian McKellen picked up the Screen Actors Guild award for 'Outstanding Performance by a Male Actor in a Supporting Role'. Ian also won the somewhat unlikely Best Fight category in the MTV Movie Awards alongside Christopher Lee, who was voted Best Villain; while the 'cave tomb battle' was voted Best Action Sequence. The film was chosen as Best Movie, as it was by readers of the UK film magazine *Empire*, who also named Elijah Wood as Best Actor and Orlando Bloom (above) as Best Debut.

In the three major film award stakes, *The Lord of the Rings* raked in a healthy number of nominations: four Golden Globes, eleven BAFTAs (British Academy of Film and Television Awards) and thirteen Academy Awards.

After being passed over by the Golden Globes, *The Fellowship of the Ring* was rewarded with five BAFTAs: Best Film, the Audience Award (voted by movie-goers), Best Achievement in Special Visual Effects (naming Randall William Cook, Alex Funke, Jim Rygiel, Mark Stetson and Richard Taylor), Best Make-up/Hair for Peter Owen, Peter King and Richard Taylor (pictured right, with his wife and business partner, Tania Rodger); and the David Lean Award for Direction was presented to Peter Jackson.

Whilst many fans were understandably disappointed by the limited recognition the movie received at the Academy Awards, the film nevertheless garnered four Oscars: for Best Music, Original Score (Howard Shore), Best Cinematography (Andrew Lesnie), Best Effects and Visual Effects (for Messrs Cook, Rygiel, Stetson and Taylor) and Best Make-up for Peter Owen and Richard Taylor – adding a second Oscar to his two BAFTAs!

There were other, less commercially significant, rewards too: Peter Jackson was made a Companion of the New Zealand Order of Merit in the New Year's Honours List and partner and fellow-scriptwriter Fran Walsh became a Member of the New Zealand Order of Merit. Peter was also voted New Zealander of the Year, eliciting this response from the *New Zealand Herald*: 'Too obvious, you could say, too populist, you might

to that Sunday morning in November 1995, when I was lying in bed and decided to call my agent and ask who held the rights to *The Lord of the Rings* ... well, if somebody had told me then "You're starting something you're not going to get out of until the year 2003" then I'd probably have said "No!"'

Talking to Peter later, with the first film an unquestioned triumph, he adds only this: 'With my track record and the fact that I'd never previously made a really successful commercial film, it seems fairly unbelievable that we should be in this position... But then, everything about this project has been about breaking the rules; everything about it has been nonconformist – which I think is kind of neat!'

think, too easily swayed by the marketing blitz of *The Lord of the Rings*, you could argue. You could, but consider this. Jackson deserves the recognition precisely because, despite the hype, the acclaim and the money, he has retained the best of what makes a New Zealander. His is an unassuming, home-grown brilliance. His feat of welding a creativity, which began with a childhood passion for filming plasticine dinosaurs, to a business brain in which he ran the biggest movie project ever, is as stupendous as Frodo's quest through Middle-earth... That he has done it all in New Zealand, down to the last hair on the hobbits' feet, has underlined his commitment to the country he could easily have abandoned years ago for the bright lights of Hollywood... The fact he could make *The Lord of the Rings* at all reveals his standing in the toughest market of them all, ahead of a galaxy of Hollywood directors. The fact he could do it allegedly wearing one or other of his two pink shirts, usually matched with shorts and sometimes bare feet shows his unaffected Kiwi style.'

Several months before the opening of *The Fellowship of the Ring*, when the film was far from finished, I asked Peter whether – had he known what lay ahead – he would ever have embarked on the project? He laughed, thought for a moment and then replied: 'Ask me if I'm pleased I've done it and the answer would be "Absolutely, yes!"'; but if you could crank the clock back

Of course, the pressure is still on. Peter is hard at work completing the trilogy and, in a sense, expectations are now even greater. But there is the reassurance that, having seen *The Fellowship of the Ring*, cinema-goers are as eager – maybe more so – to savour the remaining instalments. However amazing – even 'unbelievable' – that may seem, it's how it is. And, yes, it really is 'kind of neat'!

Acknowledgements

'What I want to read is the *biography* of this movie!' Dave Golder, editor of the magazine *SFX*, was interviewing me on the publication of *The Lord of the Rings: Official Movie Guide*. I rashly replied that my next book (*this* book) was going to be exactly that!

After all, telling the life-story of a movie is not such a far-fetched notion, since every film results from the combined talents of many people's lives. Just how many people were involved in creating *The Lord of the Rings* can be seen from the fifteen minutes or so of credits at the end of each of the pictures. Cumulatively, across the three movies, the roll-call of talent is staggering.

I have met, talked and corresponded with many of those people and a number of those who began as interviewees have become close friends. However, as I started writing, I quickly realized that it would take a book considerably longer than this one – several

volumes, maybe – to fully tell the biography of this extraordinary cinematic achievement.

So, it is, perhaps, better to think of it as of a series of 'Scenes from the Life of…', or, maybe. 'Conversations with Close Friends and Associates of…'

However, you view it, this book has only been possible because the following people gave unstintingly of their often frantically-busy time, bore my questions with patience and good-humour and offered helpful comments and generous encouragement. In thanking them, however, it should be remembered that for every one whose voice is heard in the pages of this book, there are at least a hundred others who have also made their own individual and vital contribution to the making of *The Lord of the Rings*.

Janine Abery, Gino Acevedo, Matt Aitken, Greg Allen, Bob Anderson, Dan Arden, Sean Astin, John Baster, Len Baynes, Sean Bean, Warren Beaton, Freyer Blackwood, Jan Blenkin, Orlando Bloom, Richard Bluck, Melissa Booth, Costa Botes, Billy Boyd, Philippa Boyens, Tanya Buchanan, Brent Burge, Jacq Burrell, John Caldwell, Grant Campbell, William Campbell, Jason Canovas, Norman Cates, Annie Collins, Randall William Cook, Claire Cooper, Matthew Cooper, Frank Cowlrick, Carolynne Cunningham, Chris Davison, Ngila Dickson, Jason Docherty, Don Donoghue, Meredith Dooley, Rose Dority, Peter Doyle, Terry Edwards, Dean Evans, Daniel Falconer, Xander Forterie, Megan Fowlds, Alex Funke, Savannah Green, Chris Guise, Winham Hammond, Thorkild Hansen, David Hardberger, Emma Harre, Harry Harrison, Ben Hawker, Luke Hawker,

Mark Hawthorne, Chris Hennah, Dan Hennah, Ian Holm, Belindalee Hope, Mike Horton, John Howe, Bill Hunt, Peter Jackson, Stu Johnson, Mark Kinaston-Smith, Peter King, Martin Kwok, Jon Labrie, François Laroche, Alan Lee, Christopher Lee, Virginia Lee, Andrew Lesnie, Xiaohong Liu, Tracy Lorie, Peter Lyon, Janis MacEwan, Mary Maclachlan, Grant Major, Brian Massey, Caroline McKay, John McKay, Ian McKellen, Peter Mills, Dominic Monaghan, Shanon Morati, Viggo Mortensen, John Neill, Tim Nielsen, John Nugent, Stephen Old, Jabez Olssen, Mark Ordesky, Barrie M. Osborne, Miranda Otto, Peter Owen, Craig Parker, Suzana Perič, Rick Porras, Joanna Priest, Daniel Reeve, Stephen Regelous, Pip Reisch, John Rhys-Davies, Christian Rivers, Miranda Rivers, Tania Rodger, Tich Rowney, George Marshall Ruge, Patrick Runyon, Jim Rygiel, Chuck Schuman, Lynne Seaman, Jamie Selkirk, Andy Serkis, Kiran Shah, Richard Sharkey, Howard Shore, Peter Skarratt, Heather Small, Andrew Smith, Wayne Stables, Richard Taylor, Sue Thompson, Craig Tomlinson, Rob Townshend, Michael Tremante, Caroline Turner, Liv Tyler, Karl Urban, Adam Valdez, James van der Reyden, Ethan Van der Ryn, Brian Van't Hul, Jenny Vial, Fran Walsh, Marty Walsh, Chris Ward, Moritz Wassmann, Andrew Wickens, Lisa Wildermoth, Jamie Wilson, Elijah Wood, Katy Wood, Annette Wullems.

Although featured in the foregoing list, a very particular expression of thanks is due to Ian McKellen for having found the time to contribute a foreword to this volume.

I am also most grateful (for all manner of help, advice and inspiration) to Dave Golder, Sarah Green and Phil Clark (of *New Zealand Post*), Michelle Fromont, Richard Holliss, Jean Johnston (Film and Television Co-ordinator, Capital Development Agency, Wellington City Council), Elliott Kirton, Sandra Murray and Sarah Swords.

At HarperCollins: to David Brawn for commissioning *and* believing in this book (even as it continued to evolve!); to Chris Smith for his enthusiasm and stoicism in seeing it through to press; Emma Coode for always being there to answer the phone and deal with author paranoia; and, above all, to Jane Johnson, my endlessly patient and ceaselessly encouraging editor, without whose support, wisdom and affection, I would, undoubtedly, have fallen headlong into the Cracks of Doom!

My personal thanks go to Emma Gillson for her painstaking transcription of long hours of interviews containing much riddling 'Ring-talk'; and to Ian D. Smith, for proof-checking with an eagle-eye second only to Gwaihir the Windlord! To my agent, Vivien Green, for helping to keep my chin above water and for reminding me to smile; and, above all, to my partner, David Weeks, for being the loyalest of companions on the road that goes ever on and on…

THE LORD OF THE RINGS
THE TWO TOWERS™

THE JOURNEY CONTINUES DECEMBER 18